GALLATIN

GALLATIN

America's Swiss Founding Father

NICHOLAS DUNGAN

NEW YORK UNIVERSITY PRESS

New York & London

NEW YORK UNIVERSITY PRESS
New York and London
www.nyupress.org

Frontispiece: Courtesy of Lola Haener

Library of Congress Cataloging-in-Publication Data
Dungan, Nicholas.
Gallatin : America's Swiss founding father / Nicholas Dungan.
p. cm. Includes bibliographical references and index.
ISBN 978-0-8147-2111-7 (cl. : acid-free paper) — ISBN 978-0-8147-2112-4 (e-book)
1. Gallatin, Albert, 1761-1849. 2. Statesmen—United States—Biography.
3. Geneva (Switzerland)—Biography. 4. Swiss Americans—Biography.
5. United States—Politics and government—1783-1865. I. Title.
E302.6.G16D86 2010
973.4092—dc22 [B] 2010021007

New York University Press books are printed on acid-free paper, and their binding materials
are chosen for strength and durability. We strive to use environmentally responsible
suppliers and materials to the greatest extent possible in publishing our books.

Manufactured in the United States of America

10 9 8 7 6 5 4 3 2 1

IN MEMORIAM PATRIS MEI

CONSULTI • PHILOLOGI • HELVETII • AMICI

CONTENTS

FOREWORD

Gallatin in Diplomacy

THE United States of America and Switzerland celebrate together the life and contributions of Albert Gallatin.

Swiss-born Albert Gallatin became one of America's most accomplished diplomats, following his eminent tenure as secretary of the Treasury of the United States. He stands in the pantheon of American international envoys alongside Benjamin Franklin and Thomas Jefferson. Without doubt his greatest accomplishment was the successful completion of the complex and tortuous process that led to the Treaty of Ghent, which put an end to the War of 1812 and gave the United States its genuine independence.

Gallatin was a highly skilled negotiator. Born, raised, and educated in Geneva, he retained a certain Swiss personality throughout his life, while wholly dedicated to the interests of his adopted America. He was, as a result, ideally placed to deal with Europeans who needed to understand America's motivations and, in return, to shape Americans' understanding of how best to approach the sensitivities of their European counterparts. This combination of listening diplomacy, cultural awareness, and a focus on diplomacy in action was highly effective in his day and continues to be entirely pertinent to international relations in our own time.

Our two countries, often described as sister republics, do indeed share the same values and principles. Together we work toward greater international cooperation and reinforcing the international system based on democracy and respect for human rights.

Micheline Calmy-Rey
Federal Councilor
Head of the Swiss Federal Department of Foreign Affairs

FOREWORD

Gallatin in Finance

ALBERT GALLATIN, a legendary Swiss American, was the secretary of the Treasury of the United States from 1801 to 1814 under Presidents Thomas Jefferson and James Madison. He remains the longest serving Treasury secretary in U.S. history. The Geneva-born Gallatin stayed true to his roots by displaying a strong work ethic, frugality, and realism throughout his career. He distinguished himself as a financial expert and participated in the founding of the Ways and Means Committee of the House of Representatives. When he became secretary of the Treasury, he was urged to dismantle the financial system that Alexander Hamilton had put in place. Despite a longstanding rivalry between the two men, Gallatin acknowledged the genius of Hamilton's system and instead reinforced it. During his first years in office, he focused his efforts on paying down the public debt. This enhanced the credit standing of the young United States of America. As a result, Gallatin was able to finance the Louisiana Purchase through a bond issue. This doubled the size of the country. Some have questioned whether his policies were too restrictive for an emerging economy with high growth potential. In reality, his fiscal conservatism and administrative excellence meant that the United States of America could meet its challenges even in the face of European conflicts and the War of 1812, which sorely tested public finances.

His lessons of prudent policymaking and sound financial management have stood the test of time. As medium-term fiscal sustainability has to be restored, Gallatin teaches us that public debt reduction requires unwavering political commitment to fiscal discipline. The legacy of Albert Gallatin remains relevant today.

Dr. Philipp M. Hildebrand
Chairman of the Governing Board
Swiss National Bank

Acknowledgments

Daniel Haener made this book possible: both as deputy consul general of Switzerland in New York and as a friend, he propelled the project and sustained me with his determination, his enthusiasm, and his inspiration; I am forever in his debt. André Geissmann helped make this book happen: unflappable, indefatigable, organized—and cheerful—he proved to be the ideal research assistant. Their wives, Lola and Alejandra, graciously put up with a lot of Gallatin in their lives.

I am especially grateful to Micheline Calmy-Rey, federal councilor and head of the Department of Foreign Affairs of the Swiss Confederation, and to Philipp Hildebrand, chairman of the Swiss National Bank, for their encouragement. Within Swiss diplomacy, my thanks go to Ambassador Christoph Bubb and Ambassador Urs Ziswiler and to Norbert Bärlocher, Ornela Julita, Katharine Kuepfer, Katharina Litchman, Yves Morath, Pascal Prinz, Guillaume Scheurer, Lukas Sieber, and Marianne Stäger.

Ambassador Benedict von Tscharner, chair of the Foundation and the Museum of the Swiss Abroad and author of a slim Gallatin biography for Swiss readers in three languages, was generous with his advice, introductions, and guidance, and I cannot thank him enough. Jacques de Saussure provided encouragement and access, through David Foldi, to interesting correspondence. François Jacob was pleased to receive me for a private visit of the Institut et Musée Voltaire at Les Délices. I am very thankful to Jean-Charles Giroud, director of the Bibliothèque de Genève, for his keen interest in the book and the two hundred fiftieth anniversary of Gallatin's birth. The letter in chapter 1 from Gallatin to Horace-Bénédict de Saussure offers new insights and has never been published before; I found it in the archives of the Bibliothèque de Genève thanks also to the assistance of Barbara Roth, Isabelle Jeger, Christine Tourn, and Dominique Jolliet.

At the New-York Historical Society my friend Louise Mirrer, the president, was most encouraging, as was Jean Ashton, the director of the

Library Division. André Geissmann and I are grateful to Maurita Baldock, Tammy Kiter, and Ted O'Reilly in the library. At the New York Society Library, I wish to thank Mark Bartlett and all his staff, in particular Arevig Caprielian, Laura O'Keefe, and Carolyn Waters. At the Library of Congress, Bruce Kirby was very helpful, as were Frederick Augustyn and Jennifer Brathovde. Daniel and Lola Haener and I were warmly received for a private visit of Friendship Hill by James Tomasek, arranged by his wife, Kitty Seifert, both of them highly knowledgeable professionals from the National Park Service.

Patricia Schramm of the American-Swiss Foundation, Beat Reinhart of the Swiss Society, and Maximilian Angerholzer of the Richard Lounsbery Foundation were all very kind in manifesting their interest in this project.

For their willingness to read the manuscript I wish to thank Christopher Dungan, Isabelle Dungan, Daniel Haener, Alexander Lotocki de Veligost, Charles Scribner, and Gregory Vail, as well as Erin Bauer for her editorial assistance and Adam Duker for his comments on Calvin. I have been supported throughout this process as in so many other ways by a superbly bracing and tactful group of family members and friends. I shall not name you all: you know who you are and how much you mean to me.

My last acknowledgment is an expression of my gratitude and my esteem to Steve Maikowski, the director of New York University Press, and to the NYU Press team who worked on this project, including Gabrielle Begue, Emma Cook, Despina Papazoglou Gimbel, Andrew Katz, Brandon Kelley, and, last but most certainly not least, Deborah Gershenowitz, who edited this book with unfailing good humor, professionalism, and (to use one of Gallatin's favorite words) perspicuity.

INTRODUCTION

Getting to Know Gallatin

ALBERT GALLATIN, born in Geneva and raised in the Swiss and French-speaking tradition, came to America in his youth and, in a lifetime of public service to his adopted country, contributed to the welfare and independence of the United States as fully as any other statesman of his age. After a patrician upbringing in a distinguished family and the finest education that Europe could provide, Gallatin immigrated to New England, lived on the frontier, taught French at Harvard, and settled in the rough lands of western Pennsylvania. He entered local politics as a representative of the common man and soon joined forces with the nascent Republicans, who were rallying to the leadership of Thomas Jefferson in the cause of states' rights and individual liberty, inspired by the example of the French Revolution, against the Federalists, who favored a strong central government and the authority of the state on the British model. Gallatin was elected by his fellow Pennsylvanians to the legislature of his state, then by the legislature (as the procedure then was) to the U.S. Senate, then by his constituents once more to the federal House of Representatives. Capitalizing on a talent, rare among his peers, for the analysis and management of public finance, which he had displayed from his earliest days in the legislature, Gallatin proposed and partook in the founding of the Ways and Means Committee of the House, developed as a challenger to Alexander Hamilton as the country's best expert in government finance, and acceded to the leadership of the Democratic-Republican Party in the House of Representatives. In the election of 1800, when Thomas Jefferson had emerged as the clear choice of the people, but the election was thrown for constitutional reasons to the House of Representatives, Gallatin organized and implemented the plan that secured the presidency for Jefferson after thirty-six ballots. Jefferson rewarded Gallatin with the position for which he was clearly most qualified, secretary of the Treasury. Gallatin systematized the government's finances even more thoroughly than

Hamilton had done, paid down substantial portions of the national debt, and financed the Louisiana Purchase, which doubled the size of the United States. When Jefferson, caught between the conflicting demands of Britain and France, insisted on an embargo of American shipping and, later, when Madison entered into the War of 1812, upsetting Gallatin's prudent financial management, Gallatin nonetheless stayed on to manage the Treasury and finance the young American government through some of its darkest days. He then embarked on a new career by leading a mission, on behalf of President Madison, to settle, through diplomatic rather than military means, America's disputes with Britain and to put an end to the War of 1812. After a two-year odyssey through European capitals and chancelleries, Gallatin steered the American delegation and its British interlocutors to an agreement that was signed as the Treaty of Ghent. This was not an achievement only of diplomacy or international law but of statesmanship, for it permitted the United States to stand for the first time as an equal to Great Britain. Thereafter, although for the rest of the nineteenth century the sun never set on the British Empire, the United States retained unquestioned mastery of its own destiny and its own hemisphere, free from British interference or control. Following this diplomatic triumph, Gallatin returned to Europe as American minister—now known as ambassador—to France, under the Bourbon Restoration of King Louis XVIII. As a senior statesman esteemed throughout Europe, the most seasoned American to act as an envoy of his country since Benjamin Franklin, Gallatin by his very presence enhanced the prestige of the United States even as he conducted largely laborious negotiations on the less earth-shaking matters of trade agreements and border definitions with the governments of France, The Netherlands, and Britain. After his embassy in France, Gallatin became minister to Great Britain and negotiated treaties with His Majesty's government that reduced, prevented, or postponed further matters of dispute between Britain and the United States. Returning to America, he began an entirely new career, based in New York, as a public intellectual and independent elder voice of reason. Gallatin participated in the founding of New York University and was elected the first president of its council. He accepted the presidency of John Jacob Astor's National Bank of New York and played an instrumental role in solving the financial panic of 1837. He became president of the New-York Historical Society and founded the American Ethnological Society, while achieving recognition as one of America's foremost experts on Native American ethnology and linguistics. He spoke out in favor of a more responsible management of America's finances and economy, and he decried the expansion of American territory through conquest, protesting against the annexation of Texas by force of arms. All the while, Gallatin remained devoted to his wife and family of a daughter and two sons, held fast to a small number of friendships—but of the highest level: Jefferson, Astor, von Humboldt, Lafayette, Madame de Staël, and others dating from his earliest youth, particularly Jean Badollet. He died in New York at the age of eighty-eight and was buried in his wife's family vault in Trinity Churchyard at Broadway and Wall Street. Such were the vast achievements of but one man from his birth in 1761 to his death in 1849.

THE INSPIRATION FOR THIS BOOK

Edward Gibbon tells us that the idea of writing *The History of the Decline and Fall of the Roman Empire* came to him as he "sat musing amidst the ruins of the Capitol, while the bare-footed friars were singing Vespers in the Temple of Jupiter."[1] I can claim no such grandiose inspiration, but the idea for this book did germinate among monuments. I was walking in front of the White House in Washington, DC, and then in front of the building of the Treasury Department next door. On the Pennsylvania Avenue side of the Treasury building is the statue of Albert Gallatin depicted on the cover of this book. I looked afresh at the statue and read the inscription on the plinth; it set my mind to wondering more about the man. My family has Swiss roots, so I was aware of Gallatin but not well acquainted with his story. I turned and walked back toward Lafayette Park, noting the statues of Lafayette, Rochambeau, von Steuben, and Kosciusko in the four corners of the park. I realized that I was walking among America's European Founding Fathers: French, Polish, Prussian, and, in the case of Gallatin— in front of his Treasury building but within eyeshot of the square—Swiss. As president of the French-American Foundation, I participated in the celebrations of the two hundred fiftieth anniversary of the birth of Lafayette in 2007. I attended the dedications of refurbished statues, I listened to authors present their books, and I gave a lecture at the New-York Historical Society titled "The Legacy of Lafayette and Lessons for the French-American Relationship." These occasions represented important opportunities to remind Americans that they and their country are historically and culturally rooted in Europe, to commemorate the contribution of the Europeans who helped to build America, and to reinforce relations, in a world in which people have difficulty in keeping their bearings, between the two fundamental components of Western civilization, Europe and North America.

Now I asked myself whether Gallatin's own story would represent such an opportunity for remembrance and *rapprochement*. A bit of research after I returned to New York revealed that the two hundred fiftieth anniversary of Gallatin's birth would occur on January 29, 2011, and that, remarkably, there had been no full-scale biography of Gallatin published and broadly distributed in the United States since the nineteen-fifties. I determined that I wanted to write a new biography of Gallatin in time for his two hundred fiftieth birthday. I took the idea to my friend Daniel Haener, then deputy consul general of Switzerland in New York, who was acquainted with the work I had done on Lafayette and is a true believer in the value of the European-American relationship. He at once grasped the potential of the book and of an anniversary project around it. So then did his colleagues.

THE QUANDARY OF GALLATIN'S OBSCURITY

As we continued our discussions and as I pursued my research, an intriguing question came back again and again: Why had Gallatin been forgotten? Why was he obscure? What had happened to make history lose sight of him? He had been a senator and a congressman, had served as secretary of the Treasury under two presidents, had negotiated the end of the War of 1812 and secured for America its genuine independence, had been U.S. minister to France and to Great Britain, was present at the creation of New York University and the American Ethnological Society, had succeeded in banking, and had become an influential public intellectual at an age when most men retire and rest. He was prominent in his own time and deserves esteem in our day. Yet Gallatin passed into relative oblivion in the latter half of the nineteenth century after his death in 1849. On the surface, there were some fairly easy explanations for his absence from the assembly of honored Americans. He was, as his fellow Americans sometimes maliciously reminded him, a foreigner; he had not been born on American soil, even before independence. He had a French accent throughout his life. Unlike certain contemporaries who immigrated to America, such as Hamilton, he did not have an English education; his was the erudition of continental Europe, heavily influenced by France. His specializations, finance and diplomacy, were poorly understood by the average American and his contribution in those fields harder to grasp; with the exceptions of Benjamin Franklin and Alexander Hamilton, Americans have few early heroes who were not generals or presidents. Gallatin was intellectual in his approach; he was modest; he was content to let his accomplishments speak for themselves. It would have offended his dignity to boast. He therefore wrote no multivolume memoirs, nor did he author any weighty narration of his times. He left a voluminous correspondence but no autobiography. He sought neither fame nor glory from history, merely recognition from his peers and from his family, so he did not spend years fashioning an image that he could bequeath to posterity. People would think of him what they liked; he knew what he thought of himself. He was compelling but not charismatic, persuasive but not personable, sincere but not sentimental. His was not the personality that through gaiety, gravitas, or magnetism would immediately change the atmosphere of a room; he might change your life in a quiet, one-to-one conversation, rather than a public performance. His achievements were impressive, but they were complex; they could not speak for themselves. He was a European aristocrat of the eighteenth century, reticent and refined; he was hard for Americans to relate to, especially in the twenty-first century.

What This Book Seeks to Achieve

It was based on these observations that I decided to write this book. It is not designed to be an exhaustive recital of Gallatin's every move from birth to death. I have not investigated the inner workings of the many technical matters with which he had to deal over the decades. I hope that others will. There is room in this man's life and career for more doctoral theses than have been written about him. I have also excluded incidents that may have taken up much of Gallatin's time but add little to the understanding of who he was. Rather, the book attempts to explore the elements of his life that are most revelatory and illustrative: the development of his career, his contributions as a statesman, his self-realization as a man of ideas—but also his hesitations, his shortcomings, his aimlessness, his blind spots and blind alleys, his moments of not being sure quite what to do next. I point out and discuss some of these instances in the text that follows, and I describe others without comment, for you to judge for yourself. For all his accomplishments, here is a man who was intensely proud and private but at the same time intensely honest and human. He was a first-class analyst, but he was also empathetic, with sensitivity to his own and others' feelings. The purpose of the book is to help him come alive, to bring his story to a new audience in a new era, and to present him in such a way that his qualities as a man and his colossal contributions as a statesman may be recognized in our own day both as lasting, so long as we shall make the effort to remember them, and as relevant, so long as we shall have the wisdom to comprehend them.

This book tells the story of Gallatin's life and times in nine chapters that divide evenly into three sections: Gallatin's rise to maturity (chapters 1, 2, 3), his achievements at the pinnacle of power (chapters 4, 5, 6), and his accomplishments as a senior statesman (chapters 7, 8, 9). Within each of the three sections, in turn, the three chapters—and Gallatin's life—follow a parallel pattern: the first chapter of each third of the book (1, 4, 7) traces an upward slope of Gallatin's aspiration and achievement; the next chapter of each third (2, 5, 8) sees Gallatin facing setbacks and uncertainty; the third chapter of each third (3, 6, 9) consists of Gallatin extricating himself from those dilemmas and ascending to an even higher level of accomplishment. He rises, falls, and rises again. And he does that repeatedly. In the first set of three chapters, Gallatin receives all the benefits of his Genevan background and education, then seems to waste the opportunities of his youth and of America, only to emerge triumphant as leader of the House of Representatives and Jefferson's right-hand man. In the second set of three chapters, Gallatin acquits himself with brilliance as secretary of the Treasury under Jefferson, then endures enmity and frustration as secretary of the Treasury under Madison, only to emerge triumphant as the man who was of the essence in negotiating the end of the War of 1812 and offering America its genuine independence. In the last set of three chapters, Gallatin commences as an appreciated and effective senior statesman as minister to France, then miscalculates in domestic politics and takes on a rather desultory diplomatic assignment, only to emerge as a respected public intellectual carving out a new career from the age of seventy onward. Even if Gallatin had not accomplished all he did, it is worthwhile merely watching the man progress from stage to stage, through ups and downs, doubts and misgivings, errors and strokes of brilliance, on an exceptional human journey that resulted in recognition in his own day but too little recollection thereafter. I am proud to make his story available to you now. I hope you will enjoy sharing in the adventure of his amazing life and agree that America owes Albert Gallatin recognition as its Swiss founding father.

A SON OF GENEVA, 1761–1780

ALBERT GALLATIN came from an old and noble family. As far back as 1258 AD, fully five hundred years before Albert Gallatin was born, the family's aristocratic status was recorded in a document preserved until this day. In it, the abbess of the convent of Bella Comba, located in that region of northern Italy and southern France called Savoy, acknowledged receipt of a bequest from "Lord Fulcherius Gallatini, Knight."[1] In 1319, Guillaume Gallatini, knight, and his son Humbert bore witness to a princely contract. In 1334, Humbert's son, Noble Jean Gallatini of Arlod, pledged his fealty to the local lord and in his will of 1360 provided for his tomb in the local church. In 1402, Noble Henri Gallatini, grandson of Humbert, settled at Granges, in Savoy, about halfway between Geneva and Lyons. Henri's son, Noble Jean Gallatini of Granges, received the distinction, in an attestation from 1455 signed by Louis, Duke of Savoy, of the appellation *"dilectum scutiferum nostrum"* (our beloved equerry),[2] one of the duke's principal courtiers.

A son of that same Jean Gallatini—also named Jean—not only served as an equerry to Philibert, Duke of Savoy, but acceded in 1498 to a position as one of the duke's private secretaries, with the title of Viscount. Later, Pope Leo X appointed him an apostolic judge. In the year 1510, this Jean Gallatin was accepted and registered as a "citizen of Geneva." Only the patrician inhabitants of Geneva enjoyed the right of citizenship, and such citizenship constituted in Geneva the only patrician status.

GENEVA: A PROUD CITY BOTH SWISS AND INDEPENDENT

Geneva could claim as proud a past as the Gallatins themselves. The earliest inhabitants settled in Geneva in about 4500 BC. Geneva's first mention in literature came in the opening lines of Julius Caesar's *Gallic Wars*: writing of the Helvetians—the Swiss—Caesar identified the western end of their territory as the Lake of Geneva where it emptied into the River Rhone. Geneva was both a bridge and bulwark, a crossroads and a fortified city. Geneva's earliest cathedral—the seat of a Christian bishop—was built around 350 AD, and in 443 the city became the first capital of the Burgundians. Annexed to the kingdom of the Franks in 534, it returned to Burgundy in 888 and joined the Holy Roman Empire in 1034. Throughout the Middle Ages, Geneva was an important center of medieval fairs and markets. The Medicis of Florence began banking in Geneva in 1425.

From the eleventh to the fifteenth centuries, the bishop of the diocese of Geneva was also the lord of the town and a prince of the Holy Roman Empire. But the Dukes of Savoy coveted Geneva and increasingly achieved political and ecclesiastical control. The Genevans, to assert their independence, signed a treaty with the Swiss cantons of Bern and Fribourg in 1477. A new and stronger union with Fribourg in 1519 was overturned by the Duke of Savoy. In December 1525, the duke convened the General Council of the citizens of Geneva at weapon-point. The meeting became known as the "Council of the Halberds," to identify its having been held under duress. The duke compelled the council to vote against closer ties with the Swiss cantons and in favor of the authority of the Catholic bishop. The duke also insisted on receiving veto power over the appointment of lord mayors. Following the Council of the Halberds, those Genevans who deprecated fealty to Savoy and instead advocated closer confederation with the Swiss, known as Confederates, decided to resist. They first convinced the ruling councils of Bern and Fribourg to enter into a new pact of confederation and mutual assistance with Geneva. With the assurance of that double Swiss alliance in hand, the Confederates then persuaded their fellow Genevans to opt for a treaty with their Swiss allies rather than accept submission to the Duke of Savoy. The General Council of Geneva ratified that treaty in February 1526. The Duchy of Savoy, distracted at the time by other priorities in Italy, failed to oppose the decision with any force. At a stroke, therefore, Geneva provided for its military defense through the alliance with the Swiss cantons and achieved significant political autonomy in its external affairs. Geneva thus acquired a sense of itself as both Swiss and independent—a sentiment set to last for centuries thereafter.

The Confederates, having secured freedom for Geneva from external interference, then turned their attention to the reform of its internal government. During the years from 1527 to 1534, the Confederates introduced institutional changes that served to tighten their hold on power, consolidate the control of the city in the hands of a chosen few, and eliminate the authority of the bishop who represented the interests of Savoy and regulated religion in Geneva. Rather than deferring to the General Council of all citizens of Geneva, the Confederates created a Council of the Two Hundred and a more selective Council of the Sixty and provided for cross-membership between the two. In 1528, the Confederates abolished the electoral college established earlier by the Duke of Savoy, and they stipulated that candidates for lord mayor, limited to eight in total, would thereafter be selected by the Council of the Two Hundred. In 1530, the Confederates empowered the Council of the Two Hundred, rather than lord mayors, to name members of the government, known as the Small Council. In this way the Small Council and the Council of the Two Hundred became ever more interlocked: members of the Council of the Two Hundred chose the Small Council, which itself chose members of the Council of the Two Hundred. The Confederates may not have set out to create a tightly knit Genevan governing aristocracy over the coming centuries, but that is what this system ultimately produced.

During this period, the Confederates also reformed the justice system, instituted new courts, and created new judicial officers. The government increased its involvement in religious matters, which led to growing confrontation with the bishop. The civil authorities finally stripped the bishop of his supreme element of power, the right to pardon crimes. In retaliation, the bishop excommunicated the city of Geneva and removed his episcopal seat from the town. The Genevans asked the Catholic Church to appoint new ecclesiastical representatives, but the Church failed to respond. On October 1, 1534, the Council of the Two Hundred, of which Jean Gallatin was a member, together with the lord mayors, declared the bishop's seat vacant, took over the bishop's powers, and thus secured Geneva's internal independence from the dominance of Savoy. Soon thereafter, Geneva issued its own coinage and began styling itself a republic.

Geneva from the Reformation to the Enlightenment

In those years of rapid change, Geneva did not merely recast its civil institutions; it also altered its religion. The German Reformation had begun in October 1517 when Martin Luther's ninety-five theses were nailed to the door of the Castle Church in Wittenberg. Luther wished to see the extravagances of the Catholic Church give way to a more direct relationship between humanity and God. The first area beyond Germany to which the Reformation spread was Switzerland. Under the impulsion of Ulrich Zwingli, the Reformist pastor of the Grossmünster in Zurich, that canton adopted Protestantism in 1525, followed by Bern in 1528. Geneva, under the influence of its Bernese ally, gradually converted, as members of the Council of the Two Hundred and the population at large turned their back on Catholicism. In August 1535, the celebration of Mass was suspended. Geneva formally adopted the Reformation in May 1536.

It is often thought that John Calvin brought the Reformation to Geneva, but in fact Geneva had prepared the way for Calvin's reforms. Before Calvin became the patriarch of the Reformed tradition, he was a French humanist, born in the somewhat harsh and forbidding province of Picardy, north of Paris. He had trained as a lawyer but broke from the Catholic Church around 1530. He fled to Basle, in Swiss territory, and there he published the first edition of his *Institutes of the Christian Religion* in 1536. In August of the same year, shortly after fleeing France, Calvin was traveling from Basle to Strasbourg when he was forced to take a detour in order to circumnavigate a battle. This detour led Calvin to Geneva, where he met Guillaume Farel, a zealous evangelical French reformer who had already converted Neuchâtel to Protestantism. Farel directly threatened Calvin with divine imprecation if he refused to stay and lead the Reform in Geneva. Convinced both by Farel's plea for assistance and the curse that would befall him if he declined to remain, Calvin acquiesced. Given Farel's insistence, one might presume that Geneva was ripe for their reforms. As it turned out, the Genevans, who had just won independence from Savoy and strengthened control over their own internal affairs, refused to accept the independent ecclesiastical ordinances that Calvin and Farel sought to impose. Consequently, the Genevan civil leaders expelled them both from the city in 1538. Farel moved to Neuchâtel, and Calvin spent the next three years in Strasbourg.

Following Geneva's conversion to Protestantism, it lost its Catholic ally Fribourg, so Bern was its sole source of Swiss support. Geneva, having rejected the reforms of Calvin and Farel, therefore chose to adopt the Bernese model of Reformation. Yet after Calvin's departure and without his leadership, the Reform in Geneva lost momentum, and factions within the city began to militate for the return of the Catholic bishop. Consequently, the Genevan Reformers called Calvin back in September 1541 and agreed to accept his ecclesiastical ordinances and submit to the religious authority of Calvin and his fellow pastors. Calvin thereupon returned to Geneva and remained until his death in 1564.

Calvin brought both his legal training and his religious zeal to bear on Geneva. With the formal adoption of his *Ecclesiastical Ordinances* in the autumn of 1541 he reorganized the church and established four types of church officers: pastors, doctors, elders, and deacons. The *Ordinances* were approved by the Small Council and adopted by the General Council of Geneva's citizens. Calvin established a consistory, which included both ministers and elders, to monitor both the doctrine of the church and the discipline of the people. He emphasized preaching, discipline, education, and charity. He provided a new catechism and liturgy. Religious reform required the enforcement mechanism of the civil government. Not only were prostitution, debauchery, drunkenness, and bawdiness disallowed; there was also a prohibition on singing, dancing, games, and the wearing of jewelry, gold, or silver, as well as limitation of funeral expenditures and imposition of the requirement that Genevans walk on the streets rather than ride in carriages. Debts of bankrupts were passed on to their children, who could not occupy a public office until those debts were repaid. Most saints' days and other holy days were abolished.

Jean Gallatin died in 1536, the year Calvin first came to Geneva. Later in the sixteenth century, his grandson Claude continued the family tradition by serving as a lord mayor and secretary of state of the Republic of Geneva.

After Calvin's death, the House of Savoy returned to trouble Geneva's independence. Once more, Geneva responded by reinforcing its Swiss alliances, especially with the two most powerful cantons, Zurich and Bern. Savoy countered by intermittent siege and warfare. In December 1602, on one of the longest nights of the year, Savoy mounted an invasion of Geneva by sending soldiers to scale the city walls and charge the city gates. Roused from their beds, the citizens of Geneva dropped the portcullis at the New Gate, repulsed the invaders, and earned fame throughout Europe for their grit and glory in thwarting the *Escalade*. Louis Gallatin, a member of another branch of the family, gave his life for his city at the *Escalade*.

Yet the seventeenth century did not stay so happy: Geneva lost nearly a quarter of its population to the plague, smallpox, and famine. Then, in October 1685, Louis XIV, the Sun King, revoked the Edict of Nantes, which had allowed French Protestants, the Huguenots, full religious and civic rights. A wave of Huguenots migrated to Geneva, adding thousands to the population and bringing new industries: leatherworking, gold and silver smithery, and, above all, watchmaking. Thereafter, Geneva enjoyed exceptional peace and prosperity well into the eighteenth century. The city distinguished itself in watchmaking, calico cloths, and a new industry, banking, fueled by the borrowing needs of the French kings.

During the seventeenth and eighteenth centuries, four Gallatins became lord mayor, one of them first lord mayor on five occasions. By this time, four branches of the Gallatin family lived in Geneva. One family member, François Gallatin, in his will in 1699, established the Gallatin Trust to provide for members of the family in need of financial help. The Gallatin family was now equal to any and had married well with others: Sarasins, Navilles, Pictets. Both the Gallatin family and Geneva had reached their zenith.

ALBERT GALLATIN'S FAMILY AND EDUCATION IN GENEVA

Into this family and in this city Albert Gallatin was born on January 29, 1761. He came into the world in his parents' house in the Old Town, number 7 rue des Granges, where it intersected with the rue du Cheval Blanc. The impressive four-story stone structure boasted wide windows and broad façades in each street. Albert's father, Jean, was engaged in the commerce of watches. His mother, Sophie Albertine Rolaz, came from Rolle, about halfway along the north shore of Lake Geneva toward Lausanne. Jean and Sophie had their first child in 1756, a daughter named Susanne, but she suffered from an incurable nervous disability. Five years later the couple had a second child, this time a boy. He was baptized on February 7, 1761, nine days after birth, in the medieval Church of Saint-Germain, less than a minute's walk from his parents' house, and given the Christian names Abraham Alfonse Albert.

Jean, Albert's father, was actually a partner of his own father, Abraham, in the trading of watches. Abraham lived in the countryside just across the mouth of the lake from Geneva, at Pregny, with his remarkable wife, Louise Susanne Vaudenet, a friend of the French philosopher Voltaire, whose estate lay only one town away in Ferney, and of Frederick II, the landgrave, or count, of Hesse-Cassel, whose Hessian mercenaries later fought alongside the British and the Tories, against the continental patriots and the French, in the American War of Independence. In 1764, Jean, Albert's father, became a member of the Council of the Two Hundred, but he died prematurely the following year. Albert was only four years old. Albert's mother, Sophie, attempted to carry on the watch trade, but with her invalid nine-year-old daughter and her very young son, she was soon overwhelmed. Susanne, the little girl, was sent to live at Montpellier, on the French Mediterranean coast, where she could receive full-time medical treatment. Sophie's closest friend was an unmarried lady about forty years of age named Catherine Pictet. Miss Pictet was a cousin of the late Jean Gallatin, and after Jean died in the summer of 1765, Catherine Pictet persuaded Sophie Gallatin that she and her son would both be better off if Albert moved in with Miss Pictet, which he did in January 1766, around the time of his fifth birthday. He only saw his sister, Susanne, once after his father's death. Susanne died in Montpellier by the time she was twenty. Sophie continued in the watch business, but whether from the strain of early widowhood or some other cause, she died in March 1770 and left Albert an orphan at the age of nine. By then he had been living with Miss Pictet for four years, and he always thereafter considered Catherine Pictet as if she had been his natural mother.

Between Miss Pictet, his grandparents at Pregny, and a close-knit extended family, Albert lived a perfectly happy childhood. Miss Pictet gave him all the love and attention she would have devoted to a son of her own—he was her only care or responsibility. She home-schooled Albert until it was time for him to leave for boarding school, and all the while the Gallatin Trust, because of François Gallatin's foresight and generosity in 1699, provided for Miss Pictet's expenses in raising Albert and, later, for the fees of his education at school.

Geneva had long valued the merits of education. A civic-minded citizen, François de Versonnex, founded the first educational establishment in Geneva more than a century before Calvin, in 1420, on the street now known as the rue du Vieux Collège. Calvin desired a new school, and on June 5, 1559, the *Leges Academiae Genevensis,* or By-Laws of the Academy of Geneva, were announced in the Cathedral of Saint Peter. A magnificent new Renaissance building was built around an open quadrangle between 1558 and 1562. More than two hundred years later, the Academy remained the principal educational institution in Geneva.

Albert left Miss Pictet's in January 1773, when he was twelve years old, to become a boarding student at the Academy. The Academy was divided into a lower school, known as the College (in the French sense of a preparatory school), followed by an upper school, which was the Academy proper. Normally boys attended the lower school, the College, from age six to age fifteen. They learned to read and write French and Latin in the first three years, and thereafter virtually all teaching, from the age of nine, was in Latin. Albert Gallatin had the distinction, however, of having been schooled at home by Miss Pictet, so he had acquired a well-rounded education that his comrades in the College might have missed. When he became a boarder in January 1773, he entered the College only for the final year, as a kind of preparatory year for the Academy; he and his classmates then moved on together to the upper school, the Academy itself.

Gallatin followed the curriculum of the department of philosophy, which included humanities and science. He read Latin and Greek litera- ture and took courses in geography, history, French composition, elocu- tion, mathematics, and physics. Gallatin's course outline of his physics class with Mr. Le Sage ran to five handwritten columns describing four- teen notebooks subdivided into about a hundred topics. Beyond students' classroom work, they learned equitation and the use of weaponry.[3]

The eighteenth century was the Age of Enlightenment. Two leaders in Geneva served in particular to diminish the influence of strict Calvinism and advance philosophy and the natural sciences. Jean-Alphonse Turret- tini, a church minister and professor at the Academy, promoted the con- cept of tolerance and helped soften some longstanding doctrine in the ear- lier part of the century. Jean-Robert Chouet, a professor at the Academy and a lord mayor, advanced a series of reforms that revitalized the Acad- emy, its curriculum, and its teaching staff. Both Turrettini and Chouet fa- vored the philosophical questioning laid out in the *Discourse on Method* of René Descartes, as well as the experimental system of scientific examina- tion. Geneva transitioned from a doctrinal and dictatorial Calvinism to a more liberal-minded humanism.

When Gallatin was at the Academy, a number of his professors, like other distinguished minds living and teaching in Geneva at the time, were figures of legend. Louis Bertrand taught mathematics and was a geologist; he was a disciple of Euler, who had himself studied in Berlin. Gallatin also knew Jean Sénebier (he and one of Gallatin's uncles had gotten married to sisters): Sénebier came from one of the French Huguenot families that had fled to Geneva, became the head of the Geneva Library, compiled the *Literary History of Geneva,* wrote widely on scientific matters, and was a member of various intellectual organizations in Europe. The man who was to become known as the father of Swiss history, Johannes von Müller, was also teaching privately as a tutor to the Tronchin family in Geneva at the time. Although Müller was not a professor at the Academy, Gallatin knew him as well.

The outstanding figure of them all was Horace-Bénédict de Saussure, the rector—headmaster—of the Academy of Geneva when Gallatin started the upper school in 1774. Saussure was by this time the most celebrated of the intellectuals of the Geneva Enlightenment. When only twenty-two years old, he was named chair of philosophy at the Academy and gained fame as a botanist, naturalist, and geologist. He invented the hygrometer, a device that measures humidity in air, and went on to found the Society of

Arts of Geneva as well as the newspaper *Le Journal de Genève,* for which he wrote. But most of all Saussure achieved renown for his exploration of the Alps, until then feared as an area of danger and demons. He viewed Alpinism as a scientific quest, and from his first attempt to climb the Mont Blanc at Chamonix in 1760 until he finally reached the peak years afterward, he was a heroic figure, larger than life.

Solitary study was the custom at the Academy, but Gallatin formed several enduring friendships during his tenure there. One friend was Etienne Dumont, who later moved to England: he became a follower of the British social philosopher Jeremy Bentham and edited many of his works. François d'Ivernois established himself in England as well and became a British citizen, lawyer, scholar, and Knight of the Realm. Still another friend was Henri Hentsch, who, a few years after finishing at the Academy, founded a private firm that became Lombard Odier, the famous Geneva banking house. Jean Badollet, from a less aristocratic background than the others, was a fellow student of Gallatin's in the study of English. And Henri Serre was fascinated by the liberal ideas fomenting in politics at the time, both in Europe and America. It was with Serre that Gallatin was to leave Geneva for America, while Badollet (who they had hoped would join them at once) was to follow later.

Gallatin moved back home to live with Miss Pictet in April 1778, more than a year before he completed his studies at the Academy. Around the time he finished his final year, in May 1779, Miss Pictet began to notice Gallatin's "desire for independence."[4] We have no record from Gallatin of his feelings at the time, and he never spoke ill of Miss Pictet, then or later. Still, we may surmise that, for a young man who had been in boarding school, returning to the home of his foster mother at age seventeen, though it may have been comfortable compared to Spartan school lodgings, nonetheless must have felt confining. By this time, Miss Pictet was more than fifty years old and had been living on her own while Gallatin was away. Miss Pictet's letters to Gallatin in later years reveal her as entirely dedicated to Gallatin's welfare but often scolding him, reminding him of his faults and failings, and at the same time clinging and demanding affection. We do not know for certain when Gallatin first considered leaving Geneva, but it is not implausible that Gallatin, Badollet, and Serre were already contemplating some such plan as they finished their studies at the Academy. Certainly if they were to leave together, each would have had to complete his studies successfully. Gallatin finished first in his class in Latin translation, mathematics, and natural philosophy. But he was worried about Badollet. He therefore took it upon himself to write a letter to their schoolmaster, the great Horace-Bénédict de Saussure, on the very day of their final exams, which Saussure was to administer orally to each individual student:

Sir,

I am very perturbed to bother you so often with visits and letters, but I know how kind you are and so I am taking the liberty of writing to you in order to ask for your indulgence, not for myself, though I might have done, had I not got my fever to go down, such that I will be able to take my exam today.

Within the list of students that I had the honor to bring to you on Saturday, there was one named Badollet, with a cross next to the name, because I was unsure whether he would be able to take his exam. He is a young man with great insight and taste for mathematics and physics; but he has nothing, he is obliged to feed and house himself, to pay for his own upkeep, such that he has to give four lessons a day, which has prevented him from spending as much time as he would like on philosophy and forced him to do just the required homework, which he has kept to, as you have been able to notice since he has only missed one of your lessons this whole year and always answered when called on. With that in mind, I have no doubt that despite the little time he has had, he would have done a very fine examination: but unfortunately, for the past fortnight, he has had severe lower back pains, owing either to kidney stones or rheumatism, which have made it impossible for him to do any work. . . .

He is too shy to ask for any extensions, so I am writing to you without his knowledge to request that you quiz him on statistics, which is the subject he knows best. I would like him to do well on his exam because that will encourage him in the study of philosophy, in which he will certainly do well. I am relying on [you], one of the most outstanding Men of Science of our time, and hoping that you will not refuse this favor requested by one of your greatest admirers, who will one day attempt to follow in your footsteps. As I am doing this completely unbeknownst to Badollet, I would request that you not mention it to him at the exam. Would you mind, Sir, if this is not too much trouble, indicating a brief answer, orally, or in writing, to the person who will bring you this note? I have the honor to be, with profound respect, your very humble and very obedient servant.

A. Gallatin[5]

The letter is remarkable in at least three ways—and revelatory of aspects of Gallatin's character. First, Gallatin is standing up for his friend without asking anything for himself, although this apparent generosity may conceal the desire to ensure that Badollet passes his exams so they can leave together as graduates. Second, Gallatin is quite bold toward an authority figure in asking Saussure for a sign of assent. Third, Gallatin proclaims a high ambition, to follow in Saussure's footsteps. These three traits—indirectness, audacity, and a thirst for success (but often without knowing what form that success might take) recur frequently in Gallatin's behavior in later years.

GALLATIN FACES HIS OPTIONS FOR THE FUTURE

After Gallatin graduated from the Academy, he continued to live with Miss Pictet and indeed tutored her nephew, Isaac Pictet, including, we are told, some coaching in English. Whether or not Gallatin, Badollet, and Serre had already begun to entertain a plan to leave Geneva, the time had come for Gallatin to make some choice about his next step in life.

He could have gone into the service of the Republic of Geneva. The Geneva where Albert Gallatin grew up had reached a population of just under twenty-five thousand, of whom about two thousand "citizens of Geneva" were entitled to vote. It was a republic but by no means a democracy. At the top rung of the social and political ladder stood the "patricians," who controlled the government. The patricians included the political parties known as *Négatifs* and *Ultra-Négatifs,* so called because they argued that the aristocratic government retained the right to negate the majority vote of the General Council, which comprised citizens and bourgeois and numbered two thousand men. Lower down the ladder, a third of the population were the "inhabitants" of Geneva, immigrants mainly from Switzerland and Germany who held jobs in trade and menial labor and who had been granted residence permits against payment of a fee. Inhabitants' children who were born in Geneva were known as "natives." Neither inhabitants nor natives held any political rights. The Gallatin family, given their social standing and political traditions, were established *Négatifs* and thoroughly aristocratic and conservative in their views and traditions. This carried over into their relationships, such as the friendship that Albert's grandmother Madame Gallatin-Vaudenet enjoyed with Voltaire, a great philosopher but also a darling of Europe's princes, and with the Landgrave of Hesse-Cassel.

During the eighteenth century in Geneva, ordinary city dwellers and citizens largely excluded from power increasingly called for a greater voice in their government, which the *Négatifs* granted only partially and reluctantly. Had Gallatin entered public service, he would have been caught in the tension between his conservative family tradition and the progressive political currents then growing in the city.

As to the professions, Gallatin had no particular desire to attend law school: lawyering in Geneva was not then a lucrative occupation and was mostly of an administrative nature. He had no real aptitude for theology; that would have been a specialization he might have pursued earlier at the Academy. But this was the Enlightenment, and even though a number of his contemporaries went on to become pastors, the Calvinist influence exercised no particular religious ascendancy on him—and indeed, he displayed no attraction to religion at any stage of his life. He excelled in science and could perhaps have become a doctor, but once more there was no natural affinity. There remained the possibility of going into business. His grandfather's watch trading held little appeal, and it is not clear that there was enough substance to it to constitute a genuine career option for Gallatin.

In the absence of immediate prospects in Geneva, Gallatin could consider opportunities abroad. As we have seen, a number of his friends ended up moving to England. The Swiss had lived and worked outside their native land for generations. Such an expatriate option was further legitimated by two Genevans who achieved fame or fortune in neighboring France during Gallatin's youth: Jean-Jacques Rousseau, the philosopher, and Jacques Necker, the financier. Each was to become a model of sorts for Gallatin in later years.

Rousseau was one of the most influential philosophical and political voices of the eighteenth century. The son of a watchmaker, he was a progressive thinker who clashed frequently with the elitist Voltaire. Although Rousseau lived mostly in France, or in other parts of Switzerland, he proudly styled himself a "Citizen of Geneva." Rousseau considered that man was purest in a state of nature—this gave rise to the misstatement of his views that man was a "noble savage"—and that society corrupted men, even though they needed to live in society for their mutual benefit. To counteract this corrupting effect, men should institute government that diminished injustice and reflected the general will. Education, instead of relying on discipline and compulsion, should be based on encouragement and stimulation. These ideas were embodied in his novel *Émile* and his treatise *The Social Contract.* Rousseau was among the first philosophers to emphasize individual rights and justice, even at the expense of order and authority. In literature, he was one of the earliest Romantics, who looked inward to know themselves by their feelings, rather than adhering to an external standard dictated by logic and tradition. Adopted by the French as one of their own, Rousseau was entombed in the Pantheon in Paris. Rousseau was a hero of Geneva, and Gallatin, like his friends, cannot have been indifferent to Rousseau or his political, philosophical, and personal example. Some of Gallatin's choices in later years, particularly an attraction to life in the wilderness, reflected the possible influence of Rousseau on his thinking.

Jacques Necker was a Genevan of another stripe. Of Prussian descent, he became a citizen of Geneva himself but spent most of his career in Paris as a banker amassing great wealth. In order to move into public life, he secured a position as a director of the French East India Company. He was designated the Resident of Geneva in Paris, essentially an ambassadorial post. He defended the mercantilism—intervention by the state in the private economy—that had characterized France since the time of Louis XIV and his finance minister Colbert and opposed the laisser-faire policies of the current finance minister, Turgot. In this way, he positioned himself to be appointed director general of finances to King Louis XVI. Necker was the very model of a Genevan who by his ambition and accomplishments made his career abroad a success—and, like Rousseau, he did it in France. Gallatin emulated Necker later in his career when he became the equivalent of the finance minister, secretary of the Treasury, in the United States.

Gallatin also shared with Necker a more personal distinction: he was surrounded by strong women. Necker married Susanne Curchod, who, despite being described as starchy later in life, had been sufficiently seductive to win the heart of young Edward Gibbon, the author of *The History of the Decline and Fall of the Roman Empire.* Of his father's refusal to consent to their marriage, Gibbon famously wrote, "I sighed as a lover, I obeyed as a son."[6] Jacques and Susanne Necker's daughter Germaine, not far from Gallatin's age, became famous throughout Europe as Madame de Staël, a wild genius and accomplished author.

Gallatin knew that for many generations members of his family had distinguished themselves in the profession of arms. Louis fell at the *Escalade,* but there were others. Voltaire even joked in a letter to the Count d'Argental that the Gallatins had been getting themselves killed in the service of the French since the time of King Henri IV, a couple of centuries before. More recently, François Gallatin died at the Battle of Ostend in 1745, another Gallatin gave his life at the Battle of Marburg in 1760, and among Albert Gallatin's cousins several were serving in Swiss regiments or in the forces of foreign sovereigns, including the British Crown. Given all that we know about Albert Gallatin, even up to this stage in his life, a military career is among the least fitting. He was of average height and build, but he was a soldier neither by temperament—far too philosophical and academic—nor by choice. Still, that did not stop his grandmother, the formidable Madame Gallatin-Vaudenet, from proposing that he should take a commission as a lieutenant colonel in the service of her friend the Landgrave of Hesse-Cassel. Perhaps a few years of toughening up and field experience would be just what he needed. But the prospect filled him with horror, from a practical and perhaps a moral point of view, especially as the Hessians were fighting against American independence. He shot back at her that he would never serve a tyrant—and she gave him a slap on the ear for his disrespect. Gallatin's rejection of his grandmother's admonishment in such terms certainly contains a Rousseauian echo—a preference for the general good over the will of the ruler; and resistance to autocratic authority was very much in the spirit of the epoch in Geneva. But Gallatin at the time still held the views of a *Négatif*.[7] In the coming years, as his political philosophy evolved, he defined his positions less by resistance to authority than by an attraction to moderation. He preferred pragmatism to ideology. Even as he eventually entered politics in a camp that opposed strong central government control, he remained wary of the potential tyranny of the people. In the same pursuit of moderation, Gallatin, throughout his life, always preferred peace to bellicosity. So while it is tempting to interpret his riposte to Madame Gallatin-Vaudenet as a first statement of a political creed, in fact it more probably reflected an act of personal rebellion against an overpowering figure of family authority and, perhaps, a sense of dread at the prospect of a soldier's life.

THE DECISION TO LEAVE HOME AND SEEK HIS FORTUNE

As Gallatin thought about his future, he was also conscious that he had no family fortune to fall back on. Someone from so aristocratic a family in a larger country might have owned houses and estates, but for a "citizen of Geneva" to amass such properties was not easy at home. In accordance with the Genevan custom, the inheritance he was entitled to would be his only on his twenty-fifth birthday. Badollet and Serre had between them no money at all. Gallatin and the others settled on their ambition: they wanted to make money. They would seek their fortune. It was difficult to see how to do that in Geneva, so they decided to go abroad. There is no indication they meant to leave forever. Perhaps they would strike it rich quickly, come back to Geneva with their newfound wealth, and live happily ever after. At eighteen or nineteen years old, anything seems possible.

What was perhaps more extraordinary than the idea of leaving in the first place was the idea of leaving for America. Rousseau and Necker had both succeeded in neighboring France. Others of their schoolmates went to England, a perfectly logical choice if one sought a Protestant country with greater individual freedom. On the other hand, why not think big? They were not planning the first-ever Atlantic crossing. America still had lots of wilderness, to satisfy the Rousseau in them, but it had been settled by Europeans for more than a century and a half. They had met some Americans in Geneva as well. Franklin Bache, the grandson of Benjamin Franklin, the Penns of Pennsylvania, and Francis Kinloch and William Smith from South Carolina had all completed their educations as eighteenth-century gentlemen in Geneva.

Gallatin and Serre planned their departure together, and Badollet was almost certainly part of the plot because he was expected to join them for the journey, though he did not finally leave when they did. The young men decided to say nothing of their plans. They may have been entering their manhood, but they were not long out of short trousers, and if Madame Gallatin-Vaudenet could still slap her grandson, imagine their families' reaction to a harebrained scheme such as this one. There was also the conundrum of Miss Pictet. Knowing how sensitive she was, Gallatin would have been hard-pressed to tell her he was leaving her. He loved her as his mother, and she loved him as her son. He knew he would break her heart— and crumple his own resolve. And lastly, there was a girlfriend, "*une amie*," referred to only once in Gallatin's surviving correspondence but someone it would be hard for him to leave. Again, how to explain? Better a clean break all round than the tears and trials of an attempted, and maybe even a failed, departure. In short, they said nothing because to say something was still worse an alternative.

On April 1, 1780, at the age of nineteen, Gallatin and Serre left Geneva, in the expectation that Badollet would follow later. Their friend Henri Hentsch took responsibility for telling the families what had happened. For money, Gallatin and Serre had one hundred sixty gold Louis, about the equivalent of eight hundred silver dollars, all of Gallatin's savings. They headed almost due west for the French port of Nantes, a distance of three hundred seventy miles. They would have had to hire horses, stay in inns, and pay road tolls. Depending on how much they chose to hurry, crossing the whole of France took them several days if not indeed more than a week.

Consternation prevailed in the Gallatin family. But the family had to wait for news, and for a mailing address, until the young men had crossed France and posted a letter back to Geneva. The family's reaction was impeccable. They were hurt and bewildered by such a rash act—and they did not hesitate to say so. At the same time, they were supportive and respected Albert's decision. They did not chase him across France, they did not order him to come home, they did not expel him from the family. Albert Gallatin's legal guardian—an older male relative responsible for Albert's inheritance until his majority at age twenty-five—wrote him a lengthy letter on May 21, 1780, setting out, in sympathetic but brutally frank terms, how the family felt. He stressed their grief at Gallatin's lack of trust, when his family had done so much for him and could have done so much more to smooth the way, had he only taken them into his confidence. His guardian expressed the family's worry that he had too little money to get by, that he would find America unmanageably expensive, and that his skills were ill suited to the challenges he would face trying to live off the land or in a trade. Gallatin's guardian asked somewhat sarcastically how Gallatin would earn a living if all these ventures failed: "by giving lessons? What a pitiful solution." He even admitted a fear that Gallatin's natural indolence—his inclination to dream and to read—would prevent him from getting ahead. He also criticized Albert sternly for his cruelty toward Miss Pictet.[8]

Miss Pictet was in despair. She wrote to Gallatin more than a month after his departure, in late May, to scold him for leaving. She could not understand how he did not trust her enough to tell her of his plans. She blamed herself for something, but she was not quite sure what:

> One loves as one can, all hearts are not made to love the same way, and perhaps I was lacking in what it took to secure your affection. In fact I am far from bothered to think that you love me only a little; if you loved me too much, the idea of my suffering would upset your happiness, which is the first and dearest of my wishes.

In this same letter, she said, "You see I am not yet cured of the habit of giving you advice, even though I know you do not like it and you only believe in your own judgment."[9]

Despite the family's consternation with Gallatin, they did everything they could to secure letters of introduction and send him money. Miss Pictet wrote a letter to Francis Kinloch, who had left Geneva and was by now a member of the Continental Congress in Philadelphia:

> Although I have not had the privilege of making your acquaintance, I have heard too much of your integrity and kindness to refrain from asking you a favor that is absolutely vital to my happiness in life. Two young men from this city, named Gallatin and Serre, dissatisfied with the amount of their wealth, which indeed is not large, and having got it into their heads that they should seek their fortune themselves, with a bit of additional enthusiasm for Americans, have set off for Philadelphia. They are both full of honor, right thinking, well behaved, and have never caused any trouble to their families, who are very sorry to have seen them go. I implore your kindness for them both. Gallatin, whom I love as my own son, having brought him up since his earliest childhood, must have been recommended to you by Mr. Müller. They both have talent and knowledge, but I believe that they know nothing about business or farming, which is how they imagine they will make their fortune.[10]

The family also asked the Duc de La Rochefoucauld to secure a letter of introduction for the young men from Benjamin Franklin, then the American minister in Paris. Franklin wrote back saying, "I enclose the letter you desired for the two young gentlemen of Geneva. But their friends would do well to prevent their voyage."[11] America was in the throes of a revolutionary war. Miss Pictet then wrote to Gallatin to say that she has just received this, or another, letter from Benjamin Franklin, conveyed to her by Johannes von Müller, but went on to tell Gallatin of her worry that he would be confronted with pirates and bandits and the great poverty caused by wartime conditions.[12] She continued to write throughout May and early June of 1780. Some of her letters did not reach him for more than a year.

Meanwhile, at Nantes, Albert Gallatin and Henri Serre secured passage not to Philadelphia but to Boston. They sailed on the *Katty,* an American ship whose captain—a man called Loring—Gallatin described as dishonest, stupid, and superstitious. They waited and waited for a favorable wind. They had used up fully half their money to cross France, pay for their passage to America, and buy tea they meant to resell in Boston. While they were waiting, Gallatin wrote to Badollet from Pimbeuf, the port town about eight leagues south of Nantes where they were moored. He asked Badollet why he had not written and hoped he would follow soon. He told Badollet he had an address in America, care of bankers in Philadelphia, and spoke of the correspondence from his family: "I have received letters so kind that they almost crushed me and in which I am also promised money and recommendations if I carry on. . . . We have nothing more to worry about; we've been promised our plans won't be obstructed if we want to keep to them. Hentsch has done a great job. Goodbye; the mail is going. . . . Serre sends his best. He's asleep."[13] They sailed from Lorient on May 27, 1780.

GALLATIN CARRIES GENEVA WITH HIM
TO THE NEW WORLD

Who was this Albert Gallatin who then crossed to the New World? In every way, he was a product of his family, of his city, and of his time. He knew the family genealogy by heart, from Fulcherius Gallatini through all the equerries, lord mayors, and branches down to his day. At the end of his life he was still able to comment on the family tree and the family coat of arms.[14] He knew the history of Geneva as his own, and he carried with him his city's character as his own: Swiss and independent. He knew that throughout the centuries, this fiercely proud city on a hill had, by self-reliance and astute alliances, gained, lost, and then regained its freedom, through conquests, wars, the Reformation, famine, plague, and the *Escalade*. Gallatin was a creature of this City of Calvin, the home of the Academy, the source of the Geneva Enlightenment. He carried with him examples from his family and his city: Rousseau, Necker, and Horace-Bénédict de Saussure. He was European and aristocratic and highly educated, but he was also Swiss and diligent and resilient.

Moreover, the Gallatin who left Geneva was a person fully formed. All his principal characteristics were already in place. During the rest of his life he acquired few new traits or tastes. The traits and tastes he took with him reflected his Genevan upbringing. As an intellect, he was more of an analyst than a theorist. He preferred an examination of the facts over adherence to any ideology. This was the mentality of the Geneva watchmaker in his personality. In future years, that pragmatism allowed him to face personal and political setbacks, but it also meant that he failed to stand on principle and eschewed intimacy with colleagues. In addition, just as he defied his family's authority, he was not inclined to defer to any figure of authority— even, later, the president of the United States. Just as he was not intimidated by Horace-Bénédict de Saussure, he was not awed by other figures of greatness. This was the proud and independent Genevan in him. He did not need validation of his worth from others, but, by the same token, he often neglected throughout his career to provide the validation of worth to others that they craved more than he. This detachment isolated him and created enemies who felt snubbed by the European aristocrat too grand, in their view, to offer them displays of respect. He was in fact proud and private, but they viewed him as arrogant and aloof. The same spirit of pragmatism and independence, at multiple turning points later in life, led Gallatin to make decisions based so much on his own view of what was the right answer for himself at the time that he missed opportunities to capitalize on circumstances. He often operated so close to the facts and so much alone that he sometimes underestimated his own role in history. He would have benefited from a greater ability to step back, view the big picture, and articulate strategy—including for himself and his career. His lack of interest for the larger context and his own place in it perhaps explains why he kept no diary and wrote no history of his own. As far as his tastes were concerned, Gallatin retained his love of reading throughout his life but was immune to other attractions and pursuits: he appears to have had no interest in the theater, music, or the visual arts, food or wine, sport or games. He lived in America without ever becoming American in his habits or his mode of thinking. He retained a French accent and elaborate syntax in his speaking and his writing until the end of his days. He never revered America with a near-religious faith as so many Americans did. He did not wax romantic about the concept of liberty. And he made no patriotic speeches, nor did he wrap himself in the flag. Until the end of his life, he was often considered a foreigner.

So as Gallatin said farewell to Geneva, he in fact brought to America all the marks of his Genevan background, upbringing, and education—and he retained those characteristics, both positive and negative, until the end of his life. Even as he went on to serve his adopted country and secure its own ever-greater independence in a long and distinguished career, he remained what he was the day he left home: a son of Geneva.

[2]

AMERICAN BEGINNINGS, 1780–1793

GALLATIN had many reasons to regret his departure from Geneva. He upset his family. He and Serre were seriously short of money, even if more had been promised. The first mate of the *Katty* demanded an exorbitant sum as a freight charge to carry their tea. He stole some of their clothing and money. They had salt beef to eat and contaminated water to drink on the passage across. Yet the excitement of adventure, the exhilaration of independence, the expectation of opportunities all outweighed any residual reluctance. They had a few close encounters with corsairs who chased their ship, but otherwise the crossing was placid, lengthy, and boring. They landed a month and a half after setting sail, on July 14, 1780, at Cape Ann, Massachusetts. The following day, they left Gloucester, Massachusetts, on horseback and rode to Boston, where they took up lodgings at a house kept by a Frenchman named Tahon.

Over the coming months Gallatin and Serre tried to sell their tea, but they had no luck: the Revolutionary War was continuing, and economic activity was depressed. They had wanted to go to Philadelphia, where the people to whom they had letters of introduction were meant to be. It was where their money had been sent and where letters from home would arrive. But the dug-in positions of the Revolutionary War made traveling to Philadelphia problematic if not unthinkable. So the painstaking efforts of the Gallatin family to get them off to a good start served little avail while they were marooned in Boston.

In September 1780, Gallatin sent a long letter to Badollet in Geneva:

> Boston is a city about of about 18 thousand souls, built on a peninsula that is longer than it is wide. I think it is bigger than Geneva, but there are gardens, meadows, and orchards in the middle of the town, and each family generally has its own house. . . . A few straight streets, no impressive public buildings, and a vast harbor defended by islands that leaves only two small openings, which would make the town impregnable if attacked. That's about all I have to say about Boston. The inhabitants are neither

refined nor honorable nor educated; they are quite full of themselves, as are the French, who are thoroughly detested by the Bostonians born here. We're very bored in Boston. There are no public amusements, and there is a lot of superstition, so that on a Sunday you can't sing, or play the violin or cards or bowls, and so on. I can tell you we really need you here to be able to enjoy ourselves. In the meantime, give us some news and tell us what's going on in Geneva politics. I'll make it worth your while by telling you something about this country.[1]

Gallatin then continued with an analysis, gleaned only since his and Serre's arrival in mid-July, of the organization of Massachusetts and its political system. With multiple inaccuracies, doubtless due to hearsay and incomplete information, he described the number and types of counties and towns, the institutions of representative government, and the police and justice system and then turned to a brief analysis of the economy (agriculture, shipbuilding) and mentioned a college and a library in nearby Cambridge, Massachusetts, but which he had not yet been able to visit. Already upon arrival, Gallatin began to be captivated by the structures of government and the economy in America.

DISCOVERING THEIR AMERICA

Still, Gallatin and Serre's purpose in coming was to make their fortune, and this sojourn in Boston was not advancing that plan. At Tahon's establishment they met a French-speaking Swiss woman married to a Mr. de Lesdernier, who had been a farmer in Russin, near Geneva. The Lesderniers had already been in America for thirty years and had lived in Nova Scotia. A couple of years before, the French-speaking population had risen up against the British, who controlled that Canadian province, but they had failed and fled. The Lesderniers had a son who lived in Maine—which then belonged to Massachusetts—at a place called Machias, on the Bay of Fundy, about as far north as one could go and still be in the territory of the United States. Without prospects in Boston and with no pathway to Philadelphia, Gallatin and Serre decided to accompany Mr. and Mrs. de Lesdernier to Machias in late September. Hoping to turn a profit, Gallatin and Serre exchanged their tea for rum, sugar, and tobacco to sell in Maine, and they left for Machias with Mr. de Lesdernier on October 1, 1780.

For the trip to Maine, a small vessel carried them from Boston up the Atlantic coast. Gallatin said that this was in fact a riskier journey than the one that had brought them across the Atlantic. They reached their destination after two weeks, but they were in for a bit of a shock. Machias was five miles inland from the sea, not a port town at all. It was inhabited by about one hundred fifty families in log cabins spread over ten square miles. The military garrison, Fort Gates, consisted of fewer than two dozen soldiers and a couple of cannons. The people had no currency—money was scarce, and barter was the rule when self-sustenance was not—but there were no valuables, such as fur or fish, to barter against. Gallatin ended up taking payment for their rum, sugar, and tobacco in the form of a note payable, drawn on the treasury of the state of Massachusetts for four hundred dollars. The exchequer of the state was in such a condition that he could not redeem it for full value, and he ended up selling it for one hundred dollars, an early lesson in government finance.

Gallatin and Serre wintered in Machias, lodging with a Colonel Allan and with the Lesderniers' son, a bachelor and good company. They went up to Passamaquoddy Bay on the Canadian border with Colonel Allan, and at one point Gallatin was left in charge of some soldiers, volunteers, and Indians as well as a military installation consisting of a piece of temporary construction and one cannon. This was the closest Gallatin ever got to any kind of military service, and he saw neither action nor enemy.

They lasted a year in Maine, mainly making their living as woodcutters, and despite the Rousseauesque attractions of the wild, Gallatin had no desire to spend another winter in the place. They certainly had not come closer to making their fortune. They originally hoped to buy land, but farming was difficult and they were far from a population of buyers. The barter economy provided no opportunity for trade and in fact had cost Gallatin money. The Battle of Yorktown in October 1781 marked the virtual end of the military portion of the War of Independence and the defeat of the British and Tories, together with the Hessian mercenaries of the Landgrave of Hesse-Cassel. Gallatin and Serre returned to Boston around this time, in the autumn of 1781, and they fell back on their French as a way to make a living: they hired themselves out as French teachers to Bostonians who wanted to learn the language. Just as Gallatin's guardian had predicted, they ended up trying to make a living by giving lessons.

As summer arrived in 1782, they had already been in America for almost two years and certainly had come no closer to making any sort of money, much less a fortune. Miss Pictet, who by now knew that they were in Boston and not in Philadelphia, continued her efforts at securing introductions, including writing from Geneva to Dr. Samuel Cooper, the pastor of the Brattle Street Church in Boston and a member of the Corporation of Harvard College, whose grandson had studied in Geneva. Two years earlier, at the very time that Gallatin and Serre arrived in Boston, the Harvard overseers had decided to offer French as an optional course for students whose parents were prepared to pay an extra fee for those lessons. Dr. Cooper found Gallatin—it would have been more enterprising of Gallatin to make the first approach to Cooper—and offered him a position teaching French. On July 2, 1782, the Corporation of Harvard College voted to make Gallatin a French instructor and give him the use of the library, a room in the College, and meals in the common room if he wished to pay for them. Thus Gallatin's first genuine job in America, after two years of drifting, was as a French teacher at Harvard.

He had about seventy students and quickly reverted to the methodical ways he had learned at the Academy of Geneva. His carefully preserved notes contain the names of his pupils, including some of the sons of the great New England families of the time: Amory, Pyncheon, and Otis among them. It was said of Gallatin then that he lived frugally and simply, and indeed, he made no obvious mark on society in Boston. William Bentley, a theology student, became his best American friend. Miss Pictet wrote to him at the time:

> You tell me your health is good; I find you have put it to a terrible test, and even though your life is less difficult than when you were a woodcutter in Machias, the amount of lessons you are obliged to give seems to me a very tiresome and boring thing. I hope you will have become a bit less difficult and less subject to boredom.[2]

In July 1783, after three years in America and a year at Harvard, Gallatin received a certificate signed by the president of Harvard College, Joseph Willard, the professor of divinity Edward Wigglesworth, and Dr. Cooper himself attesting to Gallatin's excellent performance and integrity.

Gallatin continued to seek opportunities to achieve business success, and his principal goal remained to make money by buying land that could then be farmed, developed, or sold at a profit. During the spring of 1783 in Boston, Gallatin met a Frenchman named Jean Savary de Valcoulon, from Lyons. Savary was entranced by the American revolutionary struggle, and for that reason he became the collection agent for another Frenchman, René Rapicault, who had provided money and matériel to the state of Virginia during the Revolutionary War. Now that the war was over, Rapicault sought repayment.

Savary, as his agent, journeyed to the United States with the intention of collecting Rapicault's debts from the government of Virginia in the state capital, Richmond. Savary arrived in America in the port of Boston, where Gallatin met him. Because Savary spoke no English at all, he needed an interpreter and someone who could follow through with the Americans as he set out to collect Rapicault's debts from the Virginia government. Savary was alert, as well, to other opportunities to make money. By now Gallatin had achieved near fluency in English, though he still had a very strong French accent, so it was agreed that Gallatin should become Savary's interpreter and traveling companion from Boston to Richmond. Henri Serre still had teaching obligations in Boston—he had carried on tutoring individual students—and intended to join them later. America was finally at peace and independent of British rule, allowing travel throughout the thirteen colonies. It appears that Savary was paying the bills and setting the pace. From Gallatin's point of view, the journey with Savary represented the potential to form a business partnership and, after three years confined to Massachusetts and its territory of Maine, the opportunity to see the America he had come for in the first place.

Gallatin and Savary left Boston and journeyed to Providence, Rhode Island, where Gallatin admired the quality of the buildings and the trading atmosphere, and visited the college, which had only twelve students. He was not able to see the president of the college, but he did have a discussion with the sole professor, who said they would be delighted to have a French teacher there and, though they had almost no funds to pay him, would be glad to try to drum up local support. Gallatin communicated this opportunity back to Serre. From Providence, Savary and Gallatin went on to have dinner in Newport, which Gallatin found well situated and pleasant. They sailed down the coast past Long Island in the company of a disagreeable Frenchman and reached New York City, which Gallatin found oppressively hot in mid-July. He remarked that there were quite a few soldiers, sailors, and refugees in New York. He found the girls in New York less attractive than in Boston. Neither he nor Savary had a single romantic adventure on the way from Boston to New York. Like many a tourist before and since, Gallatin and Savary went to the theater during their visit. They moved on to Philadelphia, then the capital of the United States. Apparently Savary was in no hurry to reach Richmond. For Gallatin, this journey represented the real beginning of his broader American experience, and he must have been delighted at the chance to spend time in the capital city.

Serre joined them in Philadelphia as planned, and they came to a reckoning of his and Gallatin's expenses since they had reached America.

Together they had spent about sixteen hundred dollars, and of this Serre had provided only about three hundred. So, splitting the expenses evenly, Serre still owed Gallatin around five hundred dollars. Since Serre's family had refused to send him any money at all, he gave Gallatin a note payable for his portion of the expenses. He then left Philadelphia with another Swiss, named Mussard, to sail for Jamaica. In fact, Serre died there of a fever the following year. His five-hundred-dollar debt to Gallatin was acquitted by Serre's sister, who left the sum to Gallatin in her will fifty-three years later, even though Gallatin never asked for repayment.

Less than a year after Gallatin and Serre had left home, in January and February 1781, popular uprisings occurred in Geneva, against the power of the Small Council. A new law entitled natives as well as country dwellers to achieve the status of citizen. During the troubles, rebels occupied the town. The patricians called on their neighbors—King Louis XVI of France, the Swiss Republic of Bern, and the king of Sardinia—to intervene. In July 1782, the combined forces of these three allied powers overturned the occupying forces, but the broadening of citizenship remained in force. After a placid and prosperous eighteenth century up to that point, the city, and particularly the patrician *Négatifs* who controlled the Small Council, had been seriously shaken up.

GALLATIN DECIDES TO MAKE AMERICA HIS HOME

Gallatin, by this time, had been more than three years in America; and the United States had come into being after victory in the War of Independence. Even if the country worked imperfectly under the Articles of Confederation, it was a land at peace and, at least in domestic affairs, in control of its own destiny. When Gallatin left Geneva in 1780, he thought only of making his fortune and displayed no special interest in the spirit of the American Revolution. Now, with the upheavals in Geneva and the *Négatifs* clinging to a form of autocratic power, Gallatin felt the time had come to renounce Geneva and adopt America. His letter to Badollet from Philadelphia on October 1, 1783, marks a significant turning point in his views and his intentions, the first occasion on which he articulates a vision of himself in America:

> My dear friend, I have just received your letter of March 20 which in some ways gives me the greatest pleasure, but in apprising me of the difficult circumstances of our beloved homeland it also succeeded in removing

any hope I might have of settling there. No, my friend, it is impossible for a sensible and virtuous man, born the citizen of a free state, and who has come to taste the love of independence that exists in the freest country of the universe; it is impossible, I say, for this man, whatever his youthful prejudice might have been, to go anywhere and play the part of a tyrant or a slave, and as I do not see any other status to choose from in Geneva, I find myself obliged to renounce once and for all those dear walls of my birthplace, my family, and my friends, unless a new revolution should change the state of affairs. You see by what I just said that my family's way of thinking has no influence on mine and that I have changed what I think since I left Europe. It is perfectly easy when one is surrounded by people who all think the same way to get into the habit of thinking as they do. . . . So that is enough to justify my having been a *Négatif* at age nineteen when I left Geneva. But at three thousand miles' remove one has a much healthier judgment. . . . That is what little by little produced a major change in my opinion following my arrival in America. I soon became convinced that, in comparing the government of America with that of Geneva, the latter was founded on incorrect principles.[3]

Gallatin continued with a technical disquisition on Geneva's lack of the representative virtues he found in the American form of government and predicted that the aristocratic institutions of government in Geneva would not last. Gallatin stated clearly that he was opting in favor of America as an alternative to the system in place in Geneva, not because he believed that the American system displayed absolute advantages over all other possible systems. Gallatin continued the letter to Badollet with news of his travels and explained that he would be going on to Virginia. He advised Badollet to write to him nonetheless at Philadelphia and said, "Only to avoid confusion do I keep the title 'Citizen of Geneva,'" although it seems unlikely that there was going to be a plethora of Albert Gallatins receiving mail through the Philadelphia post office. Gallatin also told Badollet of his plans, which he formed with Savary and during their stay in Philadelphia, to buy land in the Ohio River valley, two or three thousand acres in Virginia, especially when he received his inheritance. He did his homework, for he explained to Badollet the relative advantages and disadvantages of land and prices in the different states. Rousseau echoes throughout the letter: "the countryside, which is our favorite pursuit." Gallatin affirmed his choice of a new home: "Having abandoned Geneva, so to speak, I cannot have hesitated on the choice of the homeland I should then select, and America seemed to me the best country in which to settle given its constitution, its climate, and the resources available there." He renewed his invitation, many times repeated since his arrival in America, for Badollet to join him: "You say that Dumont is keeping you back, but what is keeping Dumont back?" He then admonished Badollet not to make any commitments that would prevent him coming in the following year, or at latest the year after that. Inspired by the troubles in Geneva, Gallatin proposed that if some of their compatriots wished to combine their funds, he would, after his time in Virginia, put together a plan for a settlement, under his leadership or at least his initiative, of Genevans in the New World. And then he pleaded not to let the letter come into the possession of his family, not because he wished to hide his political views or because he wanted to keep from his uncles his plan to settle in America, but because of the effect of his decision on Miss Pictet: "if it were known, [it] would cause too much grief to my gentle mother, Miss Pictet, who is the sole link that still binds me to Geneva."

He signed off the letter by assuring Badollet that anyone who owned land in America was entitled to citizenship and was entitled to vote, or to be voted for if he was worthy. Then he specified the ship, the *Comte de Duras* bound for Bordeaux, which carried his letter. Thereafter comes an addendum, a curious memento of those days, dated November 12, saying that the ship had sunk at the mouth of the Delaware River but that the crew escaped safely and returned his letter to him, which he posted again, a day before leaving Philadelphia for Virginia.

Between the original date of the letter and its final posting, Savary granted Gallatin a one-quarter interest in one hundred twenty thousand acres of land in Monongalia County, Virginia, for which Savary bought warrants during a trip they made to Baltimore. At long last Gallatin had taken a step on the way to realizing his ambition to own land in America. Gallatin pledged to pay for his portion once his inheritance came through. Aside from the interlude in Baltimore, Savary and Gallatin remained in Philadelphia until mid-November, when they journeyed on to Richmond, Virginia, the state capital. This was where Savary intended to collect René Rapicault's claims against the Commonwealth of Virginia. Gallatin got to know many of the state officials as he communicated on Savary's behalf in English. And for the first time in America (at least since his commendation certificate from Harvard), he was recognized for his abilities—and captivated by the charm of the place. Writing later of this first encounter with Richmond, and subsequent stays in the following six years, Gallatin said,

I was received with that old proverbial Virginia hospitality to which I know no parallel anywhere within the circle of my travels. It was not hospitality only that was shown me. I do not know how it came to pass, but everyone with whom I became acquainted appeared to take an interest in the young stranger. I was only the interpreter of a gentleman, the agent of a foreign house that had a large claim for advances to the State; and this made me well known to all the officers of government and some of the most prominent members of the legislature. It gave me the first opportunity of showing some symptoms of talent, even as a speaker, of which I was not myself aware. Everyone encouraged me and was disposed to promote my success in life. To name all those from whom I received offers of service would be to name all the most distinguished residents at that time at Richmond. I will only mention two: John Marshall, who, though but a young lawyer in 1783, was almost at the head of the bar in 1786, offered to take me into his office without a fee and assured me that I would become a distinguished lawyer. Patrick Henry advised me to go to the West, where I might study law if I chose, but predicted that I was intended for a statesman and told me that this was the career which should be my aim.[4]

John Marshall later became chief justice of the United States. Patrick Henry twice served as governor of Virginia, including from 1784 to 1786, when Gallatin sojourned in Richmond.

Gallatin and Savary stayed in Richmond throughout the end of 1783 and into February 1784 and then went to Philadelphia to prepare for a journey to "the West." They left Philadelphia in March 1784, crossed the Allegheny Mountains overland to Pittsburgh, the former Fort Duquesne, and traveled down the Ohio River from Pittsburgh to inspect the land for which he and Savary held their warrants. The land was actually in Virginia, in an area that is today West Virginia. They had journeyed from Pittsburgh on the Ohio River through the southwest corner of Pennsylvania, Fayette County, into the northwest corner of Virginia, Monongalia County. They concluded that Fayette County in Pennsylvania would be more suitable than the land just south in Virginia: Fayette had never been invaded by Indians since it was settled in the mid-eighteenth century, whereas Monongalia County had been the victim of Indian raids as recently as during the Revolutionary War. In addition, in Fayette Country, George's Creek joined the Monongahela River and might become a canal, as inland waterways were built, that could join that area to Richmond—such a route would be the straight line east to west from Richmond to their lands that Gallatin and Savary had not been able to take in their circuitous journey north, then west, then south.

In an attempt to get started in business in the area, Savary and Gallatin struck a deal with a local farmer, Thomas Clare, to set up a store on his three-hundred-acre farm near George's Creek. Gallatin opened the store and stayed on until the end of 1784.

The great General Washington, victor of the American War of Independence, was also a vast landowner in Virginia. He passed through the area around George's Creek with his nephew in late September 1784. Washington planned to build a road across the Allegheny Mountains and met with local inhabitants to help him decide on the right location. Gallatin attended, as he had been surveying lands in the region. They gathered in a one-room log cabin which served as the office and dwelling of the local land agent. Washington sat down at a pine table, and all the others stood around him, except for those who sat on the sole bed in the room. Washington questioned all the men, and as Gallatin listened to their explanations he quickly identified the appropriate location for the road. He interrupted Washington's inquiries to say that it was obvious enough that *this* was the right route for the road that Washington wanted to build. Washington gave him a cold, hard stare in remonstrance for this breach of decorum. But a few minutes later Washington looked at Gallatin and said, "You are right, sir." Washington slept on the cabin's one bed that night, and Gallatin slept on the floor. Washington made inquiries as to who this foreign-born surveyor was, who had peremptorily cut him off in his questioning, and was briefed on Gallatin's background. Thereupon, Washington offered Gallatin a job as his land agent in the area, but Gallatin declined because he soon meant to be a major landowner himself.

In late 1784 and early 1785, Gallatin and Savary wintered in Richmond and journeyed to Philadelphia. When winter was over and the weather permitted, they returned to the West country. Gallatin continued to urge Badollet to join them. In the spring of 1785, they set out again with a group of about fifteen experts whom they had recruited, until they reached a place on the Ohio River that Savary named "Friends' Landing." Gallatin carried on surveying on his own that summer, and while he was gone, Savary's operations at Friends' Landing were ambushed by Indians and had to be abandoned. They went back to the familiar and safer George's Creek, and in October 1785, more than five years after arriving in America, Albert Gallatin ceased to be a citizen of Geneva: he took the oath of allegiance to the Commonwealth of Virginia at the Monongalia County Courthouse in

Morgantown, Virginia. The United States were still governed by the Articles of Confederation; there was no central government, so citizenship was conferred by each state. In November, Savary and Gallatin rented from their friend Thomas Clare a house on five acres of land for a five-year term and thus acquired a permanent base in Pennsylvania, just above the Virginia line.

On January 29, 1786, Albert Gallatin reached the age of twenty-five and was entitled to his inheritance. First, however, he had to establish to his relatives in Geneva that he was still alive! After the Indian attack at Friends' Landing, his family had feared his death. They appealed to Thomas Jefferson, the American minister at Paris, to inquire of his whereabouts and well-being. This was the first time that Jefferson heard of Gallatin in any capacity, a remarkable way to make the acquaintance of someone whom he was to know intimately for forty years to come. Jefferson wrote to John Jay, then the secretary of foreign affairs, as the position was known under the Articles of Confederation. Jay placed an advertisement in the *Pennsylvania Packet* in May 1786, but by this time Gallatin had reestablished direct contact with home.

Gallatin's inheritance proved less than expected. Despite the four branches of the Gallatin family having spread so wide in Geneva over several centuries, Gallatin was in fact the last male of his branch—and, along with the Comte de Gallatin, one of the few surviving Gallatins at all. Consequently, he inherited both from his grandfather Abraham Gallatin of Pregny and from his uncle. Their estates turned out to be mainly composed of indebtedness, and in Calvinist Geneva, as has been mentioned, the inheritors were expected to make good on the debts of their forefathers. So instead of inheriting close to a hundred thousand dollars, after discharge of the debt he was left with only twenty thousand. For the time being, however, upon coming of age, Gallatin received about five thousand dollars in cash, remitted to him through the banking firm of Robert Morris.

GALLATIN LOOKS TO SETTLE DOWN AND MAKES A START IN POLITICS

Two developments then occurred which affected Gallatin's life in Pennsylvania for virtually the rest of his life. The very next month, in February 1786, he went back, earlier than usual, to the West country and bought a four-hundred-acre farm, not in Virginia but near George's Creek in Fayette County. He finally fulfilled his ambition to become a landowner in his own right. He named the property Friendship Hill. As if in honor of that friendship, Jean Badollet, who must have reached his own majority around the same time, at last responded to Gallatin's repeated pleas and came to join him in western Pennsylvania, where he took up residence nearby Friendship Hill.

Gallatin's project seemed ill fated, however, and several circumstances conspired against it. In the summer of 1786, Gallatin learned that Henri Serre had died in Jamaica. The Indians continued to harass the settlers, even in Fayette County, and this slowed the flow of pioneers to the area. Farming in this remote woodland was not easy. It was a lonely existence and, like his other projects since arriving in America, had the look not of a false start but of a promising start leading nowhere thereafter. Yet as in any country setting, with nature all around, there was always work to do. Gallatin returned to Richmond for the winter of 1786, went back to the West in the summer of 1787, and was at Friendship Hill with friends during Christmas of 1787. He then set out, in January 1788, for a trip north, which was to take him up to Maine. This was his first voyage outside the Richmond–George's Creek corridor for three years. Gallatin kept a sketchy diary that recorded his movements but not the purpose of the trip. The itinerary has the look of a sentimental journey to all the places he previously visited in America, so it may be that one purpose, at least, was to reconnect with his American acquaintances whom he had not seen for several years. Gallatin spent three weeks in Philadelphia in January, then went to New Jersey, up to Hartford in Connecticut in February, and then to Boston. He paid a sentimental visit to Wachusett Hill, which he had first climbed in 1780 upon arriving in America nearly eight years before. His friend William Bentley was by now an ordained church minister in Salem, Massachusetts, and was delighted to find Gallatin alive and not slain by the Indians. At Ipswich, Gallatin had dinner with two of his former French students from Harvard, Amory and Stacey. He proceeded in full winter weather at relatively breakneck speed up to Maine and back to Boston by February 27, 1788. A week later he was in New York. He returned to western Pennsylvania and spent the summer of 1788 at Friendship Hill.

In mid-August 1788, Gallatin went to Uniontown, Pennsylvania, the seat of Fayette County, to attend his first political meeting. Just as the state was divided by the Allegheny Mountains, so also there was a political divide between east and west. The Articles of Confederation had, during the past decade, shown their weaknesses, and the adoption of a federal Constitution had become a matter of debate but also of necessity. In June 1788, New Hampshire ratified the proposed Constitution, ensuring its adoption. At the same time, a significant portion of the people and a number of political figures, including in western Pennsylvania, feared the return of a quasi-monarchical strong central government, as indeed the Federalists were wont to prefer. One solution circulating was to require the adoption of a series of amendments to the new Constitution which, taken together, would constitute a bill of rights of the ordinary citizen. The countywide meeting in Uniontown in August 1788 was meant to nominate delegates to a statewide meeting to be held in Harrisburg the following month to discuss and present such amendments. John Smilie, a longstanding local political fixture who had opposed the Constitution, was chosen to go to Harrisburg as the first Fayette delegate. The second, then twenty-seven years old, was Gallatin: far more highly educated and far more worldly than his neighbors but sharing in their views on political independence (they as Pennsylvania rustics, he as a devotee of Rousseau), Gallatin was a logical if unconventional choice. The meeting at Harrisburg convened on September 3, 1788, and adopted a petition to the Pennsylvania state legislature to call for a new convention to revise the Constitution, while advising that the people of Pennsylvania should "acquiesce in the organization" of the federal government. Gallatin's draft resolutions coming into the meeting stated more dramatically that revision of the Constitution was necessary "in order to prevent a dissolution of the Union," but after four days of deliberation the meeting as a whole adopted milder language. The Pennsylvania legislature never acted on the petition. Notwithstanding the lack of political importance of the meeting, it represented, from Gallatin's standpoint, his first exposure to statewide politics and to constitutional debate; it gave him visibility beyond Fayette County; and it may have tempered his initial views, formed in the backcountry of western Pennsylvania, about the strength of popular sentiment against a strong central government under the new Constitution.[5]

After the Harrisburg meeting, Gallatin went back to Friendship Hill and stayed there through the winter of 1788. By the spring of 1789, he had probably not been in Richmond for close to a year and a half. During his previous stays there, he had lodged at a boarding house on Seventh Street owned by a lady named Mrs. Jane Batersby Allegre. As Miss Jane Batersby, she had married William Allegre, with a French name and of Huguenot descent. They had two daughters and a son. William Allegre died young, and his widow opened a boarding house. One of her lodgers had been a French-man named Louis Pauly, and he fell in love with Mrs. Allegre's daughter Jane, who married Louis Pauly against her mother's wishes and without her consent, a scandalous act in that place and time. For some years, Gal-latin had lodged at the boarding house, and he had been struck by Mrs. Allegre's other daughter, Sophie. Now, setting out from Friendship Hill on March 12, 1789, for a long-overdue return to Richmond, he made up his mind to seek Sophie's hand in marriage. He arrived in Richmond on April 1, 1789, nine years to the day after he left Geneva. He learned that Sophie was visiting her sister, Jane, and her brother-in-law, Louis Pauly, at New Kent, at a distance of something like thirty miles from Richmond. He sped to New Kent and spent a total of two weeks there. Clearly he and Sophie had been in love for some time, but neither had confessed it to the other. When Gallatin proposed, far from playing hard to get, Sophie told him the next day that she was his and that she would have been his long before if only he had asked on his latest trip or even an earlier one. She said she had always thought he loved her and had been surprised to have no news from him for more than a year.

Savary had been supposed to keep the communication channel open, following a letter Gallatin had sent to Sophie some time before, but she was unwilling to open up to Savary lest Gallatin had changed his mind. Mrs. Allegre found out that Gallatin was at New Kent and ordered her daughter home to Richmond, so Gallatin brought her back himself. Gal-latin recounted to Badollet, in a letter from Richmond of May 4, 1789, what happened when he asked Mrs. Allegre to marry Sophie: "She was furious, roughly refused me and nearly ordered me out of her house. She doesn't want her daughter dragged around the borders of Pennsylvania with some uncouth man who mutters English like a Frenchman and who was a schoolteacher in Cambridge."[6] This only increased Gallatin's resolve. In addition, he found out that Mrs. Allegre's view of Friendship Hill had been poisoned by reports she had heard from a person named Perrin, who had been part of Gallatin's household there. Ten days after sending that letter to Badollet, Gallatin married Sophie, with Gallatin and Savary paying the marriage fee, and the newlyweds took their honeymoon at their in-laws' house at New Kent. Mrs. Allegre had lost two daughters to Frenchmen, as she saw it, both without her consent. Sophie wrote to her mother in tender and respectful terms from New Kent asking forgiveness, saying that Gal-latin had great qualities, despite the fact that he was not handsome. From New Kent they went to the "borders of Pennsylvania": he took his bride home to Friendship Hill. Sadly, Sophie died that October 1789. Albert Gallatin buried his wife in an unmarked grave at Friendship Hill.

During the summer and early autumn of 1789, while at Friendship Hill with Sophie, Gallatin continued his political activity. The Pennsylvania state legislature called a convention to revise the constitution of the state, but Gallatin was convinced that the legislature, in so doing, was itself acting unconstitutionally since constitutional revision was provided for through another legal route. Gallatin drafted a letter to a number of politicians in western Pennsylvania, including one delegate to the convention, whom Gallatin asked to cancel his participation. On this occasion, far from defending the right of the people to change their mode of government at any time, Gallatin argued in favor of respecting legal and institutional precedent:

> Alterations in government are always dangerous, and no legislator ever did think of putting, in such an easy manner, the power in a mere majority to introduce them whenever they pleased. Such a doctrine once admitted, . . . instead of establishing on solid foundations a new government, would open the door to perpetual changes and destroy that stability so essential to the welfare of a nation; as no constitution acquires the permanent affection of the people but in proportion to its duration and age. Finally, those changes would, sooner or later, conclude in an appeal to arms,—the true meaning of those words so popular and dangerous, *An appeal to the people.*[7]

Ironically, not only did Gallatin's objections to the constitutionality of the convention fall on deaf ears, but he himself was elected, on October 12, 1789, along with John Smilie, as a delegate from Fayette County to the state constitutional convention in Philadelphia. Dropping his opposition, he bowed to the will of the state legislature to hold the convention and of his electors that he should attend. He set out from Friendship Hill late, because of Sophie's death, and arrived in Philadelphia two weeks after the convention had begun, on December 7, 1789. The convention met through February 1790. Gallatin explained later,

> The convention of 1789 was the first public body to which I was elected, and I took but a subordinate share in its debates. . . . But the distinguishing feature of the convention was that, owing perhaps to more favorable times, it was less affected by party feelings than any other public body that I have known. The points of difference were almost exclusively on general

and abstract propositions; there was less prejudice and more sincerity in the discussions than usual, and throughout a desire to conciliate opposite opinions by mutual concessions. The consequence was that, though not formally submitted to the ratification of the people, no public act was ever more universally approved than the constitution of Pennsylvania at the time when it was promulgated.[8]

From his first experience as an elected official, therefore, Gallatin was impressed by, and inclined toward, the type of harmonious compromise that could get the public business done. Although he did not participate actively, Gallatin worked assiduously on the issues during the constitutional convention, including writing to John Marshall in Richmond for advice on points of constitutional law. But although state politics represented a new set of interests for Gallatin, this activity fulfilled none of his previous American ambitions and certainly would not make him a rich man.

In addition, Gallatin remained inconsolable after the loss of Sophie and uncertain about what to do next. To add to his sources of woe, Geneva was in upheaval, for on July 14, 1789, the Bastille was stormed and the French Revolution began. Its effects quickly spread to Geneva. As a result, ten years after his arrival in America, when Gallatin felt least successful in having sought his fortune in the New World, when he most wanted to go home to Geneva, the disastrous economic and political situation in Geneva, combined with his own lack of funds from his investments in America, made it impossible for him to return. On March 8, 1790, nearly six months after Sophie died and two weeks after the close of the constitutional convention, Gallatin wrote a letter from Philadelphia to Badollet in Fayette County that demonstrated his sadness and confusion:

You surely feel as I do that staying in Fayette Country can't be pleasant for me, and you know that I would even like to get away from America. I've made every effort to make a success of this venture, but every day brings new problems. It is absolutely impossible for me to sell my land in Virginia at any price, and I don't know how I would make a living in Geneva. Without even going into my age and my habits and my laziness, which would be just as much of an obstruction to whatever I might be required do as a job in Europe, there is also the current situation of our country. The revolutions in the politics and especially the finances of France have had such an impact on Geneva that the businessmen are without credit and without customers, the craftsmen without work and in misery, and everyone in difficulty.[9]

He went on to say that he really should go back and be at Miss Pictet's side, if only he could be self-sufficient and make a living on his own; but at the same time he would rather live in America near his best friend, Badollet, his only friend to have known Sophie, than live far away without that friend. Yet as close as he wanted to be to Badollet, he also said that they must be independent of each other. Gallatin was lonely and desolate. Finally he wrote to Miss Pictet on April 7, 1790, to tell her of his wife's death more than half a year before. She replied at the end of June, and then, in a further letter dated July 1, 1790, in which she said that she shared his sorrow with all her heart, she also described the effects of the "precarious state of France" on life in Geneva. On this occasion, therefore, she left to him the choice of whether to return, rather than imploring him to come home, and added, "If you think you will be happier by spending a few more years in America, you would do well to stay there."[10]

MAKING HIS MARK IN THE PENNSYLVANIA LEGISLATURE

With no choice but to remain in America, Gallatin became more and more active in Pennsylvania politics. His fellow Fayette countrymen appreciated his participation in the state constitutional convention to which they had elected him, and in October 1790 they once again elected Gallatin, this time to the House of Representatives of the Commonwealth of Pennsylvania under the new constitution that emerged from the constitutional convention in which he had taken part. This meant more time in Philadelphia, away from the sad memories of Friendship Hill. He threw himself into the business of the legislature and was twice reelected, so that he sat in the state legislature for three consecutive annual sessions. Gallatin's own words best describe his tenure in the legislature:

I acquired an extraordinary influence in that body, the more remarkable, as I was always in a *party* minority. I was indebted for it to my great industry, and to the facility with which I could understand & carry on the current business. The labouring oar was left almost exclusively to me. In the session of 1791–1792, I was put on 35 Committees, prepared all the reports and drew all their bills.

I failed, though the Bill I had introduced passed the House, in my efforts to lay the foundation for a better system of education. Primary education was almost universal in Pennsylvania, but very bad; and the bulk of school masters incompetent, miserably paid & held in no consideration, . . . and the object of the Bill was to create in each County an Academy. But there was at that time in Pennsylvania, a Quaker and German opposition to every plan of general education.

The spirit of internal improvements had not yet been awakened. Still the first turnpike road in the U. States was that from Phila. to Lancaster. This, as well as every temporary improvement in our communications, road & rivers and preliminary surveys met of course with my warm support. But it was in the fiscal department that I was more particularly employed; and the circumstances of the times favoured the restoration of the finances of the State.

The report of the Comee. of Ways & Means of the Session 1790–1791 . . . was entirely prepared by me, known to be so, and laid the foundation of my reputation. I was quite astonished at the general encomiums bestowed upon it and was not at all aware that I had done so well. It was perspicuous and comprehensive: but I am confident that its true merit and that which gained me the general confidence was in its being founded in strict justice, without the slightest regard to party feelings or popular prejudices. The principles assumed, and which were carried into effect, were, the immediate reimbursement and extinction of the State Paper money, the immediate payment in specie of all the current expenses or Warrants on the Treasury (the postponement and uncertainty of which had given rise to shameful and corrupt speculations), and provision for discharging without defalcation every debt and engagement previously recognized by the State. In conformity with this, the State paid to its creditors the difference between the nominal amount of State debts assumed by the United States and the rate at which it was funded by the Act of Congress.

The proceeds of the public lands, together with the arrears, were the fund which not only discharged all the public debts but left a large surplus. The apprehension that this would be squandered by the Legislature was the principal inducement for chartering the Bank of Pennsylva., with a capital of two millions of dollars of which the State subscribed one half. This and similar subsequent investments enabled Pennsylva. to defray out of the dividends all the expenses of Govt. without any direct tax, during the forty ensuing years and till the adoption of the system of internal improvement which required new resources.[11]

Gallatin's work in the Pennsylvania legislature presaged multiple elements of his future career: his specialization in finance, his insistence on reduction of the public debt and the repayment of all monies due, his preference for a central bank that safeguarded public funds from the whim of the legislature, his parliamentary role as secretary or scribe, his interest in education, and his belief in the importance of infrastructure, then known as internal improvements. Gallatin's preference also emerged to act "in strict justice, without the slightest regard to party feelings of popular prejudices." Lastly, he might have mentioned that he was viewed as outstanding in finance issues because few others adopted that specialization.

In addition to his legislative duties, Gallatin was drawn into a matter of local politics that later took on national dimensions. Alexander Hamilton, secretary of the Treasury in President George Washington's administration, had enacted by Congress an excise tax on whiskey. The farmers of western Pennsylvania grew grain, and the lack of roads meant that they could not bring this bulky crop, either as harvested or ground into meal, to market in the East. So they distilled the grain into whiskey and sold that or, more often, bartered it for other goods. An excise tax on whiskey was anathema because it fell on the farmers as a group but not on others and so was unequal; and it required them to make payment in money, whereas they seldom had cash. Gallatin defended the western farmers' point of view in the legislature, and during the summer recesses of 1791 and 1792, when he returned to western Pennsylvania, he also acted as clerk at protest meetings against the excise tax in Brownsville and Pittsburgh. Although he neither originated nor vigorously supported these protests, and although they were not criminal, the words used were violent in their tone. He did not protest loudly against them. Later, he was required to defend his actions, and he presented a conditional mea culpa:

> I was one of the persons who composed the Pittsburg meeting, and I gave my assent to the resolutions. It might perhaps be said that the principle of those resolutions was not new. . . . I might say that those resolutions did not originate at Pittsburg, as they were almost a transcript of the resolutions adopted at Washington [Pennsylvania] the preceding year; and I might even add that they were not introduced by me at the meeting, But I wish not to exculpate myself where I feel I have been to blame. The sentiments thus expressed were not illegal or criminal, yet I will freely acknowledge that they were violent, intemperate, and reprehensible. For, by attempting to render the office contemptible, they tended to diminish

that respect for the execution of the laws which is essential for the maintenance of a free government; but, whilst I feel regret at the remembrance though no hesitation in this open confession of that *my only political sin,* let me add that the blame ought to fall where it is deserved [on the people who attended the meeting].[12]

In December 1792, Gallatin received a letter from Geneva dated the previous spring telling him that his grandfather had died, as had his grandfather's only daughter, Gallatin's aunt. His grandmother had slid into advanced senile dementia. The inheritance from his grandfather was the source of the debts that reduced Albert Gallatin's own assets. From Philadelphia he wrote to Badollet on December 18, 1792, that he was considering a brief return to Geneva to tend to his personal affairs. He would go back for no other reason than to see Miss Pictet, he said, except that he knew that his leaving again would grieve her more than his absence.[13] In fact, there was a letter on the way to him from Miss Pictet in Geneva, dated November 6, 1792, to say that she only wanted him to do what was best for him, and if that meant staying where he was, she would not tell him to return to Geneva. And, she added, she would do so "even less at this time when we hardly even know whether we shall have a homeland." She went on to describe the "bloodshed and carnage" in France—the Paris Commune and the end of the French monarchy had occurred in late summer and autumn of 1792:

> complete anarchy: they have destroyed all religion, all morality, all law, and while they go on and on about the rights of man, they have violated every one of them and persuaded the people that absolute equality might exist. For a long while we were merely observers of these horrors that have been committed, without imagining that we could become involved, especially as they only designated kings and the powerful as enemies. But about six weeks ago, one of these hordes of brigands took possession of Savoy, where they encountered no resistance. The Genevans, seeing troops and artillery moving ahead, took a defensive position and requested assistance from our neighbors and allies the Swiss, who provided it forthwith. It is surely because of the aid from the Swiss and the firmness and courage of the Genevans that we have not been attacked.[14]

By the end of 1792, Albert Gallatin had been in America for over twelve years. He had bought land, but he had not made his fortune. He had fallen in love and married, but he had been bereaved of his wife and sweetheart. He had taught and interpreted French, met influential people, and traveled the country, but he had established himself in no profession. He had wanted to return home to Geneva, but conditions had militated against that. His time in America looked a lot like a dozen years of drift. But his recent performance in Pennsylvania politics was about to lead to unforeseen opportunities.

[3]

THE SENATE AND THE HOUSE, 1793–1801

DESPITE Gallatin's desire to return to Geneva to settle his personal affairs and see Miss Pictet, he did not in fact go back to Geneva that spring. This was not the result of the revolutionary events in his birthplace but because, quite unwittingly and to some degree unwillingly, Gallatin was elected a senator of the United States.

The system for choosing members of Congress under the original Constitution was, with respect to the House of Representatives, direct election via universal suffrage, as exists today. But the Constitution provided that senators, as representatives of the states and not direct representatives of the people, would be elected by the members of the legislatures of each state. In all states except Pennsylvania, the upper and lower houses of the state legislature met together in one body to elect their U.S. senators. In the Commonwealth of Pennsylvania, the state senate insisted that the upper and lower houses sit and vote separately, although simultaneously. Since the state senate was smaller than the state assembly, this stipulation increased the power per vote of the state senators. This led to a deadlock in replacing Senator Maclay from Pennsylvania, such that one of the Pennsylvania seats in the U.S. Senate stood empty for two years,. The issue was much debated in the Pennsylvania state legislature, and Gallatin expressed the view in speeches there that it was unjust for six state senators thus to block Pennsylvania from exercising one of its votes in the U.S. Senate while the other states all had two each. At long last, it was agreed that the two Pennsylvania state bodies would meet together and vote for Senator Maclay's replacement. Gallatin proposed General Irvine, a former Revolutionary War commander and member of the Continental Congress. Gallatin did not seek his own election to the seat, nor did he encourage his political allies to nominate him. However, when a caucus meeting was held to designate a candidate, Gallatin's name was placed in nomination. As Gallatin himself said, he had acquired extraordinary influence in the legislature and had been active on all major issues, especially on questions related to finance. Nonetheless, Gallatin protested that there were candidates far better qualified than he was and even questioned his own eligibility to run. He was concerned—and stated his concern—that he did not fulfill the constitutional requirement that a senator must have been a citizen of the United States for nine years at the time of his election: Gallatin became a citizen of Virginia in October 1785, so he was well short of meeting the requirement in February 1793. The caucus, when it met again, discarded that objection and put Gallatin forward as their candidate. The contest to replace Senator Maclay turned out to be between Gallatin and Henry Miller, a Federalist from York County, situated in the southeastern part of the state. Simply because of Gallatin's preeminence in the lower house, and because he was a fair-minded but convincing champion of the interests of the western part of Pennsylvania, this combined assembly, even though it had a Federalist majority, elected Gallatin as U.S. senator from Pennsylvania by a vote of forty-five to thirty-seven on February 28, 1793, in Philadelphia. Gallatin himself said of this election, "It was my constant assiduity to business and the assistance derived from it by many members, which enabled the republican party in the Legislature, then a minority on a joint ballot, to elect me and no other but me of that party, Senator of the United States. This choice made in February of 1793 was contrary to my wishes and opinion."[1]

Gallatin was thus elected to the Senate in February 1793, but the next Senate session was not scheduled to convene until December of that year. Despite being a senator-elect of the United States, Gallatin retained his seat in the Pennsylvania legislature and carried on with his state-level responsibilities throughout the spring of 1793. On March 9, he sent a letter from Philadelphia to Badollet back in Fayette County. He wrote that he had to set aside plans to go to Geneva, so as to be sure of being in Philadelphia in December when the Senate convened. He wrote to Thomas Clare back in Fayette County that he would not be able to come back to Friendship Hill for the summer of 1793 as he had been tapped for a committee on the impeachment of a state official, and that task had to be completed and the committee's report presented to the Pennsylvania legislature on August 27, 1793.

A MEETING OF HEARTS AND MINDS

Although Gallatin's committee work was set to continue over the summer, the Pennsylvania state legislature adjourned its sessions in late spring or early summer. Among Gallatin's friends in Philadelphia were Alexander J. Dallas and his wife, Maria. Dallas, then the secretary of state of the Commonwealth of Pennsylvania, had been born in Jamaica and brought up in

Edinburgh and London; Maria was from Pennsylvania. The Dallases invited Gallatin to join them on a four-week trip to Albany, in upstate New York. They journeyed overland by stagecoach from Philadelphia through New Jersey to New York City, where they spent several days. They were invited to the house of Commodore James Nicholson, a prominent anti-Federalist and distinguished former naval officer. Among the party was Nicholson's daughter Hannah, then twenty-five years old. Maria Dallas invited Hannah and several other young women to join the summer boat ride up the Hudson River. Gallatin was smitten. From Hannah's standpoint, Gallatin constituted a very suitable match: thirty-two years old, he had been elected a U.S. senator from the very same political persuasion as Hannah's eminent family, he was highly intelligent if not especially handsome, he was gentle and sincere even if dreamy and indolent. Gallatin went back to Philadelphia after the Hudson River excursion but quickly returned to New York to woo Hannah.

By July 30, 1793, Gallatin was able to write to Badollet to say that he had asked for Hannah's hand and believed "the business to be fixed." Hannah had been courted earlier by Thomas Paine, the famous author of *Common Sense* and *The Age of Reason*, so—like Jacques Necker before him, who had married Edward Gibbon's flame—Gallatin the finance expert from Geneva captured the heart that had enchanted one of the great English writers of the Enlightenment. In Gallatin's letter to Badollet, he described Hannah as "neither handsome nor rich, but sensible, well-informed, good-natured, and belonging to a respectable and very amiable family, who, I believe, are satisfied with the intended match."[2] Indeed, beyond the Commodore's own naval pedigree, eighteen men in his family had served in the navy. Hannah's mother was Frances Witter, whose father, Thomas Witter, had been born in Bermuda and had become a successful merchant in New York.

Hannah was born in New York on September 11, 1766. She was the second of James and Frances Nicholson's six children, a close-knit group of five sisters and one brother. Her older sister, Catherine, married Colonel William Few, who had been the first U.S. senator from Georgia and was leaving the Senate as Gallatin entered it. The next eldest after Hannah, named Frances like her mother, was also married. Her husband, Joshua Seney, was a U.S. congressman from Maryland. Next came James, twenty years old and the only boy; then Maria, aged seventeen, who was charming and pretty and whom Gallatin adored; and lastly a little sister, Jehoiadden, just ten years old. This was to be the family that Gallatin had never until then had.

With the betrothal in place, Gallatin continued to work in Philadelphia on his legislative duties and to look ahead to the wedding, which they planned for the following winter of 1794 in New York. In the meantime, Gallatin wrote regularly to Hannah, and she to him. Commodore Nicholson and his wife had raised their daughters to be strong and well-educated women, and Hannah said she looked forward to learning from Gallatin. In reply, he said that while he could teach her history and French, he had much more to learn from her than she from him. Despite his patrician upbringing in Geneva, Gallatin was nonetheless in many ways ill prepared to take his place in society. He said he had been apathetic about everything except politics and counted on her to make him more polished and well mannered. Their letters also take a political turn—coming from that family, she certainly knew politics—and he replied with his analysis of America in the current international situation, views that reflect his Geneva roots as to the value both of peace and of independence from foreign domination:

> I believe that, except a very few intemperate, unthinking or wicked men, no American wishes to see his country involved in war. As to myself, I think every war except a defensive one to be unjustifiable. . . . As to the present cause of France, although I think that they have been guilty of many excesses, that they have many men amongst them who are greedy of power for themselves and not of liberty for the nation, and that in their present temper they are not likely to have a very good government within any short time, yet I firmly believe their cause to be that of mankind against tyrants, and, at all events, that no foreign nation has a right to dictate a government to them. . . . I wish Great Britain and Spain may both change their conduct towards us and show that they mean to be our friends, but till then no event could be more unfavorable to our national independence than the annihilation of the power of France.[3]

Hannah was the first person besides Badollet to whom Gallatin could talk about anything and everything. His letters to her open up to a range of thoughts and emotions that demonstrate how happy and fulfilled he was at last.

In the late eighteenth century, Philadelphia was the most populous city in the United States, the federal and the state capital, a major commercial center, and an important port. People and products from many foreign places passed through Philadelphia, including, in 1793, refugees from Haiti. About two years before, Toussaint Louverture, the son of an African chief and a freed slave from the French colony of Saint-Domingue (Haiti), who was both literate and imbued with the ideas of the Enlightenment, began what was to be a lengthy rebellion in that island: an uprising of slaves, freed slaves, mulattos, and some whites against European authority. In the summer of 1793, Toussaint Louverture's successes in Haiti caused many French people to flee Haiti and head to Philadelphia. One of the scourges of Haiti was yellow fever, and many of the new French arrivals to Philadelphia were infected with the disease. This led to one of the most destructive epidemics to occur on North American soil, and around one-tenth of the population of Philadelphia died in just the first month after the fever arrived. Given Philadelphia's political and commercial importance, this was a dire development.

Gallatin was in Philadelphia as the yellow-fever epidemic broke out. He was still involved in the impeachment of a Pennsylvania official, which had retained his attention in the state legislature. On August 29, 1793, Gallatin wrote to Hannah that, given the outbreak of fever, were it not for that impeachment process, then under way, the state legislature might already have disbanded and its members have left Philadelphia. Four days later, on September 2, 1793, he wrote that his friend Dr. Hutchinson, who had tended to many of the sick, lay dying; Dr. Hutchinson succumbed to the epidemic on September 6, 1793. The legislature agreed to adjourn on that same day, and Gallatin sped to New York on September 7, 1793. He intended to stay only a short time and then go out to Fayette County, but he fell ill himself after three weeks in New York with precisely the symptoms of yellow fever. The panic, if not the fever, had spread to New York, and the concern was that if Gallatin's illness were known, he might be quarantined with other infected persons in temporary hospitals set up on one of the islands in New York Harbor. Colonel Nicholson insisted that Gallatin move into his house—a brave and generous gesture to his future son-in-law—and Gallatin stayed there, was nursed, and recovered. Gallatin and Hannah, living under the same roof, decided to get married earlier. Two months after Hannah's twenty-sixth birthday, on November 11, 1793, they became husband and wife in New York.

GAINING AND LOSING HIS SEAT IN THE SENATE

Less than a month later, on December 2, 1793, Gallatin was back in Philadelphia to take his seat in the U.S. Senate. On the very first day of the Senate session, soon after Gallatin took his oath of office, John Adams, the vice president of the United States and therefore president of the Senate, read out a petition that had been sent by nineteen citizens of York County, in eastern Pennsylvania, the jurisdiction where Gallatin's Federalist opponent in the February election, Henry Miller, came from. The petition objected to Gallatin's election as senator on the ground that he had not been a citizen for nine years at the time he was elected. This was an entirely natural political move on the part of the Federalists from York County. Their candidate had been the runner-up to Gallatin in the senatorial election in the Pennsylvania state legislature the previous February, with thirty-five votes to Gallatin's forty-five. Gallatin himself had openly raised the issue of his ineligibility for the office. If Gallatin were disqualified, York County's native son Henry Miller might take his place in the Senate. So it made perfect sense for the York County citizens to submit their petition to the Senate seeking Gallatin's disqualification.

Gallatin was the junior senator from Pennsylvania, having just assumed office. The senior senator was the Federalist financier Robert Morris, through whose banking house Gallatin had received his inheritance. Morris told Gallatin that he had been asked to present the disqualification petition but that he refused to do so and intended to remain strictly neutral on the issue of Gallatin's election. A bit more than a week later, Vice President Adams referred the petition to a committee of Federalists whom Gallatin considered dead set against him. Accordingly, on December 31, 1793, the committee issued the Rutherfurd Report, stating that at the time of his election, Albert Gallatin had not been a citizen of the United States for nine years. Gallatin himself was quite unperturbed by this development, as he wrote to Badollet around this time:

> I believe I wrote to you, at the time of my being elected a Senator, that the election would probably be disputed. This has, agreeable to my expectation, taken place, which arises from my having expressed doubts, prior to my election, whether I had been a citizen nine years. The point as a legal one is a nice and difficult one, and I believe it will be decided as party may happen to carry. On that ground it is likely I may lose my seat, as in the Senate the majority is against us in general.[4]

Although Gallatin had been the object of an unfavorable committee report, until the Senate as a whole voted him out, he was a fully fledged U.S. senator. So he decided to act like one. Early in January 1794, he asserted his strong suit, the management of government finance, to the annoyance of Alexander Hamilton, President Washington's secretary of the Treasury. Gallatin thus did nothing to endear himself to the Federalists at the very moment when his fate was in their hands.

The first Congress after the adoption of the Constitution and the election of President George Washington established three departments of the executive branch: State for diplomacy, War for defense, and the Treasury for finance. There was, however, no other domestic department except Treasury, which therefore assumed all the domestic responsibilities of the executive branch. President Washington was elected in early April 1789 and inaugurated later that month, but it took until September 1789 for Congress to establish the Treasury, whereupon Washington appointed his longtime aide Alexander Hamilton as the first Treasury secretary. Hamilton took up his duties in mid-September 1789 and provided his first report on the public credit in January 1790. He faced daunting tasks in creating a new financial system and looked to the English example of William Pitt for guidance. In the ensuing years, Hamilton established the good credit of the United States by insisting that the federal government assume the debt, principal and interest, previously incurred by the states under the Confederation. He oversaw the founding of the first Bank of the United States. He established a system of taxation to raise revenue for the federal government, including tariffs on foreign trade but also the excise tax on whiskey that upset the farmers of western Pennsylvania. In short, Hamilton created from virtually nothing a functioning financial system for a national economy. In 1790 and 1791, he communicated to the House of Representatives two reports on the public credit, a report on manufactures, a report on duties on imports, and a report on the establishment of the U.S. Mint. The act establishing the Treasury Department had specified that the Treasury secretary should report on the Treasury's activities to the Senate or the House of Representatives when they so required. Thus, it had not been formally worked out what kind of information the Treasury would supply to Congress or how often. Gallatin was a stickler for financial oversight and intensely uncomfortable with this system, which gave considerable leeway to the president and the secretary of the Treasury. Gallatin thought Hamilton, an arch-Federalist, would be inclined to cultivate his position at the Treasury along the lines of the British government, in which the First Lord of the Treasury was the prime minister. Gallatin also supported an appropriations system whereby monies made available to the executive branch by Congress should be designated for a specific purpose and spent only for that purpose, rather than allocated to the head of the department for general use.

Despite the fact that the legitimacy of Gallatin's election to the Senate was being contested, on January 8, 1794, he introduced a motion in the Senate, in keeping with his views on sound financial management, calling for detailed reports in four broad categories for every year since 1789: (1) outstanding domestic debt divided into six categories, (2) domestic debt that had been redeemed, again under specific categories, (3) foreign debt, similarly broken down into categories, and (4) actual receipts and expenditures for each branch of the government, the comparison of expenditures to appropriations, and a statement of the balances remaining in each Treasury account. This was in one sense a clever move because it reinforced the power of the legislature over the executive, so senators could adopt the motion—even if they were Federalists in the same party as the secretary of the Treasury. In addition, the motion originated from a senator who had distinguished himself by his fiscal capabilities in his previous legislative experience. Notwithstanding the uncertainty surrounding the validity of Gallatin's sitting in the Senate, the senators adopted his motion on January 20, 1794. From the Treasury point of view, however, this was outrageous: it questioned the probity of Hamilton's management, put an extra burden on him and on the Treasury staff, and diminished the Treasury's independence. Hamilton rebuffed the request by making reference in a letter to the president of the Senate on February 22, 1794, to the effect that foreign affairs and the yellow-fever epidemic, together with the press of business generally, made it difficult to respond to "unexpected, desultory, and distressing calls for lengthy and complicated statements" that should not be demanded of a Cabinet officer "unless the officer was understood to have forfeited his title to a reasonable and common degree of confidence."[5] Hamilton, obviously offended, never provided to the Senate the information that Gallatin's motion demanded. In fact, only when Gallatin became secretary of the Treasury himself, seven years later, was the requirement for an annual report from the Treasury to Congress enacted. Gallatin was soon voted out of the Senate, and the motion, although voted by the Senate, simply went unheeded after his expulsion.

If Gallatin had not raised his potential ineligibility for the Senate at the caucus meeting back in February 1793, very probably nobody else would have done so. As it was, however, for a week in February 1794, the Rutherfurd Committee heard from seven witnesses, including Gallatin, and then the full Senate debated for another week, with Gallatin participating again. Technical and historical arguments failed to persuade, such as the view that nobody had actually been a citizen of the United States for nine years in 1793 or that the colonists had complained that King George III had obstructed the naturalization of the foreign born (so the Senate should not do that now). Gallatin also tried the ploy of saying that the petition was not a sufficient accusation for him to have to give up his seat, so he declined to go to the expense of mounting a full defense. Vice President Adams said that in a tie vote, he would break the tie in Gallatin's favor. But Benjamin Hawkins of North Carolina, who had been expected to vote for Gallatin, departed from Philadelphia, and Robert Morris, Gallatin's colleague from Pennsylvania, rescinded his pledge of neutrality. Gallatin was voted out of the Senate by fourteen to twelve, a vote entirely on party lines, with no tie to be broken.

After the vote, Gallatin wrote to Thomas Clare in Fayette County:

[O]n the subject of my seat in the Senate, . . . I have lost it by a majority of 14 to 12. One vote more would have secured it, as the Vice President would have voted in my favor; but heaven and earth were moved in order to gain that point by the party who were determined to preserve their influence and majority in the Senate. The whole will soon be published, and I will send it to you. As far as relates to myself I have rather gained credit than otherwise, and I have likewise secured many staunch friends throughout the Union. All my friends wish me to come to the Assembly next year.[6]

With hindsight, we are entitled to question whether Gallatin approached his brief tenure in the Senate with the care and seriousness it deserved. If he had indeed not desired to occupy the office of senator, he could have insisted on excluding himself as a candidate. He could have claimed that his own personal doubt concerning his eligibility for office was enough to prevent him, in good conscience, from running. To accept the office while continuing to protest that he did not seek it, or did not even want it, or was not even eligible for it, smacks of vanity or insolence. Having taken his seat and seen its legitimacy contested, because of protestations he himself had been the first to make, a sense of respect for the institution would have required that he at least deign to mount a full defense. In addition, it would have been more seemly to wait until his fate as a senator was decided before pressing demands on the Treasury secretary from the opposing (and majority) party for information that seemed excessive at the time. In the instance, Gallatin looked, and acted, needlessly confrontational, particularly by inducing the Federalists to increase pressure on Hamilton, even under the guise of polite parliamentary procedure. He may have felt that he gained in reputation with his allies, but he was also beginning to make enemies.

WESTERN PENNSYLVANIA ONCE AGAIN

Out of the Senate, indeed out of politics, and out of a job, Gallatin now needed both an occupation and money. The only place he knew to look for either was in the West. He took Hannah back to New York, where she stayed on with her family, while he returned to Philadelphia to prepare to cross the Allegheny Mountains. He sold his land in Virginia, to the same Robert Morris who had just treacherously voted him out of the Senate, for four thousand Pennsylvania pounds, payable in three installments over three years; he told Hannah that Morris was the only buyer in the market. Having settled his affairs at Philadelphia, he set out with Hannah for Friendship Hill in early May. A New York City lady born and bred, and hence unlikely to take to the ways of the West, Hannah was about to find out with Gallatin how wild the West could be—much more violent and dangerous than anything either had experienced to date.

Over the course of 1794, the local uprisings of 1791 and 1792 against the excise in Pennsylvania were far outdistanced in their hostility by the Whiskey Rebellion. In June 1794, Congress gave state courts jurisdiction over cases involving the excise taxes on whiskey, but not over past cases in which the whiskey distiller had incurred a penalty. Federal marshals served notices on distillers throughout the West for the outstanding penalties to be enforced. This inflamed local passions and resulted in meetings around the western part of the state during the summer, meetings in which the question was whether to defy the authority of the federal marshals and, by extension, the federal government. Fayette County decided to obey the law at a meeting in Uniontown on July 20, 1794, which Gallatin attended and at which he and his friend Smilie counseled moderation and obedience to the law. Other counties, however, rose up in insurrection. Tensions built over the summer, and at a jittery meeting in Brownsville on August 28, 1794, Gallatin's life was very much in danger. He remained calm, gave a lengthy speech to the meeting the next day again in favor of obedience to the law, and prevailed against an old enemy, a Pennsylvania politician named David Bradford who had wanted to defy the federal officers and whose mad jealousy Gallatin had fanned by treating him with scorn but who could have incited the country men to violence at any moment. The Whiskey Rebellion was finally quelled when President Washington sent thirteen thousand militiamen into western Pennsylvania, with Alexander Hamilton in the vanguard, in a show of force that went unopposed by the western Pennsylvanians, that displayed the power of the new U.S. government to compel its citizens to obey its laws, and that, as a show of force, constituted a singular victory for the Federalists.

Gallatin had indeed lost none of his prestige among his constituents, and in the elections of October 1794, he found himself in the exceptional position of being voted into two offices simultaneously. As he had expected, his friends in Fayette County returned him to the state legislature of Pennsylvania. On the same day, the western district of Pennsylvania, without his being aware of it in advance, elected him as their congressman in the U.S. House of Representatives. Shorn of his Senate seat, he decided to fulfill both mandates. Then the western Pennsylvania elections were contested. As Gallatin recounted,

> [In October 1794] I was reelected Member of the State Legislature in Fayette County for the ensuing session: and, on the same day I was, without my knowledge, elected Member of Congress for 1795–1797, by the western district of Pennsylvania, . . . in which I did not reside; the only instance of the kind I believe that has ever occurred.
>
> [In December 1794] the House of Repr. & the Senate of Pennsylvania, in clear violation of the Constitution, (but a most fortunate circumstance for me), set aside all the western elections under pretence of the late insurrection. The same members were immediately reelected, and the election for Congress was not questioned.[7]

The Pennsylvania legislature was scheduled to meet in January 1795, whereas the next session of the federal House of Representatives was not set to convene until December 1795. Gallatin and Hannah returned from Friendship Hill to New York in late 1794. She stayed on with her family, while Gallatin went back to Philadelphia to take his seat in the state legislature. In his first speech, Gallatin reviewed his role in the Whiskey Rebellion, starting with the summer uprisings of several years before. That was the occasion on which he confessed his earlier assent to violent language to have been his "only political sin."

In addition to his duties in the state legislature in Philadelphia, Gallatin was occupied during much of 1795 with increasingly dire news from Geneva. He wrote a long letter to Badollet on December 28, 1794, to relate that Geneva was caught up in the convulsions resulting from the Reign of Terror and the French Revolution, that it was torn between the French and the Swiss and was the scene of bloody fighting among inhabitants. Already some Genevans had emigrated. Gallatin sent Badollet a summary of the latest revolutionary developments, prepared by their former schoolmate François d'Ivernois in London, including a proposal to buy land and provide a place of settlement in America to which the Genevans could immigrate as a group. D'Ivernois also proposed to relocate the Academy of Geneva to the United States, and he wrote to Thomas Jefferson, Gallatin, and others to that effect. Gallatin made an exploratory trip through New York State in April, purportedly to look for suitable land for the Academy, but as he wrote to Hannah with his overall impression, he felt that New York was controlled by a small number of families and that the people therefore were less independent than in Pennsylvania, that property there was too expensive, and that, whether from "prejudice, or habit, or whatever you please," his preference was still with western Pennsylvania.[8] He then returned to Philadelphia, where he was promptly summoned as a witness before a grand jury on behalf of the government, which was prosecuting for treason individuals who had been involved in the Whiskey Rebellion.

In other news from Geneva that summer, Gallatin learned that Miss Pictet was ill and unlikely to recover. He was not proud of the way he had treated her, and he wrote to Hannah, "I have not behaved well."[9] In September, Gallatin was informed that Miss Pictet had died. He wrote to Hannah, "I trust, I hope at least, the comfort she must have experienced from hearing she had not been altogether disappointed in the hopes she had formed of me, and in the cares she had bestowed on my youth, will in some degree have made amends for my unpardonable neglect in writing so seldom to her."[10]

GALLATIN JOINS THE HOUSE AND GROWS INTO A LEADER

On December 7, 1795, Albert Gallatin took his seat as a member of the U.S. House of Representatives in the opening session of the fourth Congress. Aside from his brief tenure in the Senate, this marked Gallatin's first foray into national politics, where a system of parties was beginning to emerge. In 1792, Thomas Jefferson and James Madison formed the Democratic-

Republican Party—known as the Republicans or the Jeffersonians. Jefferson resigned as Washington's first secretary of state toward the end of Washington's first administration, which gave him a freer hand to oppose the Federalists. The Republicans championed states' rights and were viewed as pro-French, against the centralizing Federalists, who were deemed closer to Britain. Gallatin, when he arrived in Congress, threw himself into his duties and again played to his strengths. Within ten days of Congress convening he proposed the establishment of a committee "to superintend the general operations of finance," which was to become the House Ways and Means Committee. The resolution was adopted within four days and a committee of fourteen members appointed, including Gallatin himself. He was to assert the financial prerogative of the House of Representatives in another debate, which occurred in March 1796 on the treaty of peace that had been concluded by John Jay with the British government. "Mr. Jay's Treaty" in fact procured several years of good relations with Britain, but it had excited considerable controversy in the country. The Republicans argued that the treaty was too favorable to British interests, for example, in restricting American ability to trade cotton or sugar. It looked to the Republicans like a Federalist move to ally the new United States too closely with Britain, to the prejudice of the relationship with France that they preferred. President Washington had his own doubts about the treaty but did not think it could be improved and had no wish to enter a fresh war with Britain. He sent it to the Senate for ratification, where it barely passed. Under the Constitution, that should have been the end of the matter. But the Republicans, with Gallatin in the lead, tried to stop the treaty in the House of Representatives by refusing to allocate the money required to put the treaty into effect until the executive provided all documentation to the House. This eroded too much of the president's privilege to conduct foreign affairs for Washington to tolerate, and he refused point blank unless the House were to impeach him. The House relented and allocated the funds by a close vote, and the principle of executive authority to make treaties, and of Senate exclusivity to ratify treaties, thereafter prevailed.

Gallatin was also involved in this session on a matter of special interest to him, the sale of federal lands. An act passed to provide for organized townships in former Indian territories northwest of the Ohio River and set out how the land was to be sold.

The session ended in June 1796. Gallatin and Hannah returned to New York for the summer. The expected immigration of Genevans had not materialized the year before, but during that summer of 1795, Gallatin bought land in the area around George's Creek and formed a new trading company with a group of partners already in America who included Hannah's brother, James Nicholson. A year on, in the latter half of 1796, a number of businesses came into being there, including a glass-making business, the first in the West. They named this small town New Geneva, Pennsylvania.

George Washington, partly because opinion turned against him after Jay's Treaty, decided not to seek a third term as president. The election of 1796 followed a vituperative campaign between his vice president, the Federalist John Adams, and Thomas Jefferson at the head of the Republicans. Gallatin supported Jefferson in the western counties of Pennsylvania and also campaigned for his own reelection as congressman. Jefferson received the vast majority of votes for president in that region, and Gallatin was reelected. In the overall presidential election, Adams won, and Jefferson came second. And under the rules of the Constitution of the time, Jefferson as runner-up became Adams's vice president.

In November 1796, Gallatin published a magisterial study of the American economy. In March of that year, Jefferson wrote to Madison that the finances of the United States were beyond anyone's understanding and expressed the wish that "our Gallatin would undertake to reduce this chaos to order and present us with a clear view of our finances."[11] Gallatin's compilation was modestly entitled *A Sketch of the Finances of the United States* but in fact ran to one hundred seventy pages of detail on every aspect of the American economy, including sources of revenues, expenditures, and debts, together with close to twenty appended tables. Gallatin composed it for the education of his own political party, but it also served to assert his preeminence as an expert on government finance. Gallatin did not contest the wisdom of the federal government assuming the states' debt as Hamilton had insisted, but he condemned the concept of public debt, which "makes not the smallest addition either to the wealth or to the annual labor of a nation,"[12] and he called for the extinction of the debt as quickly as possible. This is precisely the policy he implemented when he later became secretary of the Treasury.

The second session of the fourth Congress was a short one, from December 5, 1796, to March 3, 1797, and it saw out the end of George Washington's administration. While Gallatin was in Congress in Philadelphia, Hannah had their first child, a boy. Born in New York on December 18, 1796, he was named James in honor of his grandfather. Gallatin went back to New York to be with Hannah and the baby for Christmas. He returned to Philadelphia in January but was lonely and depressed without Hannah until Congress adjourned on March 3, 1797, and he could go back to her. The highlight of that stay was probably a dinner Gallatin attended in January with the outgoing President Washington, whom he found even more "grave, cool and reserved" than usual.[13]

In the fourth Congress, James Madison acted as leader of the Republicans in the House of Representatives. When the first session of the new fifth Congress reconvened on May 15, 1797, Madison left the House, and Gallatin took his place as the leader of Jeffersonians. The Congress met through July 10, 1797, and debated the increasingly complex U.S. relationship with France, now under the rule of the Directory, which had refused to receive the American minister Charles Cotesworth Pinckney. Gallatin again dined with the president, now John Adams, toward the end of this session. He and Hannah went to New Geneva for the summer and picked up where they had left off in the autumn. He returned to Philadelphia for the second session of the fifth Congress on November 13, 1797.

During this period, the United States continued to be caught, as it had been since independence and as it was to be still for some years, between the interests of Britain and France. This was the time of the infamous XYZ Affair, when members of an American delegation in Paris were asked for outrageous bribes by French officials, including foreign minister Charles Maurice de Talleyrand. Word got back to America, inflamed public opinion, and led to the popular slogan "Millions for defense, but not one cent for tribute." In the wake of this affair, a naval conflict broke out between the United States and France which lasted from 1798 to 1800 and led to significant harassment on both sides but stopped short of outright hostilities, the so-called Quasi-War. President Adams had no more desire for warfare with France than President Washington had had in his time for warfare with Britain. But the United States was still caught between the interests of these two powers.

The U.S. government pursued a handful of measures designed to assuage the symptoms of this dilemma. One was the creation of the Department of the Navy, alongside the already-existing Department of War. Another such measure was the Alien and Sedition Acts, which sought to reduce the threat of foreign aggressors and fellow travelers within America. The Alien and Sedition Acts became law in June and July 1798, and many people thought they were squarely aimed at Gallatin, a foreigner and a Republican, deemed to be pro-French. During the debates, Gallatin kept a lower profile, but he continued to make demands on the Treasury Department for detailed data, much to the discomfiture of Secretary Wolcott.

After the close of the congressional session on July 16, 1798, the Gallatins returned to Friendship Hill for the summer. The year 1798 was to be one of personal financial setbacks for Gallatin. His partnership in New Geneva was not thriving. He had entrusted management of the company to a fellow Genevan, Bourdillon, but found his performance disappointing. Bourdillon had bought and sold on credit and thus exposed the company to debt. Robert Morris, to whom Gallatin had sold his lands and who had been reputed at one point the richest man in the United States, was bankrupt and could not pay the third installment of his purchase. Gallatin lost a thousand dollars that he had lent to Badollet for the business, and almost all the capital had been spent, while the speculation in land and house building had proved fruitless. He reproached himself for having entered into business with anybody else. In Europe, his grandfather's estate had been sold, and he had given orders, as a good Genevan, to pay off all the debts, which were considerable. This resulted in a negative equity in the estate and a cost to Gallatin of two hundred dollars, a far cry from the assets he might have expected to inherit as sole surviving male of his branch of the family. His investments in France and the Netherlands all lost money, and he calculated that the French Revolution had cost him sixteen thousand dollars. "Yet the Federalists call me a Frenchman, in the French interest and forsooth in French pay"—an easy target after the XYZ Affair and the Alien and Sedition Acts.[14] Gallatin wrote to the Lesdernier son, with whom he had lived in Machias when he first arrived in America, a full account of his life since then, with fond memories of Lesdernier's parents, adding, "I am a bad *farmer*, and have been unfortunate in some mercantile pursuits I had embraced. I have just made out to live independent, and am neither richer nor poorer than I was twelve years ago; the fact is, I am not well calculated to make money,—I care but little about it, for I want but little for myself, and my mind pursues other objects with more pleasure than mere business."[15] Dealing with business took much of his time in 1798 and 1799. But the turn of the year brought good news: the birth of his and Hannah's second son on January 8, 1800, whom they called Albert Rolaz Gallatin.

In response to the Alien and Sedition Acts, Jefferson and Madison wrote resolutions that were adopted by the Kentucky and Virginia legislatures declaring that the Alien and Sedition Acts were unconstitutional and that the individual states should have the right to determine matters that were not specifically ascribed to the federal government under the Constitution. With these resolutions, the lines were drawn between the Federalists— centralizing, pro-British, elitist—and the Republicans—states' rights, pro-

French, spokesmen of the people. Hannah accompanied Gallatin back to Philadelphia for the opening of the sixth Congress on December 2, 1799. The election of 1800 was shaping up, and the death of the uniting figure of George Washington on December 14, 1799, sharpened party differences. During this congressional session, Gallatin pursued his financial specialization, speaking out against increased government debt. The Republicans' campaign fell into place: Jefferson, now serving as Adams's vice president, was the clear choice for presidential candidate, and in May 1800 the Republicans selected Aaron Burr as his vice-presidential running mate. The first session of the sixth Congress adjourned on May 14, 1800, and by July 1800 Gallatin had produced an impressive update of his *Sketch of the Finances* of four years before. This was called *Views of the Public Debt, Receipts and Expenditures of the United States. Views,* like the *Sketch* before it, flew in the face of the Treasury's protestations that detailed figures were too hard to produce, furnished a financial platform to the Republicans in the upcoming national election, and asserted—if any such additional assertion were needed—that Gallatin was the premier financial expert in his political family.

In the presidential election of 1800, Adams was pitted against Jefferson once again. The Federalists ran General Charles Cotesworth Pinckney of South Carolina, the same man whom the French had refused to receive as American minister, for vice president. Jefferson was clearly the country's choice and won the popular vote by a massive sixty-one percent. This was the "Revolution of 1800," in which power changed hands from one political persuasion to another for the first time in the history of the young American republic. But the popular vote actually counted for nothing since the election occurred in the Electoral College. By a quirk of the Constitution, and with a lot of politicking involved, the electoral vote ended in a tie between Jefferson and Burr, both Republicans, at seventy-three votes each. In accordance with the law, this tie had to be resolved by a vote in the House of Representatives. But this was the old House, elected in 1798, in which the now-defeated Federalists had a majority. Meanwhile, as decided in the Compromise of 1790, the federal capital moved from Philadelphia to the new and thoroughly unready city of Washington, on the Potomac River. Congress met there in November 1800, but the presidential vote in the House of Representatives was deferred until the session reconvened on February 11, 1801.

Gallatin, despite the brickbats hurled at him in the form of the Alien and Sedition Acts, and very much because of his financial expertise, continued to assume the role of leader of the opposition that Madison had turned over to him. Consequently, when the time came to devise the Republican strategy for the presidential election in the House in February 1801, Gallatin was the chief organizer. Thomas Jefferson was the choice of the country, the choice of the party, and the choice of Albert Gallatin. The election process was complicated by the lingering sessions of Congress that continued past the popular election period: not only was the House the lame-duck Federalist legislature that would prove unwieldy for a Republican to manage, but Thomas Jefferson himself, as John Adams's vice president, was president of the Senate and therefore held the gavel in the upper chamber while the lower chamber decided his fate. Gallatin prepared a detailed plan of action for Jefferson that outlined all the contingencies, employed all the relevant parliamentary procedures, and took account of all the salient personalities in the upcoming election in the House of Representatives. The most important goal was to avoid a scenario in which the Federalists elected Burr or called a new election or took over executive power in the absence of a clear result. Gallatin wrote later, "The only cause of real apprehension was that Congress should adjourn without making a decision, but without usurping any powers. It was in order to provide against that contingency that I prepared myself a plan that did meet with the approbation of our party."[16] It took six days of continuous meeting to come to a decision. Finally, on February 17, 1801, Gallatin wrote to Hannah from Washington: "We have this day, after 36 ballots, chosen Mr. Jefferson President."[17]

From a low point eight years before, Gallatin had pursued his interests, emphasized his abilities, and crafted for himself a unique position as a leading financial expert on the American political stage. He built on his wearisome but worthwhile experience in the Pennsylvania legislature, achieved and then lost the status of senator of the United States, and was rewarded by his fellow Pennsylvanians with an unexpected mandate in the federal House of Representatives. Gallatin sharpened and deployed a broad set of political capacities. He evolved into a practiced parliamentarian, a sure speaker, and a redoubtable debater despite his still-strong French accent. He achieved recognition as an expert in economics and government finance unequaled in his party and perhaps in America.

[4]

JEFFERSON'S SECRETARY OF
THE TREASURY, 1801–1809

O NCE in office, President Jefferson offered Gallatin the role for which he was clearly the most qualified Republican: secretary of the Treasury. As much as he wished to accept the position, Gallatin hesitated: already ejected from the Senate by the Federalists, he was wary that the current Federalist Senate would refuse his nomination. Jefferson therefore submitted no nomination for secretary of the Treasury and instead designated Albert Gallatin for the position via a recess appointment after Congress had adjourned. Gallatin took the oath of office in Washington on May 14, 1801, but his formal nomination was not submitted by Jefferson to the Senate until January 6, 1802, when the new Congress convened, with friendly Republican majorities in both Houses. Gallatin was confirmed on January 26, 1802, nine months after he had actually started the job.

Before he began work at the Treasury, Gallatin went back to Pennsylvania to move his family from Friendship Hill to the new capital, known then as Washington City. The town planner had been the Frenchman Pierre Charles L'Enfant, a former major in the Revolutionary War. Jefferson, as secretary of state, chose the sites of the Capitol and the president's house. On January 15, 1801, Gallatin, in Washington on his own for the congressional session, described the town to Hannah: "Our local situation is far from being pleasant or convenient. Around the Capitol are seven or eight boarding-houses, one tailor, one shoemaker, one printer, a washing-woman, a grocery shop, a pamphlets and stationery shop, a small dry-goods shop and an oyster-house. This makes the whole of the Federal City as connected with the Capitol." To the east was a "large but perfectly empty warehouse, and a wharf not graced by a single vessel," and a vast swamp; and to the west, "towards the President's house," the other side of the swamp and alongside it a stream, feeding but not draining the swamp. Between the Capitol and the president's house ran a causeway called

Pennsylvania Avenue, where "not a single house intervenes or can intervene without devoting its wretched tenant to perpetual fevers."[1]

With Hannah, who was pregnant again, and their two sons—James, who was now three and a half, and Albert Rolaz, only four months old—the Gallatins made the overland journey from western Pennsylvania to Washington. They initially rented a house near the president's mansion but then found a home on higher ground, on Capitol Hill, on the road to Bladensburg, a town to the northeast, in Maryland. While they were getting settled, they were often guests of the new president, who wrote to them on June 3, 1801: "Th. Jefferson asks the favor of Mr. and Mrs. Gallatin to dine with him today; and requests that while they are arranging matters at their new quarters they will dine with him every day."[2]

JEFFERSONIAN PHILOSOPHY AND GOVERNMENT

Like Gallatin, Jefferson was an intellectual from a patrician background. He was born in Virginia in 1743, and at the age of fourteen he inherited from his father, a planter and surveyor of Welsh descent, five thousand acres of land and dozens of slaves. His mother was of the elite Randolph family of Virginia, and Thomas received a classical education in Latin, Greek, and French. He read law at the College of William and Mary in Williamsburg. Jefferson entered politics in the Virginia legislature and was principal author of the Declaration of Independence of the United States; he became governor of Virginia and from 1785 to 1789 was U.S. minister to France, where he watched the French Revolution unfold. Returning to America, he was appointed the first secretary of state by President Washington, but he resigned after disagreements with Hamilton in 1793 and returned to his country house at Monticello in Virginia until he took office as John Adams's vice president.

Jefferson was tall, stiffly erect, slightly awkward in company, yet charismatic. He lisped and disliked giving speeches; during eight years as president he delivered only two. He spent half of each day writing correspondence, and his rhetoric, especially on politics, could be irresponsible and inflammatory. He was a diehard Republican and determinedly pro-French; he affected simplicity, but he lived the life of a lord. He conspicuously lacked a sense of humor and could be exceedingly full of himself. He was quick witted, charming, and whimsical—and he adored women. After his wife's death he took her half sister, a slave, as his lover and fathered three of her children. He returned to Monticello whenever he wished and spent well over two years of his presidency away from Washington.

On March 4, 1801, Jefferson delivered his first inaugural address and poured oil on the troubled waters of the recent bitter election: "We have called by different names brethren of the same principle. We are all Republicans, we are all Federalists." He then called for "a wise and frugal Government," "economy in the public expense," and "the honest payment of our debts," precisely Gallatin's financial strategy for the Treasury. Jefferson enunciated a foreign policy, with which Gallatin could not have concurred more wholeheartedly, of "peace, commerce, and honest friendship with all nations, entangling alliances with none," an idealistic isolationism of an exceptional America aloof from the wars and vices of Europe. Also in his inaugural address, Jefferson spoke of Americans as "possessing a chosen country, with room enough for our descendants to the thousandth and thousandth generation." The principles of Republican government were meant to create the conditions by which a prosperous and open nation could be built up on the American continent, an empire of liberty and not of oppression. But the danger of the Jeffersonian system, in which Gallatin believed deeply at the time, was to rely too heavily on its own theories, to put too much faith in the abstract Enlightenment virtue of "reason" and to make its principles too plainly known. By failing to take account of human villainy and weakness, Jeffersonian high-mindedness risked making virtuous sacrifices that could then be undone by negative developments, and in foreign affairs in particular, with its attachment to peace at almost any price, it risked being manipulated by more Machiavellian statesmen pursuing interests and not ideals.

In this first changeover from one political party to another, Republicans sought to share in the spoils of the presidential election. In 1801, all officeholders of the United States were by definition Federalist appointees by Presidents Washington or Adams. Although Jefferson was little inclined to make wholesale purges, he did seek to replace some Federalist appointees. On March 5, 1801, the day after his inauguration, Jefferson nominated James Madison as secretary of state and Henry Dearborn as secretary of war. Both were confirmed by the Senate at once. Also confirmed was Levi Lincoln as attorney general, a one-man part-time position in the Cabinet. The position of secretary of the navy was offered to Samuel Smith, a powerful senator from Pennsylvania who occupied it for a short while before passing it to his brother Robert Smith. Gallatin knew Madison well already and

described his other colleagues in a letter to Hannah's sister, Maria Nicholson, of March 12, 1801: "General Dearborn is a man of strong sense . . . and
what is called a man of business. . . . I think he will make the best Secretary
of War we have yet had. Mr. Lincoln is a good lawyer, a fine scholar, a man
of great discretion and sound judgment, and of the mildest and most amiable manners."[3] Gallatin was to have his problems in the future with both
Smiths, but for the present time, the day-to-day government of the country came to reside with Jefferson, Madison, and Gallatin, soon to become
known as the triumvirate.

GALLATIN TAKES OVER AT THE TREASURY

At the time that the federal government moved from Philadelphia to
Washington, the total number of central government officials and clerks
was only about one hundred twenty-five people. Of these, nearly eighty
were the Washington staff of the Treasury, whose staff of agents around
the country numbered more than twelve hundred. In addition to being the
biggest department of government, the Treasury was, as has been mentioned, the only domestic department of the executive branch.

Gallatin conceived of the Treasury within the executive branch as the
point of financial supervision of the other departments. He viewed the
Treasury much like a European finance ministry, à la Necker under Louis
XVI or the British prime minister as First Lord of the Treasury—however
much this might align him with the position of his Federalist rival and pre-
decessor, Hamilton. Now in office, Gallatin insisted on a strict system of
specific appropriations for specific expenditures. Congress was delighted
by this increased legislative oversight of the executive branch, especially as
the new chairman of the Ways and Means Committee was Gallatin's friend
John Randolph of Roanoke, and the second-ranking member, John Hop-
per Nicholson of Maryland, was Hannah Gallatin's cousin.

Although Jefferson asked Gallatin to revolutionize Hamilton's Federalist money machine, in fact Gallatin had no dissatisfaction and only minor
differences with Hamilton's approach. Beyond a preference for specific appropriations, Gallatin questioned the value of a debt-management method
that Hamilton had adopted from the British prime minister William Pitt,
called the sinking fund. The concept was that at the time a debt was incurred, the funding for its repayment would be specified. Gallatin had
criticized this method when in Congress, for he felt it offered a false sense
of comfort by giving the impression that the funds had somehow been set

aside, whereas in reality the expected source of repayment had merely been identified.

Gallatin devoted his first year in office to understanding the workings of the Treasury and making his own assessment of the situation. During the summer and autumn of 1801, he mastered the operations of the Treasury, filled appointments to office, and determined the levels of expenditure in the other departments of the government. It took him until the end of the year 1801, when the time came to prepare the president's first annual message to Congress, to achieve a satisfactory conclusion on the levels of revenue, expenditure, and debt. At the end of 1801, Gallatin projected revenue for 1802 of $10.6 million, of which $9.5 million came from customs duties, $450,000 from land sales and the postal service, and $650,000 from internal taxes, especially the excise tax on whiskey stills that was left over from Hamilton's time. Gallatin's first priority was to reduce the outstanding debt. He calculated that by applying $7.3 million of revenue each year to debt service (interest and repayments), he could reduce the principal amount of the debt of the United States by $32 million over the eight years of two presidential terms. That would leave $45.6 million of debt, which, he calculated, in a growing budget and with a lower portion of the payments devoted to interest, could be paid off in full by 1817. Meanwhile, the 1802 budget, with revenues of $10.6 million and debt service of $7.3 million, left enough to finance the operations of the government with $3.3 million, about two-fifths of which went to the army and with the remainder split between the navy and civil expenses.

The Treasury was responsible for public lands, one of Gallatin's great interests. Jefferson appointed him to a commission, early in 1802, together with Secretary of State Madison and Attorney General Lincoln, to solve a longstanding dispute in Georgia. In 1795, the Georgia legislature had passed the so-called Yazoo Act, which allowed four land companies to sell large tracts of what were actually federal lands that were later to become parts of Alabama and Mississippi. This had fueled a speculative bubble, lost money for prominent investors, and remained a bone of contention between Georgia and the federal government. As the upshot of negotiations with the representatives of the state of Georgia, the commissioners agreed on the borders of Georgia as excluding the Alabama and Mississippi tracts, clarified that the Yazoo lands that had been sold were in fact the property of the United States, and achieved a financial settlement that provided the state of Georgia the first $1.25 million of receipts of the sale of those lands by the federal government and the next $5 million to the land companies themselves: this compromise solution solved the question of Georgia's borders and laid to rest the financial issue of the sale of lands. The agreement became known as the Yazoo Compromise.

A less contentious assignment concerned the unincorporated Northwest Territory, which ranged from the northern bank of the Ohio River to the Great Lakes. It was acquired by the United States under the Treaty of Paris with Great Britain in 1781 that ended the American War of Independence. This was the area where Gallatin had already been involved, in Congress, in the laying out of townships. So when the eastern portion of the Northwest Territory sought to enter the Union as the state of Ohio, Gallatin's opinion was important. He had long held the idea that adequate infrastructure was key to a thriving economy. He therefore proposed that one-tenth of the proceeds of the sale of federal lands in the state should be earmarked for a fund to build roads from the Atlantic coast across the whole state of Ohio. Congress reduced the percentage to one-twentieth, but the road was later built as the Cumberland Road or National Road. The provision of the Northwest Ordinance of 1787 by which a section of federal lands in towns was set aside for schools also remained in force. Thus, a year into Jefferson's presidency, on April 30, 1802, the Congress voted to admit Ohio, which joined the Union after ratification, on March 1, 1803.

INTERNATIONAL AFFAIRS

In retrospect, it is difficult to determine whether Jefferson and Gallatin's goal of detachment from foreign entanglements subsequently served to safeguard the United States from day-to-day involvement in Europe's internecine conflicts or whether it condemned the United States to remain unprepared, for more than a century and a half, every time its international engagement was required. In any event, during Jefferson's presidency, there was no escaping international affairs. For Gallatin, this specifically meant their effect on finance.

Under Presidents Washington and Adams, the United States paid an annual peace price to four countries, known as the Barbary states, located in north Africa, whose fleets patrolled the Mediterranean. These were Tripoli, Tunis, Algiers, and Morocco; the tributes, for the United States alone, had amounted to nearly $10 million. Although Jefferson was generally non-militaristic and had reduced naval appropriations, he ordered the U.S. fleet into combat with the Pasha of Tripoli, who had declared war on the United States in May 1801, shortly before Gallatin arrived at the Treasury. By the time Gallatin took up his duties, Jefferson had already decided to send a squadron to the Mediterranean to protect U.S. shipping. This hardly did the trick, and in the summer of 1802, while Jefferson was sojourning at Monticello, Secretary of the Navy Robert Smith added to the force. Gallatin preferred peace, as always, and implored Jefferson to avoid war expenditure and pay the tributes, just as many other countries did.

Still, the United States continued battling with the Barbary states until the *Philadelphia* was captured and its crew put to hard labor by Tripoli. Lieutenant Stephen Decatur, in command of the schooner *Intrepid,* freed the ship, and then, in an extraordinary act of derring-do, the American consul at Tunis, William Eaton, assembled a small force, including sixteen members of the U.S. Navy and Marine Corps, marched them across five hundred miles of north African desert, and captured Derna, thus earning the Marines the distinction of extending their reach "to the shores of Tripoli."

The major achievement of Jefferson's first term in office was the Louisiana Purchase, an issue where international affairs and the question of public lands perfectly intersected. The Louisiana Purchase is often described as the best real-estate deal in history, and it doubled the size of the United States. But its significance sharpens when set against the historical background of the development and decline of European empires in America, as well as the contemporaneous ambitions of Napoleon Bonaparte.

The first European explorer to reach the coast of what is now the United States was sent by the king of France. Whereas Columbus landed in the Caribbean, the Florentine navigator Giovanni da Verrazano, plying under the orders of King Francis I, in 1524 reached the mouth of New York Bay, where the bridge bearing his name stands today. In 1534, Jacques Cartier sailed from Saint Malo in Brittany across the Atlantic and down the St. Lawrence River, where he named a hilltop Mont Royal, which today is Montreal. In 1608, Samuel de Champlain established a permanent French settlement at Quebec. And in the ensuing century and a half, French explorers reached across America from the northwest to the southeast and down to the mouth of the Mississippi, where they founded New Orleans. At the height of *La Nouvelle France* around 1750, it comprised about one-third of the land mass of North America, including all or portions of what are today fourteen U.S. states and almost the entire eastern half of Canada, while Spain owned the area west of the Rockies. The French held their territory, however, with a population of only about seventy thousand, compared to a million inhabitants in the British colonies along the eastern seaboard. Pressure for imperial domination in North America might have occurred sooner or later between the French and the British, but it was made inevitable by the Seven Years' War from 1754 to 1763 (actually nine years), a worldwide conflict among colonial empires. In North America, France allied with various native tribes, and that portion of the struggle became known as the French and Indian Wars. On the Plains of Abraham at Quebec in 1759, General Montcalm lost New France to the British general James Wolfe. In the Treaty of Paris in 1763, France signed away all its North American holdings to Britain and to Spain, except for two small Atlantic islands, Saint Pierre and Miquelon, and two Caribbean island clusters around Guadeloupe and Martinique. France then disappeared from North America as a political power until the rise of Napoleon Bonaparte after the French Revolution.

Napoleon overthrew the Directory in the coup d'état of the "18 Brumaire An VII," the French Revolutionary calendar date for November 9, 1799. So when Jefferson and Gallatin took office in early 1801, Bonaparte had been sole ruler of France for more than a year. By this point, France exercised considerable power over Spain in Europe. Under some duress, the Spaniards agreed to the Third Treaty of San Ildefonso, signed on October 1, 1800, and initially kept secret, in which Napoleon reacquired the Louisiana Territory in exchange for assurances that a Spanish prince would be enthroned in Italy. In 1801, Napoleon planned an invasion of England, but instead France and Britain signed the short-lived Treaty of Amiens on March 25, 1802. Though billed as a "Definitive Treaty of Peace," it was to prove only a year-long truce. Governing circles in Europe were aware of transfer negotiations from the signing of the San Ildefonso treaty onward, but it took until mid-1802 for Jefferson's Cabinet to hear about it. At this point, the United States shared North America below Canada mainly with Spain, as administrator of the Louisiana Territory and Florida and the owner of the lands west of the Rocky Mountains. Jefferson was under no illusion about the importance of New Orleans, "through which three-eighths of our produce must pass to market."[4]

Napoleon originally wanted to expand the French empire again into North America. As a prelude, he sent an expeditionary force to Saint-Domingue on Hispaniola to suppress Toussaint Louverture's twelve-year uprising. With Napoleon's military campaign so close to home, news that France would be taking over the Louisiana Territory seriously alarmed Jefferson. "There is on the globe one single spot the possessor of which is our natural and habitual enemy. It is New Orleans. . . . The day that France takes possession of New Orleans," he wrote to the American minister in Paris, "we must marry ourselves to the British fleet and nation."[5] Coming from a Francophile such as Jefferson, ever wary of the British, this would have been a stunning turnabout in policy—but it was probably a provocation, meant to be shown to the French.

For Napoleon, Saint-Domingue turned into a disastrous campaign. Its commander, Charles Leclerc, the husband of Napoleon's sister Pauline, and much of his force of thirty-five thousand men died from yellow fever, the rebellion succeeded, and the French were compelled to withdraw. Thereupon, Napoleon abandoned his ambition to reestablish the French empire in North America and adopted as his priority to keep the Louisiana Territory out of the hands of the British. So he decided to sell it to the United States; but the Americans did not know this yet.

The Americans initially approached the transfer of the Louisiana Territory defensively, not as an opportunity. Their sense of danger heightened when the Spanish governor of Louisiana withdrew the right of Americans to use the port of New Orleans for transit of shipments. Federalists and the inhabitants of Kentucky and Tennessee proposed trying to capture the city by force, in essence a war against Spain and perhaps against France on American (but not United States) soil. Partly in response to these domestic pressures, Jefferson and Secretary of State Madison decided to offer to purchase New Orleans, and perhaps part of Florida, the western strip of which extended along the Gulf Coast. Nobody knew at this point what the French had acquired or what the precise borders were. The Americans had not seen the Third Treaty of San Ildefonso, and in fact the French and Spaniards had themselves neglected to specify in the treaty the exact geographical limits of what was being ceded. But at this point the focus was chiefly on New Orleans itself, not the broad territory covering much of what had been New France.

The American minister in Paris, Robert Livingston, was a distinguished official whom Jefferson had nominated and the Senate had confirmed on the day after Jefferson's inauguration. Now Jefferson and Madison sent instructions to Livingston to attempt to buy New Orleans. James Monroe joined Livingston for the negotiations; and Congress, with the cooperation of John Randolph, voted a resolution authorizing $2 million for "expenses relating to the intercourse between the United States and foreign nations" so that they would have money to offer.

On April 11, 1803, France broke diplomatic relations with Britain, put an end to the Treaty of Amiens, and returned to a state of war. On the very same day, Napoleon's foreign minister, Talleyrand, said to Livingston, "What will you give for the whole of Louisiana?" Livingston was taken unawares by the question but was not unfamiliar with the subject. He answered that he supposed the United States would pay $4 million. At this point Monroe had not yet arrived in Paris. Talleyrand rejected the offer as too low. Less than twenty days later, on April 30, 1803, the treaty by which France ceded the Louisiana Territory to the United States was signed by Monroe and Livingston. The purchase price was $15 million.

When word of the Louisiana Purchase reached America, not everyone was pleased. New England Federalists felt that it undermined the position and power of their states. Others believed that, since the borders of the territory were ill defined, the United States had bought a cat in a sack. There was also a heavy constitutional question, for there had never before been such an opportunity for the federal government to acquire territory from another established sovereign state (as opposed to Indian tribes). This engendered serious doubts in Jefferson's mind and debate within the Cabinet. Gallatin, the states'-rights frontiersman rooted in western Pennsylvania, now offered advice to Jefferson that could have been drafted by a Federalist:

> 1st that the United States as a nation have an inherent right to acquire property. 2d. That whenever that acquisition is by treaty, the same constituted authorities in whom the treaty-making power is vested have a constitutional right to sanction the acquisition. 3d. That whenever the territory has been acquired, Congress have the power either of admitting into the Union as a new State, or of annexing to a State with the consent of that State, or of making regulations for the government of such territory.[6]

In the end, for an idealistic Enlightenment president who wished to eschew international affairs, the Louisiana Purchase was an exercise in global realpolitik without compare.

Gallatin provided for the financing of the Louisiana Purchase, which unbalanced all his careful bookkeeping. The United States agreed to pay $11.25 million not in cash but in six-percent loan stock not redeemable for fifteen years. The remainder was to be spent in the United States to satisfy claims that Americans held against France. The Dutch bank Hope & Company and the British bank Barings were selected to purchase and distribute the American bonds and provide cash to the French. Gallatin got to know Alexander Baring in the autumn of 1803 when Baring came to negotiate the transaction in Washington. Gallatin also provided in his budgets for the payment of the additional debt and the interest on it. He had originally planned to be able to discharge the public debt of the United States by 1818. After giving effect to the receipts and disbursements of the Louisiana Purchase, he found it necessary to extend this deadline by only eighteen months.

Once the full implications of the Louisiana Purchase were understood, it was immensely popular and contributed substantially to the landslide re-election of Jefferson in 1804. The Twelfth Amendment to the Constitution, proposed by the Congress on December 9, 1803, provided for the separate election of president and vice president, to avoid the deadlock experienced in 1800. When the amendment was duly ratified by the states on June 15, 1804, Jefferson knew he would be reelected. His outgoing vice president was Aaron Burr, who killed Alexander Hamilton in a duel on July 11, 1804. Burr was subsequently disgraced. George Clinton, the warhorse and king-maker of New York State politics, replaced Burr as vice president in Jefferson's second administration.

Another happy outcome of the Louisiana Purchase was the Lewis and Clark expedition, authorized by Jefferson to explore new western territories. The expedition departed from St. Louis on May 14, 1804, and Gallatin's Treasury financed it—one of his smallest headaches, since the budget was minimal, although the impact was great. Gallatin, ever the son of Geneva and disciple of Rousseau, took a genuine interest in the content of the expedition itself. Lewis and Clark named a river in his honor.

MANAGING THE TREASURY, LIFE IN WASHINGTON

Gallatin handled the finances of the United States with great prudence during his first four years as secretary of the Treasury. In his report of December 9, 1805, he indicated that from April 1, 1801, to March 31, 1805, revenues had been $50,667,467 and expenditures $49,665,508, for a surplus of over a million dollars; and he included within those expenditures the payment of interest on foreign debt of $16,278,701 and the reimbursement of principal of debt of $19,281,447, both excellent measures for the finances of the United States and for its credit standing abroad. Despite the Barbary Wars, the Louisiana Purchase, and many other financial commitments during those years, he was right on target.

During Jefferson's second term, the Senate asked the Treasury to prepare a report on internal improvements, specifically public roads and canals.

The assignment took advantage of Gallatin's skill at painstaking research and leveraged his passion for geography, politics, land planning, economics, and infrastructure, providing the perfect showcase for his talents. After a year's hard work, he presented his report to the Senate on April 12, 1808. He divided it into four parts: improvements along the eastern seaboard, so as to provide for continuous inland navigation; land and water communications routes between the East Coast and western lands; canals and roads running north and northwest to the Great Lakes; and local canals and roads. He planned for a stable and supportive infrastructure for a civilized and prosperous society, and he took into account, with great finesse, the need to balance local, regional, and national preferences. Gallatin provided for the financing, including for matters we would today characterize as homeland security, and took account of the need for upkeep, maintenance, and repairs. Congress failed to adopt the plan, although parts of it were executed in later years; it stands as a model of sustainable development.

Jefferson had pet projects and pet peeves: nothing irked him more than the Bank of the United States, a single, central bank owned by external shareholders alongside the federal government. This was a Federalist project that Hamilton had adopted in 1791. Gallatin strongly supported the idea in his *Sketch of the Finances* in 1796. Against Jeffersonian ideas of state banks widely dispersed so as to avoid a monopoly of the money men, Gallatin defended the Bank of the United States on multiple occasions. As soon as the Louisiana Purchase went into effect, he ensured the establishment of a branch of the Bank of the United States in New Orleans, over Jefferson's objections—and Gallatin was furious when he learned that a collaborator of Jefferson's in New Orleans intended to establish a bank there on his own initiative. Gallatin held his ground against Jefferson again and again. Ultimately, Jefferson's objections, which were ideological, could not stand up against Gallatin's justifications, which were practical.

Gallatin worked long hours, often into the evening, during both of Jefferson's administrations. Since Jefferson was a bachelor, Dolley Madison, the wife of the secretary of state, took upon herself the role of supreme Washington hostess, which she later perfected as first lady. The Gallatins' house on Capitol Hill, however, was a center of entertainment for members of Congress, many of whom were on their own in Washington and residing in boarding houses. They were grateful for the convivial domestic atmosphere.

Hannah and her sons, James and Albert Rolaz, spent the summers at her parents' house in New York. Gallatin often made the trip with them, only to return to the sweltering capital, where he worried that he was not doing enough for the boys' education. Hannah bore their first daughter, Catherine, on August 22, 1801, but the baby died of measles and whooping cough the following April. Hannah had three more girls, though only one survived. Their second daughter, Frances, born on February 3, 1803, lived a long and healthy life. Two more sisters—Sophia Albertina, born in 1804, and Hannah Maria, born in 1807—died within a year of birth. Hannah's sister, Maria, ever an object of Gallatin's affection, visited frequently and met her future husband in Washington. Particularly when Gallatin was left on his own, he delighted in receiving distinguished visitors, and his account of the passage of the brilliant and eccentric Alexander von Humboldt in June 1804 provided both a moment of welcome relaxation and one of the most amusing letters he wrote to his wife.

INTERNATIONAL AFFAIRS INTRUDE AGAIN

Hostilities between Britain and France, which resumed after the collapse of the Treaty of Amiens, had an important effect on the United States— no longer because of the threat of European imperial incursions onto the American continent but because of the tensions engendered between Britain and France on the high seas. Napoleon crowned himself emperor on December 2, 1804, at the Cathedral of Notre Dame de Paris. In 1805, Britain convinced Austria and Russia to join a Third Coalition against France. Napoleon tried to lure the Royal Navy away from its blockade of the British Isles, so that a Franco-Spanish fleet could take control of the English Channel and allow French armies to invade England from Boulogne. It was not to be. Admiral Horatio Lord Nelson gave chase to the French fleet under the command of Admiral Villeneuve from April 1805 until he cornered Villeneuve in Cadiz. On October 21, 1805, with Nelson's missive from his flagship HMS *Victory*, "England expects every man will do his duty," Britain opened the Battle of Trafalgar. Nelson was shot at a quarter past one in the afternoon, and the French fleet surrendered in retreat. Nelson died of his wounds at half past four that day, but Britannia ruled the waves.

Napoleon thereupon renounced his strategy of a land invasion of England for which he had massed his troops at Boulogne. His only option was naval blockade, which would render British maritime supremacy ineffectual. He marched his armies from Boulogne eastward across the Continent. On the first anniversary of his coronation, he defeated Austria and Russia at the Battle of Austerlitz. Flush with victory, Napoleon issued his

Berlin Decree of November 21, 1806, which forbade the import of British goods into European countries allied with or dependent on France.

In many ways the British continued to behave as if their American cousins were unruly rebels who really still belonged within the British Empire. They evidenced this attitude in the practice of "impressment," whereby British ships stopped, searched, and seized sailors of British origin from American ships. The relatively higher wages in the U.S. Navy stimulated desertions from the Royal Navy, but impressment was widely abused and sailors taken on the thinnest of pretexts. The terms of a treaty that James Monroe negotiated with Great Britain late in 1806 compounded the complexity of relations between Britain and the United States. Congress adopted on April 18, 1806, a "Non-Importation Act" to take effect in November 1806, interdicting the import of many goods from the British Empire, which the United States actually hoped would serve as a ploy to soften British policy toward the United States. This Monroe-Pinckney Treaty, signed December 31, 1806, was designed to repeal the Non-Importation Act and replace it with a new agreement. However, the British negotiated toughly, and the terms of the Monroe-Pinckney Treaty, which were very favorable to Britain, included a provision that the United States must refuse to recognize the Berlin Decree before the treaty would come into effect. Jefferson never even sent it to the Senate for ratification, and the Non-Importation Act, which had just gone into effect, continued.

In Britain, the appropriate legal response to a decree from the French emperor was the issue by the sovereign of "Orders in Council," a measure adopted by the Privy Council without ratification by Parliament but for which the government was ultimately responsible to Parliament. The Orders in Council of November 11, 1807, issued at the behest of Foreign Secretary George Canning, forbade French trade with the United Kingdom, its allies, or neutrals and instructed the Royal Navy to blockade French and allied ports. Napoleon promptly fought back with his Milan Decree of December 17, 1807, stating that no European country was to trade with the United Kingdom. Both these measures were devastating for nations involved in neutral shipping, including the United States.

THE DISASTER OF THE EMBARGO

Jefferson fell prey to two simultaneous, seductive, self-reinforcing conclusions: first, that Bonaparte, despite his inability to invade England, would soon cripple the British; second, that the United States could disable

Britain by economic sanctions. Still, he did not want to choose between the two warring powers. So the only option was a self-imposed blockade that would return the United States to its position of benign isolation. This was embodied in the Embargo Act, which Jefferson rushed through Congress in one day, on December 22, 1807. The act went into effect immediately. It prohibited all exports from the United States, forbade American ships to sail abroad, and ordered American vessels overseas to come home or lie in port. Essentially the United States shut down all its international trade. American sailors, far from being impressed, now sought employment from British vessels. The Embargo Act was hastily drafted and required numerous corrections over many months to achieve any kind of enforcement. It failed to provide for many contingencies. It encouraged smuggling and lawlessness, particularly across the wide-open Canadian border. It hobbled the industries and ports of the United States, not least in New England. It set American against American. It required enforcement measures by the U.S. government against its own citizens—measures generally enforced by officers of Gallatin's Treasury—that, perpetrated by someone else, would have been anathema to Thomas Jefferson as violations of individual and economic freedom: whether vessels could be loaded or unloaded, how much in the way of foodstuffs could be shipped from state to state, the seizure of merchandise and property. Jefferson's embargo inflicted far more damage on the American economy than it did on Britain's. But it was his idea inspired by his ideals of an America that could stand apart from the vagaries of other countries. It was a huge self-inflicted wound, and resistance to it from citizens whose livelihood and freedoms were directly threatened by the embargo took Jefferson completely by surprise.

Gallatin opposed the embargo for both domestic and international reasons: he believed it would have no taming effect on Britain at all and would produce precisely the damage to the American economy that in actuality came to pass. Jefferson did not listen. Gallatin's pragmatism, or perhaps his sense of duty, caused him to carry on. Gallatin decided, however distasteful it may have been, to remain in his position and enforce the policy of his president and the Congress. It is surprising, maybe even disappointing, that he did not choose to resign on principle, so much did the embargo violate all his precepts of sound financial management, individual liberty, and limited central government. Worst of all, from Gallatin's perspective, the embargo cut off the revenues of the federal government, virtually all of which were duties on international trade, depressed American economic activity with unprecedented brutality, and upset in one blow the careful calculations and prudent frugality that Gallatin had implemented over the prior eight years.

When Thomas Jefferson's tenure as president of the United States is examined in the light of international relations, it becomes clear that his greatest triumph and his greatest tragedy both related to France and, more specifically, both resulted from a decision by Napoleon following a defeat. Bonaparte's losses in Saint-Domingue led him to abandon the acquisition of Louisiana and paved the way for Jefferson's triumphal purchase. Bonaparte's loss of the French fleet at Trafalgar convinced him of his inability to invade England and led to the blockades and counterblockades with Britain that ultimately trapped Jefferson between Britain and France, and so led to the embargo. Early in his term, Jefferson had written to Gallatin that their administration would be less influenced than the Federalists' by events abroad and would not be compelled to choose between the two imperial powers of France and Britain. He could not have been more wrong.

Gallatin honed in the executive the qualities he had acquired in the legislature. His responsibilities ranged from the management of the Treasury to the public lands to foreign affairs to domestic infrastructure. He showed himself every inch the analyst and technician, respectful of the facts, that he had always been. At least until the embargo, he held to his Geneva principles of frugality and avoidance of debt. But he also confronted, more than ever before, the consequences of imperfect choices. Unlike Jefferson, he retained his ideals, but he did not succumb to ideology. Whenever a practical choice needed to be made, he made the choice on its merits, not on the basis of polemical obedience or political expediency. When he felt he had to, he opposed his chief and his allies with courtesy and tenacity, but in the end he did not abandon them. Gallatin began the Jefferson administration wishing to turn from politics to policy. He was now prepared to move from policy to statesmanship.

[5]

MADISON'S SECRETARY OF THE TREASURY, 1809–1813

IMMEDIATELY after James Madison's election to the presidency was confirmed, Jefferson effectively ceased to behave as president of the United States, on the pretext that he wished to make no decisions that would bind his successor. Yet until Madison's inauguration on March 4, 1809, only Jefferson was president, and only he had the powers conferred on the president by the Constitution. Neither his secretary of state, the president-elect Madison, nor his secretary of the Treasury, Gallatin, could operate in his stead, however much they had functioned as a triumvirate together over the previous eight years. Furthermore, the catastrophic economic situation in the country resulting from the embargo caused enormous confusion in Congress, and without policy guidance from the executive branch, even the members of the administration's own Republican Party lost their bearings. President Jefferson's message to Congress in early November 1808 expressed no view on the embargo, which added to the chaos. On November 15, 1808, Gallatin wrote to Jefferson to say that he and Madison felt the Congress needed decisiveness from the president. A week later, on November 22, 1808, Congressman George W. Campbell of Tennessee, a member of the committee on foreign relations, submitted a message to Congress in the name of the president. This document became known as Campbell's Report, but Gallatin drafted it.

Campbell's Report laid out in exhaustive detail the American view, based on historical precedent and international law, of why Canning's Orders in Council were unjustifiable. They could not be defended as retaliation to Napoleon's decrees and were in "open violation" of prior British policy.[1] Even more important, the report was meant to propose positions that the Republicans in Congress could rally around: first, that the United States refused to submit to the edicts of Britain and France; second, that the United States would exclude British and French ships, products, and allies from its ports; third, that increased measures should be taken for the defense of the United States. To fill the leadership void left by Jefferson, Gallatin's position was, in essence, that Canning and Napoleon both needed to know that the United States meant business and would not be toyed with. In essence, Gallatin recommended either a ruthless implementation of the embargo or war with Britain and France at the same time. These resolutions were adopted by the House after three weeks of debate. Gallatin offered to finance a one-year war from funds in the Treasury, without recourse to new loans or new taxes. When Jefferson and Madison demurred in favor of the embargo, Gallatin asked for additional powers, as secretary of the Treasury, to carry out the embargo law, and these were provided in the Enforcement Act of January 1809. This draconian measure violated all the Republicans' traditional scruples and outstripped in its central government control anything the Federalists had ever attempted.

At the same time, in private, Gallatin encouraged the young British minister in Washington, David Erskine, who was married to an American woman and well disposed toward the United States, in his desire to improve relations with the United States. When Erskine implied that Madison might take a more pro-British, or at least a less pro-French, attitude than Jefferson had, Gallatin did nothing to disabuse him of this notion. In a series of dispatches to Canning, the British foreign secretary, on December 3 and 4, 1808, Erskine recommended that Britain take advantage of this potential improvement in relations.

Thus engaged in domestic politics and in international diplomacy, Gallatin also continued to fulfill his duties as secretary of the Treasury. Gallatin submitted his Treasury report on December 10, 1808. He began with the financial report, which was still positive because the effect of the embargo would be principally felt in the Treasury accounts of the following year. For the fiscal year ending September 30, 1808, Gallatin reported record revenues of close to $18 million and a cash balance in the Treasury projected for January 1, 1809, of $16 million, and he forecasted a surplus for fiscal 1809 of $3 million. The report then went on, under the guise of a financial presentation, to look ahead at the consequences of four international scenarios. Two implied capitulation to Britain and France, in violation of the resolutions of Campbell's Report; the other two contemplated either the continuation of the embargo or war.

Gallatin became convinced at the end of December that Congress did not have the stomach either to continue the embargo or to go to war. Different factions prevailed within the Republican Party and between the two houses of Congress. In the Senate the mood was more warlike. On January

4, 1809, the Senate adopted a bill that directed a full naval mobilization, which would end up costing the Treasury $6 million whether war came or not—all the money going on current expenses, buying nothing of lasting value. The vote by the Senate was a slap in the face to Gallatin not because it prepared for war but because it allocated funds so carelessly. While the Senate moved in one direction, the House moved in another. On February 2, 1809, the House voted to lift the embargo entirely in June; the next day it changed course, voting to do so on the very day Madison was to be inaugurated, March 4, 1809. In the end, Congress passed a Non-Intercourse Act on March 1, 1809, just four days before Jefferson's presidency ended. This ended the embargo and restored trade with everyone except Britain and France directly. The American system of checks and balances, in which the legislature is a policymaking and not just a lawmaking body, had shown just how unbalanced and ineffective it could become if one branch, in this case an enervated executive, failed to uphold its office.

A ROCKY START TO THE MADISON ADMINISTRATION

After serving as a senator and congressman and for eight years as secretary of the Treasury, Gallatin harbored no higher ambition than to become secretary of state. Madison had occupied that position throughout Jefferson's two administrations, and just as Gallatin succeeded Madison as leader of the Republicans in the House, so it appeared sensible that he might now do so as Madison ascended from the State Department to the presidency. This was certainly Madison's desire, but he kept it to himself until shortly before his inauguration. When news of Madison's choice reached the Senate, opposition was immediate. Gallatin's antagonist was the navy lobby, led by Senator Samuel Smith, his brother Robert, who was secretary of the navy, and their friends in the Senate, including Senator William Giles of Virginia. For years, Gallatin had antagonized the Smiths. Early in the first Jefferson administration, he had written to the president to criticize Secretary of the Navy Robert Smith's management of the Navy Department. "I cannot discover any approach towards reform in that department,"[2] he said, and he was especially annoyed at Robert Smith's habit of coming to the Treasury with last-minute demands for immediate cash. Now Robert Smith himself wanted to become secretary of state instead of Gallatin. Senator Giles declared that he would not vote for a foreigner as secretary of state, despite that same foreigner having held the office of secretary of the Treasury for eight years, and the cause was taken up by William Duane and his newspaper the *Aurora*. Madison attempted to satisfy them both by appointing Gallatin secretary of state while moving Robert Smith to the Treasury. Gallatin, ever disdainful of Smith, dismissed this idea by saying he could not run both departments at the same time. Madison made Robert Smith secretary of state, and Gallatin remained secretary of the Treasury. But Gallatin's assault on the Smiths was far from over.

James Madison was inaugurated on Saturday, March 4, 1809. In his address, Madison reviewed the difficulties in which the country found itself after an era of unparalleled prosperity. He blamed America's predicament on the warring powers of Britain and France, not on poor handling of its own affairs. He reiterated his commitment to the policies of Washington and Jefferson: to seek peace with all nations and neutrality between belligerents, even though that policy had conspicuously failed to operate in the interests of the United States. He finished with an appeal to God and his fellow Americans for their support, to compensate for his modest abilities in this high office. All in all it was a lackluster speech that offered no new policy ideas. The inaugural ball was otherwise: it benefited from the presence of the president's wife, Dolley Madison, who became the consummate Washington hostess and the model for future generations of first ladies.

James Madison came to the presidency with impressive credentials but insufficient qualifications. Known as the "Father of the Constitution"—a distinction which he always maintained belonged to several of the Founding Fathers and not to him alone—Madison had authored the Federalist Papers, along with Hamilton and John Jay, and had drafted the Bill of Rights, which was adopted as the first ten amendments to the U.S. Constitution. Like Washington and Jefferson, he was a Virginian from a plantation family; and he became the largest landowner in his county in Virginia. He attended Princeton (then known as the College of New Jersey) and entered politics. He and Gallatin had been colleagues in the House of Representatives and in the Jefferson administration, and it was of course Madison who had negotiated the Louisiana Purchase as secretary of state.

The problem was that Madison did not exercise power effectively. He was better suited to drafting papers and negotiating treaties than to making tough decisions that might earn criticism and enemies. He had a shortcoming that has often been attributed to American lawyers called into government service, namely, the conviction that disputes can be resolved by calling on all parties to behave reasonably in pursuit of compromise. Whereas Jefferson was too idealistic, Madison was too indecisive. Moreover, he had periods of ill health throughout his life and so was not endowed with the robust physical stamina of a Washington or a Jefferson—notwithstanding which, he lived to the age of eighty-five. Too much the technocrat, not enough the politician, small and looking old before his time, he did not have the stuff to control Congress and lead the country.

David Erskine conveyed to the U.S. government—through Robert Smith, the secretary of state—that the British Orders in Council would be withdrawn, as regarded their impact on the United States, by June 10, 1809. In response, a delighted President Madison rescinded the provisions of the Non-Intercourse Act as regarded Great Britain in a proclamation of April 19, 1809, and declared trade restored between the two countries as of June 10, 1809. The Erskine Agreement was a hugely welcome measure in the United States and boosted Madison's popularity enormously. Not only had trade resumed in March with most countries; now it would pick up again with Britain. But George Canning, the British foreign secretary, was not of this view. Canning considered that Erskine had substantially exceeded his instructions. Britain's policy at this time was to pursue global domination ruthlessly, especially as it was under constant threat from Napoleon. Canning's purpose was not to promote trade with America but to annihilate entirely America's ability to trade and its ability to fight to retain that trade. He sought for Britain the total command of the seas, not merely the ability to ply them alongside others. Canning disavowed the Erskine Agreement and did not revoke the Orders in Council. He recalled Erskine and his American wife and forthwith replaced Erskine in Washington with a new envoy hostile to America, Francis James Jackson, and his Prussian wife. Canning's disavowal of Erskine became known in the United States in July 1809 and provoked despondency in American political and economic circles. Madison had been badly outmaneuvered. He had succumbed to wishful thinking by putting his faith in Erskine, though he should have recognized that Canning was capable of a much more hard-nosed approach.

The situation could hardly have been worse for the United States—or more dissatisfactory in the eyes of Gallatin. Madison's choice as secretary of state—Robert Smith—was proving disastrous. Consequently, Madison effectively had to perform this role himself, and, despite having occupied that office for eight years, Madison was now proving inept, as his reversal by Canning showed. In addition, Gallatin, while continuing as secretary of the Treasury, had to abandon almost all his prudent policy ambitions for the financial management of the country. Although increasing trade after the end of the embargo increased tax receipts—in essence, the embargo had shown that U.S. government revenue was dependent on American international commerce—Gallatin had to shelve his desire to reimburse the national debt and create a national infrastructure in favor of dealing with the short-term effects of Congress's policy zig-zags and the British and French responses to them. Beyond that, Madison had begun his first term as Jefferson had ended his second, by ceding power to Congress. Madison created a vacuum of executive authority, then tried to compensate by restoring trade with Britain, only to end up a victim of Canning's tough approach.

GALLATIN'S FRUSTRATION GROWS

Exacerbating Gallatin's frustration was the situation with the Smiths, who, with their political friends, increasingly became known as the "Invisibles." Gallatin permanently poisoned his relations with the Invisibles when he raised the issue of financial irregularities in Robert Smith's earlier custodianship of the Department of the Navy. This went beyond his usual criticisms of lax management practices to suggest that something illicit had taken place. Secretary of the Navy Robert Smith had bought bills of exchange on behalf of the Navy Department from a firm controlled by his brother Senator Samuel Smith at good profit and little risk. Gallatin found this outrageous and confided his concerns to a political friend, who spread the word about it in order to frustrate Senator Smith's bid for reelection. The Smiths were incensed. John Randolph opened a public inquiry into the matter, but Robert Smith, now secretary of state, managed to defend himself and his family's honor reasonably well. Gallatin kept his calm, was not extravagant in his accusations, and consequently showed no remorse when the Smiths cleared their name. In essence he had discovered an irregularity which, instead of being solved quietly as an administrative issue, had been exploited for political purposes. Gallatin had not pressed it, but he had initiated it and let it run its course. There was no peace with the Smiths thereafter, and Gallatin could count on the unremitting opposition of the Invisibles to almost anything he sought to do.

As Jefferson had so often done, Madison spent the summer at his country house in Virginia. The Gallatins were invited to stay with the Madisons at Montpelier and accepted their hospitality. Hannah Gallatin and Dolley Madison were by this time good friends. The Madisons' property at Montpelier lay near Jefferson's estate at Monticello, and together they paid a visit to Thomas Jefferson. The three statesmen—the triumvirate of old—discussed the current dilemmas the country faced. During that visit, Gallatin confided at least in Jefferson and perhaps in both that he felt he was in an impossible predicament with his archenemy, Robert Smith, in the Cabinet and that perhaps he should resign. Jefferson encouraged him to stay in a letter of October 11, 1809. He emphasized the country's need for Madison and Gallatin to work together, not least in the worthy aim of reducing the national debt. Jefferson urged Gallatin to set aside any thought of leaving, focus on the next eight years, and not consider retiring before then.[3] Gallatin replied to Jefferson from Washington on November 8, 1809, to say he would not allow his wounded feelings to influence his own decision. But Gallatin desired a broader policy role—and showed his bitterness at remaining in the Treasury while a bungler had the job he wanted at the Department of State. He wrote to Jefferson,

> I cannot, my dear sir, consent to act the part of a mere financier, to become a contriver of taxes, a dealer of loans, a seeker of resources for the purpose of supporting useless baubles, of increasing the number of idle and dissipated members of the community, of fattening contractors, pursers, and agents, and of introducing in all its ramifications that system of patronage, corruption and rottenness which you so justly execrate.[4]

In the same letter, Gallatin made it clear that he knew his enemies wished to drive him from office. He was right, and they would do everything they could to that purpose.

In the midst of all this, Gallatin carried on with the work of the Treasury. He sent his annual report to Congress on December 8, 1809, one year after the Treasury report that had contemplated war or a heightened embargo. This report, for the fiscal year ending September 30, 1809, more fully included the effects of the embargo, and Gallatin was in the unhappy position of sending his first-ever report showing a deficit for the year. Whereas he had previously shown surpluses even after giving effect to the paying down of the capital amount of the national debt, on this occasion, the expenses of the government fell short of revenues by $1.3 million before any debt repayments were factored in. Gallatin asked for authority to incur a fresh loan of $4 million if military and naval spending reached the level of 1809. His financial system rested on the principle that if Congress authorized expenditure, then the Treasury had to find the money, either through taxes or through borrowing. If Congress and the executive acted in concert, this was eminently achievable. If not, the management of the Treasury became more problematic.

Ever phlegmatic, especially in his official reports, Gallatin drew attention in the closing paragraph of the 1809 Treasury report to the ineffectiveness of the Non-Intercourse Act. Madison revived the act, with its half measures of trade restrictions, against Britain after Canning's disavowal of the Erskine Agreement. It contained many exceptions, provided precious few means of enforcement, and did not prevent many violations. Consequently, Americans traded with Britain and France quite freely yet in breach of U.S. law, while the U.S. government still attempted, and spent money, to restrict that trade. Gallatin recommended either a system of restriction that could be fully enforced or the abandonment of any restriction at all.

President Madison's political convictions compounded the complexity of this problem. In the formative years of the republic, Alexander Hamilton had felt the executive should have exclusive jurisdiction over foreign affairs. Madison, with his more Republican, states'-rights, non-Federalist principles, felt that Congress needed to be involved on matters of foreign commerce, which the Constitution specified should be regulated by Congress. Madison therefore ceded executive policymaking power to Congress. But if this was to be the method, Gallatin would employ it. On December 19, 1809, Congressman Nathaniel Macon, of the House of Representatives Committee on Foreign Relations, introduced a bill, which became known as Macon's Bill No. 1, reportedly with significant content from the Treasury. It was essentially a short-term diplomatic negotiating ploy, but, given the circumstances, it needed to be adopted by Congress. Macon's Bill No. 1 imposed severe restrictions on British and French shipping and imports to the United States but authorized the president to relax these if and when France or Britain removed their restrictions; and the bill was set to expire on March 4, 1810. As a political move, it was brilliant: the bill was as tough on Britain and France as it was on the United States, it gave them every incentive to relax their restrictions, it authorized the president to decide when to relax the restrictions instead of requiring yet another legislative act and so shifted power from Congress to the executive, and it gave a short deadline to encourage Britain and France to respond quickly. The bill passed the House but failed in the Senate, where the Invisibles first emasculated it and then killed it in early 1810.

A much milder bill, known as Macon's Bill No. 2, was introduced to the House of Representatives on April 7, 1810, and finally passed in the Senate on the last day of the legislature, May 1, 1810. Macon's Bill No. 2 had no teeth and succumbed to almost every one of the restrictions of Britain and France. The bill did provide that if one of the belligerents repealed its restrictions, then the United States would restore nonintercourse with the other; in this way, the United States would be bound to choose between Britain and France based not on America's own criteria or interests but on the choice of one or both of the belligerents themselves. This was a thoroughly unnecessary renouncement of national sovereignty, exceptionally bad policy arising from a divided legislature and an empty executive. Madison had refused to intervene in the debates, did not veto the bill, and in one sense welcomed it as a legal framework within which to conduct his policies. He foresaw that Britain would be happy with the status quo and that France might wish to revoke its restrictions so as to wrong-foot Britain.

What Madison did not foresee was that, having been the dupe of Canning in the Erskine affair, he would be the dupe of Napoleon now. In response to Macon's Bill No. 2 of May 1, 1810, Napoleon's foreign minister, the Duc de Cadore, wrote a letter on August 5, 1810, to John Armstrong, the American minister to France. He communicated Napoleon's offer to revoke the Berlin and Milan decrees as of November 1, 1809, provided Britain revoked its Orders in Council. If Britain failed to make that revocation, then the United States agreed to enforce nonintercourse with Britain. Napoleon took full advantage of Congress's policy confusion and Madison's irresolution. First, Macon's Bill No. 2 provided that a belligerent must sweep away all restrictions against American shipping, but Napoleon only offered to revoke the Berlin and Milan decrees. He had also issued the Rambouillet Decree on March 23, 1810, of which Congress was unaware when it adopted Macon's Bill No. 2 on May 1, 1810; the Rambouillet Decree provided for the seizure of American property in France. Second, Napoleon was offering but not committing to revoke the Berlin and Milan decrees, and that offer was valid only provided the British revoked their restrictions. Yet Madison jumped on the opportunity of the Duc de Cadore's letter even before he received Armstrong's dispatches from Paris. On November 2, 1810, Madison issued a presidential proclamation restoring trade with France and restricting intercourse with Britain in three months' time unless Britain revoked its Orders in Council. Madison fully understood that Napoleon offered neither a binding commitment nor full compliance with the language of Macon's Bill No. 2. He took a calculated risk. It did not work. Britain maintained its Orders in Council in place.

Thus, despite Gallatin's having called for greater clarity on U.S. trade policy in his 1809 Treasury report, the year 1810 saw neither a resolution of the trade disputes with Britain and France nor a smooth policymaking process between Congress and the executive. The same frustration arose with respect to the renewal of the charter of the Bank of the United States. From the outset, in Congress and then as secretary of the Treasury, Gallatin had been a strong proponent and defender of this institution, even in the face of determined resistance by Thomas Jefferson. As Congress reconvened for a short session to last from December 3, 1810, until March 3, 1811, it was imperative that it debate and, in Gallatin's view, extend the bank's charter, which was set to expire on the twentieth anniversary of its founding on February 25, 1791. Gallatin made plain his support for the renewal of the charter in a message addressed to Congress on the last day of Jefferson's administration in March 1809 and again in January 1811. The House of Representatives conducted a lengthy debate and on January 24, 1811, voted by sixty-five to sixty-four to postpone indefinitely the decision whether to renew the charter, in essence putting the Bank of the United States in a temporary but potentially long-term suspension of its activities. In the Senate, the Invisibles had their day: on February 20, 1811, the Senate vote was tied seventeen to seventeen. The president of the Senate, Vice President George Clinton, disliked President Madison enormously and voted against the bill, thus breaking the tie and putting an end to the Bank of the United States. By this point the executive had ceded an enormous amount of power to the Congress, and within the executive, the Treasury was deprived of all the power that Gallatin's enemies could efface or extract. Gallatin was spared pointed personal abuse, but this was nonetheless a test of his power and influence. Defeat on an issue he had consistently advocated could only weaken his position.

GALLATIN PROVOKES A CABINET CRISIS

Congress adjourned on March 3, 1811, and the next day or very soon after Gallatin wrote to Madison,

> I have long and seriously reflected on the present state of things and on my personal situation. This has for some time been sufficiently unpleasant, and nothing but a sense of public duty and attachment to yourself could have induced me to retain it to this day. But I am convinced that in neither respect can I be any longer useful under existing circumstances.

Gallatin went on to say that in a government like that of the United States where power was dispersed, and in circumstances like those prevailing where the country was under constant pressure from abroad, members of the administration needed to maintain a "heartfelt cordiality." In this, Gallatin wrote, "your present Administration is defective." Policymaking was blocked, difficulties were magnified, public confidence was eroded, factions had risen up that were "equally hostile to yourself and the general welfare." Gallatin went on: "Such state of things cannot last; a radical and speedy remedy has become absolutely necessary. What that ought to be, what change would best promote the success of your Administration and the welfare of the United States, is not for me to say." And he closed, "I beg leave to tender you my resignation, to take place at such a day within a reasonable time as you will think most consistent with the public service. I hope that I hardly need add any expressions of my respect and sincere personal attachment to you, of the regret I will feel on leaving you at this critical time, and the grateful sense I will ever retain of your kindness to me."[5]

The quoted text comes from a draft, and the original letter has not survived. The fact remains that, faced with the prospect of losing Gallatin, James Madison refused to accept his resignation and instead fired Robert Smith as secretary of state. He authorized Gallatin to sound out James Monroe, then governor of Virginia, to take up that position. The remedy was indeed "radical and speedy," for Monroe was approached within a week and assumed office on April 1, 1811. Gallatin had galvanized Madison into action; this was to be a relief but only a reprieve. Smith went down fighting. The outcry in the press, the political class, and among the public was decidedly hostile. But it was far better to have Monroe at the Department of State.

Gallatin presented his 1811 Treasury report in late November and, with the effect of the resumption in trade, was able to show a surplus of $5 million for the prior fiscal year, owing to the increase in imports and the duty on them. He projected a deficit for the following fiscal year, however, of $1 million, which would therefore require recourse to borrowing. In the decade that he had served as secretary of the Treasury, fully half the public debt, more than $46 million, had been repaid. The remainder of a bit more than $45 million required $2.2 million per year be set aside in the federal budget for interest payments. All internal taxes had been abolished during Gallatin's tenure, including the tax on whiskey and the tax on salt, and a two-and-a-half-percent additional tax for a Mediterranean Fund that had been created in Jefferson's first term to pay off the Barbary pirates had since been abandoned. The management of the Treasury had been especially adept at dealing with contingencies such as the Louisiana Purchase and the embargo. A great weakness was the vulnerability of the United States to a reduction in government revenue in the event of a reduction in trade, since, in accordance with the Republican-Democrat principles of Jefferson and his party, there was at this point no tax on U.S. citizens for activities carried out inside the United States. As a consequence, and as Gallatin's 1811 Treasury report pointed out, government receipts could drop from $15 million to $6 or $8 million in case of war or adverse trade circumstances, so that war needed to be financed by loans but also perpetuated the accumulation of government debt. Gallatin had paid off debt in good years but was obliged to borrow anew in worse years. He had maintained the credit standing of the United States, but if war came, the inevitable additional expense and the probable shortfall of revenues would have to be made up by loans or taxes or sales of government land.

THE COMING OF THE WAR OF 1812

President Madison called on Congress to reconvene in Washington on November 4, 1811. Before its adjournment in March 1811, Congress had endorsed Madison's move to reinstate nonintercourse with Britain in the face of Canning's refusal to rescind the Orders in Council. This gave an unfair advantage to France since Madison maintained more open trade with France, even though the French were seizing American ships. Meanwhile, more and more acts of aggression occurred with the British. This new twelfth Congress included representatives of a younger, up-and-coming generation of Republican Democrats from further west and south. Chief among these was Speaker of the House of Representatives Henry Clay of Kentucky, who soon moved to turn that parliamentary function into a position of political power. This group of aggressive young men—who also included John C. Calhoun, Langdon Cheves, Felix Grundy, and William Lowndes—were tired of do-nothing diplomacy and pushed for war. They became known as the "War Hawks" and gathered more and more influence as the session of Congress progressed from late 1811 into the winter and spring of 1812. President Madison, who had urged war-readiness measures on Congress in his message of November 1811, nonetheless was unsure of his own position on war with Britain. He made no particular attempt to intervene in the congressional debates, even as Gallatin and the new secretary of state James Monroe carried the executive's positions to Congress. Still, it was clear that the people and their representatives wanted war, and neither Madison nor his administration intended to oppose that. On March 31, 1812, Secretary of State Monroe conveyed to the Committee on Foreign Affairs of the House of Representatives that President Madison recommended the House declare war before adjourning but should not come to a decision until the latest diplomatic dispatches were received from Europe on the *Hornet,* which reached America on May 22, 1812, without definitive news. By then, Congress was ready to adjourn, and a delegation led by Henry Clay told Madison the time had come to act. Madison complied by sending a message to Congress on June 1, 1812, asking for a declaration of war against Britain, with war against France to remain in abeyance until negotiations with France concluded. The House voted for war on June 4, 1812, and the Senate did the same on June 17, 1812. Madison signed the bill on June 18, 1812. Canning revoked the Orders in Council on June 16, 1812, two days before the American declaration of war became effective but too late to alter the course of events.

In 1812, Madison was reelected with almost no opposition and without campaigning. After twelve years of rule by the Republican-Democrats, the Federalists' support base had shrunk to the Northeast. The vice president, George Clinton of New York, died in April 1812, and his nephew De Witt Clinton was nominated as Madison's vice-presidential candidate. The Federalists supported De Witt Clinton, but Madison won in the electoral college by one hundred twenty-eight votes to a mere twenty-nine for Clinton.

The War of 1812 was known as "Mr. Madison's War," and it did not get off to a good start. Neither the country nor its armed forces were in any way prepared for a full-scale multiyear conflict. Public support waned, especially after word spread of Canning's revocation of the Orders in Council. Congress planned on an army of twenty-five thousand men, but it proved difficult to raise the recruits. With mediocre leadership, little training, and meager supplies, the American fighting force began the War of 1812 in pathetic shape. An initial campaign to invade Canada proved to be a ludicrous disaster that culminated in the surrender of Detroit to the British on August 16, 1812. Generals William Henry Harrison and Henry Dearborn received orders to take aggressive action in Canada but simply declined to move against their targets. Summing up the beginning of the war, on December 18, 1812, Gallatin wrote to Jefferson, "The series of misfortunes experienced this year in our military land operations exceeds all anticipations made even by those who had least confidence in our inexperienced officers and undisciplined men."[6]

DISASTERS BARELY AVERTED

The financial situation of the Treasury was no better than the military situation in the field. From the time war was declared in mid-1812 until the spring of 1813, the Treasury's resources deteriorated markedly. Gallatin's Treasury report in November 1812 was mild and factual and forecast a borrowing need of $20 million. Congress ultimately voted $16 million.

Congress would not listen to Gallatin or to the president. There was no longer a Bank of the United States, and Gallatin had moderate success only with the banks of the various states. In March 1813, Gallatin launched the loan that Congress had authorized. The Federalists did everything they could to make the loan fail and bring down the government. Gallatin wrote to Madison in early March that there was not enough money in the Treasury to last until the end of the month, so it would be wise to postpone payments if possible. By chance, Alexander Dallas, Gallatin's old friend from Philadelphia, had a conversation with David Parish, a financier from Hamburg whom Gallatin had met several years before through Alexander Baring. Parish believed he could secure the funding required from Europeans, including Stephen Girard, a Frenchman born in Bordeaux but who lived in Philadelphia, and John Jacob Astor, who was originally from Walldorf in Germany and whom Gallatin had also known for some years. The public and domestic banks subscribed for less than $7 million, while Parish, Girard, and Astor took over $9 million themselves. Gallatin concluded the agreement with the three of them at Dallas's house in Philadelphia on April 6, 1813. The $16 million was subscribed, therefore, not in a burst of patriotic American fervor but largely by European-born private capitalists who, rallied by a European-born secretary of the Treasury, came to the financial aid of the United States in a time of dire need mainly caused by the ineptitude of the American decision-makers themselves.

Gallatin was under attack during these years, but the family continued their life in Washington. And Gallatin did manage to take portions of the summers in New York with the Nicholson family. In Washington, Dolley Madison remained the main promoter of the social round, but Hannah Gallatin gave a ball in January 1813 that was deemed exclusive and elegant. The social life slightly bothered Gallatin, but it probably did him good. His investments in Pennsylvania provided almost no money, and he tried to be frugal in his domestic management. At one point he accepted Hannah's suggestion that it would be more prudent to buy cigars by the box, rather than twenty-five cents' worth at a time, but he smoked twice as much. Maria Nicholson, Hannah's sister, often stayed with the Gallatins, and she met her future husband in Washington. In 1809, she married Congressman John Montgomery of Maryland.

AN OPPORTUNITY FOR DIPLOMACY

As Gallatin completed the Treasury loan in April 1813, the U.S. government received an interesting proposal from the Russian emperor: Tsar Alexander I offered to mediate between Britain and the United States. Gallatin believed that events in Europe were so distracting to the British that they might welcome this intervention from a friendly power and a chance to end hostilities with the United States. John Quincy Adams was already the American minister at St. Petersburg, but it was decided to put together a fully fledged delegation for this mission. Gallatin asked to head the delegation and to take a leave of absence from the Treasury for this purpose. Madison and Monroe assented. It was not clear whether the negotiations would be long or short, but they were expected to be completed within a few months; meanwhile Gallatin would remain secretary of the Treasury and his responsibilities be assumed pro tempore by the secretary of the navy. He made painstaking preparations for his departure, leaving everything in order at the Treasury and with his family. Hannah moved back to New York with the younger children, at least for the time being, while James Gallatin, now sixteen years old, was to accompany his father, as was Peter, an African American manservant who worked for the family. The delegation also included James A. Bayard, a Federalist and senator from Delaware, who was named on April 5, 1813. The nomination of the commissioners required the consent of the Senate. Alexander Dallas asked Gallatin before he left whether he had considered the possibility that the Senate would refuse the nomination when submitted by President Madison. At this question, Gallatin merely smiled. He did write to James Nicholson on May 5, 1813, "I am well aware that my going to Russia will most probably terminate in the appointment of another Secretary of the Treasury, and in my returning to private life. If I shall have succeeded in making peace, I will be perfectly satisfied."[7] On May 9, 1813, Gallatin and his son James and the rest of the party boarded the *Neptune* at New Castle, in Delaware. They made their way out of the Chesapeake Bay, passed through a British coastal blockade by showing Gallatin's passport issued by the British authorities, and sailed into the open sea.

The ceaseless combat during the Madison administration seriously tested Gallatin's fortitude. Shortly before Gallatin left for Russia, President Madison allowed his new secretary of war, John Armstrong, the former minister to Paris, to appoint Gallatin's sworn enemy, William Duane, editor of the *Aurora,* to a position of military responsibility, and at this development Gallatin pronounced himself "disgusted." In Gallatin's mind, he had brought his European education and Genevan ethics to America and ascended to the loftiest levels of trust and power that his adopted country had to offer. He had acquitted himself with honor. He retained an awareness of his initial ideals, and at the same time, in action, he respected the realities that he encountered. Yet, even at the summits of high office, he confronted examples of venality—and personal hostility—that nothing in his upbringing had prepared him for. In response, he gravitated to where his talents would be better employed and better satisfied: instead of managing a large administration, living in the public eye, and needing to fight political battles for the smallest gain, he opted to conduct a mission that would allow him to operate more independently and withal in Europe, where he would be understood and esteemed.

[6]

THE DEBUT OF A DIPLOMATIST, 1813–1815

GALLATIN was American enough to represent his country in Europe—and European enough to excel in doing so. On Sunday, June 20, 1813, the *Neptune* reached the quarantine ground outside Gothenburg, in Sweden. Three young men accompanied Gallatin and Bayard as secretaries: the son of Alexander Dallas, George Dallas, who had just graduated from Princeton; George Milligan, an army colonel; and John Payne Todd, Dolley Madison's son from her first marriage. The next day they took a small boat into Gothenburg and stopped at the house of a Scot living in Gothenburg, named Dixon, who had previously served as American consul there. Other Americans living in Gothenburg—one from Boston, one from Philadelphia, and one from Georgetown—joined them, and Gallatin was overjoyed to meet his fellow countrymen in Sweden. On Tuesday, June 22, 1813, they returned to their ship and set sail for St. Petersburg.

While in Gothenburg, Gallatin wrote a letter to his old friend Alexander Baring, with whom he had negotiated the financing of the Louisiana Purchase. Baring was a solid ally of the United States who had previously lived in Philadelphia and had an American wife. He belonged to the British establishment and circle of power. Consequently, Gallatin offered in a first and fairly official letter to open a dialogue by correspondence with Baring—an unofficial conversation that provided valuable information on both sides as the negotiations unfolded. From Gothenburg, on June 22, 1813, Gallatin wrote to Baring Brothers,

Gentlemen,
The President of the United States having accepted on the part of the said States the mediation offered by the Emperor of Russia, Mr. Bayard and myself have been appointed, jointly with Mr. Adams, ministers, with full powers to treat of peace with such ministers as may be appointed on the part of Great Britain. We left the United States in the public ship Neptune, Captain Lloyd Jones, on the 11th of May, arrived here on the 20th instant and intend to proceed this evening in the ship on our way to St. Petersburg.

We are authorized to draw on you for our salaries and the contingent expenses of the mission, and, in order to assist us with the best mode of negotiating bills, will thank you to let us know at St. Petersburg the course of exchange between London and Amsterdam.

We will also be obliged to you to have the account and date of our arrival here inserted in Lloyd's List and some other paper, as it may give to our friends in America the earliest account of our safe arrival.

Of the fact that we are appointed to treat and on our way to St. Petersburg for that purpose, as stated in the first paragraph of this letter, I should wish your government to be informed. And we will be thankful for any intelligence connected with our mission which you may deem important and which you may feel at liberty to communicate.[1]

While Gallatin's letter made its way to Baring, the delegation continued its journey. From June 22 to 24, 1813, they sailed along the coast of Sweden and stopped at Ellsinore in Denmark to see Hamlet's garden. On Thursday, June 24, 1813, they reached Copenhagen, where they remained for six days as tourists. A week later, July 1, 1813, they embarked again and entered the Gulf of Finland on Monday, July 12, 1813. On July 15, 1813, they made landfall in the Baltic provinces of Russia and began to make their way to St. Petersburg. They arrived in the Russian capital on July 21, 1813, and went straight to the residence of the American consul, Levett Harris. The three commissioners—Gallatin, Bayard, and John Quincy Adams—began their work together. They found that the British had done nothing with respect to this negotiation but send a note discouraging third-party arbitration. The emperor, Tsar Alexander, was with his army fighting Napoleon in Bohemia. Consequently, two days later, on July 24, 1813, John Quincy Adams arranged for the commissioners to present their persons and credentials to the imperial chancellor, Count Romanzoff, in a formal ceremony in full diplomatic uniforms. But there was little to do. The explanation soon came in the form of a frank reply from Alexander Baring, who had wholly understood and acted on Gallatin's offer of a parallel dialogue and assured him that the sources of his information were at the highest level. Baring's letter was sent from London on July 22, 1813.

Dear Sir,—The letter with which you honored my house from Gothenburg has remained for a few days unanswered, for the purpose of obtaining the information necessary to enable me to make a satisfactory reply. . . .

I have taken care to make in the proper quarter the communications you desire, and, as you express a wish to be informed of any occurrences here relating to your mission, some observations may perhaps be acceptable on the dispositions of government and the public concerning it, upon which I have good reason to assure you that you may perfectly rely. . . .

I anticipated the most favorable result from the names which constituted this new commission, and felt confident that we should soon see an end of this senseless war. I was quite sure you would not leave your home without the powers and disposition to do your country this essential service, and although the *place* fixed upon for the negotiation, and the manner in which it was proposed to conduct it, considerably abated the confidence of the public, I never entertained those doubts of the sincerity of America with which those circumstances inspired others.

The mediation of Russia was offered, not sought,—it was fairly and frankly accepted,—I do not see how America could with any consistency refuse it; but to the eyes of a European politician it was clear that such an interference could produce no practical benefit. . . .

This is not the way for Great Britain and America really to settle their disputes. . . . It is sort of a family quarrel, where foreign interference can only do harm and irritate at any time, but more especially in the present state of Europe, when attempts would be made to make a tool of America in a manner which I am sure neither you nor your colleagues would sanction.

These, I have good reason to know, are pretty nearly the sentiments of the government here on the question of *place* of negotiation and foreign mediation, and before this reaches you you will have been informed that this mediation has been refused, with expressions of our desire to treat separately and directly here, or, if more agreeable to you, at Gottenburg. . . .

My hopes of a favorable result would be much increased by your coming at once in contact with our ministers.

At this point Baring explained that negotiating with plenipotentiaries instead of with ministers directly implied the giving of written instructions that had to be recorded in the ministry and made available to Parliament. Essentially he asked Gallatin to enter into more secret negotiations directly with decision-makers. His letter continued with a statement of position on the facts and his recommendations on the content of negotiations. He said, "the prevalent opinion here was that the war was a war of passion with the people of America, and that concessions would only show weakness, and never satisfy them, and that therefore no alternative was left to us but to fight it out as best we could." Baring went on to say that although it was improbable that all issues could be resolved to the entire satisfaction of both parties, nonetheless an arrangement could be made that would restore peace, even if differences subsisted; and, since the alternative was perpetual war, there was "a necessity of some settlement."[2]

BIDING TIME IN ST. PETERSBURG

Meanwhile, the American delegation, without very much to do, toured St. Petersburg in the summer. Count Romanzoff gave a dinner in their honor. In August they prepared an elaborate note, drafted by Gallatin in French (and later translated into English by John Quincy Adams), addressed to the emperor, Tsar Alexander, and stating the American position. In the latter half of August, Gallatin received and replied to Baring's letter of July 22, 1813:

> Dear Sir,—The letter (of 22d July) with which you have favored me was received on the 17th inst. [of August]. For this I return you my sincere thanks, and duly appreciate the importance of the information you have obtained, and the motives which have actuated you. Although I cannot write as freely as a person whose communications do not commit his own government, the hope that our correspondence may be of some public utility induces me to enter as far in the subject as is consistent with my situation.
>
> We have not received, as you had suggested, the information that the mediation of Russia had been refused by Great Britain, with expressions of a desire to treat with us separately and directly at London or Gottenburg.

Gallatin then explained that although Lord Walpole, then in St. Petersburg, may be the bearer of such a message, the Tsar, on learning that their mission had reached his capital, had in the meantime renewed his offer of mediation. This the Americans, given the instructions they were under, could of course not ignore. Moreover, Gallatin added, if the British genuinely insisted on refusing to accept mediation, his delegation could not enter into those negotiations without new instructions, since their mandate was to negotiate based on the mediation of the Russian emperor (though they did hold instructions for a separate, direct negotiation with Britain on a commercial treaty). Gallatin explained that when they left America, the delegation had no idea there were British objections to the mediation. "I would not have given up my political existence and separated myself from my family unless I had believed an arrangement practicable and that I might be of some utility in effecting it." He explained that he was not in a position to enter into matters of substance that would open a negotiation, but he closed with an assurance to Baring:

> I have thus freely communicated as far as our relative situation seemed to permit, being well assured that what I have said will be used for its intended purpose of assisting in promoting a restoration of peace. I know how dear this object is to you, and that we both have an equal desire that not only peace but the most friendly relations and understanding should subsist between the two countries. I can assure you that such also is the sincere and earnest desire of my government, and that nothing which can be done in that respect will be omitted on my part or on that of my colleagues. Whatever the result may be, I will preserve a just sense of your friendly conduct on this occasion, and remain with great consideration and sincere regard, dear sir, your very obedient servant.[3]

The letter was brilliantly drafted such that Baring would know, as an individual, how much Gallatin valued his advice; but because Gallatin explained that he wrote within the limitations of someone who cannot express himself otherwise than in an official capacity, Baring would be able to show the letter to his government, without it ever actually constituting a direct contact between the American commissioners and the British ministers. And from Gallatin's standpoint, he remained entirely correct vis-à-vis his own government and that of Russia. Indeed, the day after his reply to Baring, on August 28, 1813, Gallatin wrote to Secretary of State James Monroe to brief him on the correspondence and enclosed copies of Baring's letter of July 22, 1813, and Gallatin's own reply of August 27, 1813. He said to Monroe of Baring, "You will easily distinguish in his letter what belongs to him and what in fact is an indirect communication through him of the views and dispositions of his government." Gallatin closed his letter by saying to Monroe, "I need hardly add that neither Mr. Baring's nor my letter are intended for publication or even communication to Congress."[4] Finally Gallatin was able to enjoy the diplomacy he so wanted to practice as secretary of state. On August 29, 1813, the American commissioners described their arrival and official actions since then in a formal dispatch to Secretary of State Monroe.

In the beginning of October, Gallatin wrote to Count Romanzoff, telling him that if the British refused mediation, the commissioners would require new powers from the president of the United States to enter into direct bilateral negotiations. He mentioned that they would save two months of communications time by writing from London rather than papers coming from London to St. Petersburg and back to Washington. Baring also replied to Gallatin on October 12, 1813, but before Gallatin received that letter, he wrote a further letter to Baring, which young George Dallas delivered in person to Baring, as the young man was "desirous of spending a few months in England before his return to America." Gallatin wrote to Baring that he had nothing to add to his earlier reply except,

> Not a single word has since that time reached me from England, either directly or through the medium of the Russian government. No such proposition as was suggested in your letter has been made or hinted in any shape. If the determination of your government had been such as you stated, it would have been advantageous to receive it early in an official shape, as although it would have prevented a negotiation with this mission, yet we would have lost no time in transmitting the proposition to our government; whilst on the other hand the delay has prevented our return to America, and if there was a prospect of peace there will have been a useless continuance of the reciprocal injuries of war. We are now probably chained here for the winter, and this, I think, affords an additional motive in favor of the acceptance of the mediation on the part of your government.[5]

Once again, Gallatin made the appropriate distinction between the government and his correspondent, reserving his exasperation for the lack of clarity and waste of time perpetrated by the British government itself. He sent Dallas off to London with that letter and with instructions to remain discreet while in London and silent on all issues of substance.

After this outgoing mail, Gallatin received Baring's letter of October 12, 1813, in reply to Gallatin's of August 27, 1813. Baring first apologized for his delay in responding, as the people he needed to consult were out of London. He went on,

> In communicating to you the result of my endeavors I am sorry to say that they have been less successful than I could hope or than I had at one time expected. . . . We are here resolved to abide by the principle of direct

negotiation. . . . What you will think proper to do in this case—whether to wait for new powers, to return yourselves, or to come here in the expectation of those powers being sent—will remain with you to determine; perhaps, indeed, you have determined before this reaches you, as the Baltic will probably be closed for navigation by the end of this month. . . .

On the subject of the probability of an agreement between the two governments I am sensible that you must necessarily write with reserve; but, as I am under no such restraint, I will state to you fairly what you may expect here, and I do it because this may influence your determination on other points. . . . We wish for peace. The pressure of war upon our commerce and manufactures is over; they have ample relief in other quarters; and, indeed, the dependence of the two countries on each other was, as it usually is, overrated. But the war has no object; it is expensive, and we want to carry our efforts elsewhere. Our desire of peace, therefore, cannot be doubted, and you may quite rely upon it.[6]

Gallatin was probably the only American to whom any Englishman of influence—and certainly Alexander Baring—would have felt comfortable writing in such terms. Baring placed implicit trust in Gallatin as an individual and as a representative of his government. That trust encompassed not only his probity but also his judgment. Baring was entirely honest; Gallatin would understand the subtleties and realities of the situation. In this sense Gallatin was different from other Americans because he embodied both European character and American determination. He was a product of both cultures and continents but an emanation of neither.

GALLATIN'S SUFFERS AGAIN AT THE HANDS OF THE SENATE

Notwithstanding Gallatin's eminent qualifications, he once again suffered a setback from the Senate. On the very day after he wrote to Baring, October 19, 1813, Gallatin learned that his nomination the prior spring by President Madison as a commissioner to be part of this diplomatic delegation had been refused in the summer by the Senate, which was constitutionally required to give its consent to such diplomatic appointments. Not even a week earlier, on October 15, 1813, Count Romanzoff had delivered to the American commissioners a letter stating that Tsar Alexander had authorized Count Romanzoff to accept the commissioners' letters of credence. Gallatin's diplomatic mission had thus been officially recognized by Russia for only five days when he belatedly learned of his disavowal by his own government. The Senate had voted down his nomination on July 19, 1813. Voting against him were the Invisibles and the Federalists, who claimed that the additional duties of a commissioner were incompatible with his continuing responsibilities as secretary of Treasury. That may have been a fair point, but in the past the chief justice of the Supreme Court, John Jay, had been sent on diplomatic missions while retaining his office. A few days afterward, near the end of October, newspapers from the month of July arrived from America with the story. On November 1, 1813, Gallatin wrote a brief but elegant note in French to Count Romanzoff to tell him of his dismissal and confirm the newspaper reports. He added that none of the commissioners had received any official communication from the U.S. government since the time of the Senate action and that he therefore possessed no instructions or letters of recall and was not in a position to make any official communication to the imperial chancellor. He added that he would be grateful for a brief conversation in person before leaving. Count Romanzoff replied that the Senate vote was of no special consequence to him and that he would be delighted to continue with Gallatin.

Gallatin waited until November 21, 1813, to write to Secretary of State Monroe. He enclosed a copy of Baring's latest letter and said he had not heard from Monroe since June 23, 1813. Monroe had actually written to the commissioners with the unfortunate news about Gallatin's nomination on August 5, 1813, and in a personal note to Gallatin dated August 6, 1813, he deplored the action of the Senate. John Jacob Astor, Gallatin's good friend, wrote on August 9, 1813, to fill in the details. He explained that President Madison had not really known what best to do; he had not wanted to revoke Gallatin as secretary of the Treasury, although had he done so the Senate would quite certainly have approved Gallatin's nomination as a commissioner. But Gallatin had received none of these letters when he was writing to Secretary of State Monroe on November 21, 1813. In that letter, he informed Monroe that he had read in the newspapers of the rejection of his nomination and would make his way back to America when the snow dissipated enough to make the roads passable. He added that he might stop in England along the way and would bring back as much information as he could. He assured Monroe that he and Bayard would act "in perfect concert."[7]

There was nowhere to go, so Gallatin stayed on in St. Petersburg throughout the winter. He might have hoped for some word from his government or some progress on mediation from the Russians, but it was quite clear that direct talks with the British would be the only answer. He no longer had any instructions because he was no longer a commissioner nominated by the president of the United States. He was, however, still secretary of the Treasury.

Baring continued his correspondence with Gallatin and wrote to him from London on December 14, 1813, in reply to Gallatin's letter of October 18, 1813, which had been delivered to him by George Dallas. Baring stated his regret at the fruitlessness of Gallatin's mission but said the British desire for peace with the United States was strong.

> The pressure of war is diminished by the altered state of our commerce, now abundantly prosperous, and also by the political effect of the non-existence of French maritime commerce, for it is a singular result of late events that the project for the destruction of our commerce ends in the destruction of that of France. . . . But I am sure that our government will be found equally ready to put an end to the war as soon as it can be done consistently with the principles they have laid down of preferring a direct to a mediatorial negotiation.

Baring added that Lord Castlereagh, the British foreign secretary, had communicated directly to Secretary of State Monroe that Russian mediation was out of the question, so perhaps new instructions were on the way from America.[8]

Gallatin wrote to Monroe on January 7, 1814, to say that he would to leave for Amsterdam on January 21. He wrote the same day to Baring to ask whether it would be appropriate for him to stop in England and whether Baring would be so kind as to let him know one way or the other by a letter to the bankers of the U.S. government in Amsterdam. The stepson of the president of the United States, John Todd, was to deliver the letter to Baring.[9] Gallatin left St. Petersburg with his son James and his servant Peter, as well as James Bayard, on January 25, 1814, and it took six weeks to reach Amsterdam overland. It was a brutal journey in bad weather and through a great deal of snow. In Riga they were taken to the theater by the regional governor. When they arrived at Berlin a letter from the American consul in Amsterdam awaited Gallatin, saying that President Madison had appointed new commissioners to negotiate directly with the British at Gothenburg. Gallatin was not among them. They finally reached Amsterdam on March 4, 1814, after a grueling trip across a frozen European continent.

The group stayed a month in Amsterdam, and Gallatin at last received some news from home: a letter from Hannah saying that all was well.

At this point he and James had been gone for nearly ten months. Madison's failure to appoint Gallatin as a commissioner arose from no ill will, for when Madison responded positively to the British proposal for direct negotiation he had assumed Gallatin would come back to Washington to resume his duties as secretary of the Treasury. A complication arose in that regard as well, however, for the office was declared vacant after Gallatin's having been absent from it for six months. In fact, this development proved highly satisfactory. Madison then appointed Gallatin as a member of the delegation to negotiate directly with the British, on February 8, 1814, although it took some time for this information to reach him. If Gallatin was perturbed by these rather chaotic developments—on-again, off-again commissioner, secretary of the Treasury—he did not show it overly. By this time he was accustomed to the mercurial nature of politics and the difficulties of communicating across vast distances. He may even have derived some satisfaction from the discomfiture of others, since, whatever annoyance the Senate tried to perpetrate on him, he was in fact far out of its reach. He had high esteem for Madison personally but no illusions about his vacillating leadership abilities, so Gallatin could be confident that Madison would try to do the right thing, even if it took him some time to get there. While he missed his family, the company of his son James and the enforced leisure probably did him a world of good after so many years of hard work under pressure. He had made rather little progress since arriving in Europe the previous July. That was about to change.

On his arrival in Amsterdam, Gallatin learned that Baring had not yet received his last two letters from St. Petersburg. He renewed his request, in a letter to Baring Brothers, to advise whether he should stop in England on the way home and requested passports (which, in those days, were issued for separate journeys and, in this case, would be required from the British authorities for enemy nationals, Americans, to pass through the British naval blockade) for himself, his son, and his servants. Three weeks later, having received letters from Baring encouraging him to come and saying the government would be glad to have him in London, he replied on April 1, 1814, to say he was on his way. On April 9, 1814, he reached London, where he was to stay for three months.

A world-changing event occurred shortly after Gallatin's arrival when Napoleon abdicated as emperor of France on April 11, 1814, and went into exile on the Isle of Elba. With this development, Europe was at peace and had nothing more to fear from France. On April 26, King Louis XVIII of France, who had been in exile in Britain, landed at Calais, and he was restored to the throne on May 4. During Gallatin's stay in England, the world scene shifted strongly in favor of Britain, which would no longer need to exhaust itself in continental wars after a quarter century of virtually unceasing conflict.

GALLATIN REAPPOINTED, NEGOTIATIONS COMMENCE

While in London, Gallatin took the opportunity to assess the attitude of the British government firsthand. He also played tourist. He had never been to London before, so he visited the historic capital city, spent a few days in Oxford, and let Alexander Baring introduce him to the people he should know in British power circles. Madison had by now appointed a fresh delegation of commissioners to negotiate a treaty directly with the British. Gallatin thought he was part of that delegation but was not sure. Gallatin made contact with Henry Clay, the Speaker of the House, who had arrived in London from Washington, and he awaited the return of Jonathan Russell, who had been appointed both a commissioner for the negotiation of a treaty and minister to Sweden; Russell was off presenting his credentials in Stockholm. John Quincy Adams was renewed as a commissioner in this delegation as well as remaining minister at St. Petersburg. James Bayard, who had already been part of the delegation at St. Petersburg and traveled to Amsterdam with Gallatin, was off in Paris seeing the sights. During this period, Clay confirmed to Gallatin his appointment as a commissioner. Madison had waited until Gallatin's tenure at the Treasury had officially closed and then reappointed Gallatin as a commissioner. The Senate then confirmed his appointment without difficulty. On May 6, 1814, Gallatin and Bayard wrote jointly to Secretary of State Monroe:

> It is much to be apprehended that the great and unexpected events which have so entirely changed the state of affairs in Europe may have a serious effect on the nature and aspect of the war carried on by Great Britain against the United States, as well as on the proposed negotiations for peace. A convention has already been signed between France and the allies for the suspension of hostilities and for the restoration of prisoners. It is said and believed that the articles of a definitive treaty of peace between all the European powers have been chiefly agreed upon, and the treaty is expected to be concluded in a few weeks. This state of things, and the security derived by Great Britain from the restoration of the Bourbons on the throne of France and from the expulsion of Bonaparte to Elba, put at

the disposition of this government the whole of their force heretofore employed against France. . . . The complete success obtained by this country in their European contest has excited the greatest popular exultation, and this has been attended with a strong expression of resentment against the United States.[10]

Within ten days, Gallatin and Bayard informed the British government of the new commission, received in return an assurance that Britain would soon appoint commissioners of its own, and accepted the British suggestion that negotiations should take place at Ghent, in the Low Countries. On June 13, 1814, Gallatin wrote to Monroe from London to prepare him for the fact that Britain meant to teach the United States that nobody declares war on Britain without paying the price. Whatever the prospects for negotiation, Great Britain would now turn its full fighting force against the United States for whatever gains Britain felt it could achieve. Gallatin left London on June 21, 1814, and made a stop in Paris before repairing to Ghent on July 6, 1814. The other American commissioners were already there. They initially lodged at the Hôtel des Pays-Bas and then leased a three-story private mansion, the Hôtel d'Alcantara, in the expectation that they would be living in Ghent for several months to come.

The first meeting with the British commissioners took place on August 8, 1814. The U.S. delegation—Adams, Bayard, Clay, Gallatin, and Russell—included experienced diplomats and distinguished statesmen. The British commissioners were far less impressive. Lord Gambier was a retired admiral, Henry Goulburn was a young diplomat, and William Adams was an expert on the law of the sea. They could not display the same degree of negotiating flexibility as their American counterparts could, as they were nearer home and of lesser stature. Near the outset of discussions, the British, acting on instructions from Lord Castlereagh, put forward a sine qua non that the Americans found completely unacceptable, namely, that the United States should set aside the Northwest Territory in perpetuity for the Native Americans, whose sovereignty in that region would be guaranteed by Britain. They also raised issues relating to the continuance of fishing rights that Americans enjoyed in Canada under the terms of a previous treaty. The Americans wanted to discuss the rights of neutrals and the nature of blockades. The British were under orders not to discuss those questions. Britain was making progress in the land war at this stage, preparing the siege of Washington, DC, and an attack on the United States via Lake Champlain. Consequently, Monroe instructed the Americans that they might drop the question of impressment in order to secure a treaty. Impressment duly came off the agenda, but the two sides were no closer to agreement on the other matters.

On August 20, 1814, Gallatin wrote to Monroe to say that Britain's ambitions were greater and more perilous than he had warned of earlier.

> I had supposed, whilst in England, that the British Ministry in continuing the war yielded to the popular sentiment and were only desirous of giving some éclat to the termination of hostilities, and by predatory attacks of inflicting gratuitous injury on the United States. It appears now that they have more serious and dangerous objects in view. . . . It appears to me most likely that their true and immediate object is New Orleans. They well know that it is our most distant and weakest point, and that if captured it could not be retaken without great difficulty. . . . It is now evident that Great Britain intends to strengthen and aggrandize herself in North America. . . . It is highly probable that our struggle will be longer and more arduous than I had anticipated.[11]

That letter was written four days before the White House—and Gallatin's house—were burned by the British in Washington, DC.

Narrowing the Issues to Achieve Agreement

From August to October, things went from bad to worse in Ghent. On October 8, 1814, the American commissioners received a note from the British that was even more severe than their worst expectations. It referenced the questionable legality of the Louisiana Purchase and made an ultimatum on the question of Indian tribes. The British intended to increase their territory in North America, whereas the American position was that there should be no territorial changes from the period before the war started. Nonetheless, Gallatin wrote to Monroe from Ghent on October 26, 1814. He confirmed that the main basis of negotiation was the status quo ante bellum but asked for specific instructions on other issues of potential negotiations, in essence all the points between Britain and the United States: the right of the British to trade with the Indians, granted under the treaty of 1794; the presence of American naval forces on the Great Lakes; the renewal of American fishing rights under the treaty of 1783; the right of British navigation of the Mississippi; the northern boundary of Louisiana; the appropriate American negotiating position with respect to lands between the Rocky

Mountains and the Pacific Ocean; the northern border between Maine and Canada and the country watered by St. John's River; and, lastly, what the American position should be on impressment. With respect to British territorial intentions in the war on the ground, Gallatin advised Monroe that his belief still was that their "principal object" was Louisiana.[12]

On that same day, the American delegation sent a note to the British, written by Gallatin, that proposed that each side should write a draft treaty and send it to the other. The American draft was sent on November 10, 1814, and had been the source of long labor and tremendous arguments within the American delegation. The American draft adhered to the status quo ante bellum, which meant restitution of captured territory by both belligerents. That American draft eliminated or pushed into the future the negotiation of the other sticking points in the relationship that Gallatin had cited in his letter to Monroe, suggesting that they be referred to a later set of commissioners for negotiation. In this way, the American draft focused on one essential point: the restoration of peace, at a price each could pay. Within British government circles, unbeknown to the Americans, a similar debate was taking place. The Duke of Wellington told the prime minister, Lord Liverpool, that it was a mistake to demand territorial concessions from the Americans. And in the British Cabinet, the American draft treaty, which after all represented an opportunity to end the conflict, provoked a discussion of how costly and inconvenient the war was. There is no doubt that Gallatin's inventive tactic of suggesting that each side should produce a draft of a treaty that it would actually be willing to sign, rather than quibbling over points on which they knew themselves to be in discord, changed the atmosphere of the discussions. Ultimately Britain changed its tune and decided to opt for peace, whereupon the discussions with the British representatives became vastly easier. On November 30, 1814, the Americans sent a note proposing a face-to-face meeting, and the British accepted within hours. The two delegations met three times during the first half of December, and on December 14, 1814, the Americans proposed that all outstanding points of disagreement should be provided for in later negotiations, with neither side giving up its prior claims. This allowed both sides to concentrate on the provisions that should be included in the treaty, which was limited to restoring the status quo ante bellum and therefore included the restoration to each side of land captured in the conflict (by Americans in Canada, by the British in Maine, Michigan, and along the Pacific), exchange of prisoners, and the return of captured property. Both sides signed the Treaty of Ghent on December 24, 1814.

The next day, Gallatin wrote to Monroe to say that the treaty was complete and that, while the European powers stood aloof from the treaty negotiations and might have been glad to have hostilities against the United States continue, the United States had shown it could meet the British as equals. The rest of his letter briefed the secretary of state on various aspects of the treaty.

GALLATIN RETURNS TO GENEVA AND COMPLETES HIS MISSION IN LONDON

Gallatin also wrote to Hannah to tell her that the treaty was signed, that it was imperfect but the best that could be achieved. She had written to him in the beginning of December to say that she missed him terribly:

> [Y]our wife is at this moment one of the most miserable beings in existence, fondly expecting every moment to hear of the arrival of the Neptune and once more to have the happiness of embracing my dear husband & child, all at once to receive your letter telling me that in all probability you would be detained in Europe all winter, has almost broken my heart, indeed it seems more than I can bear. . . . I feel almost tempted to run the risk of a winter passage and join you in Europe.[13]

Despite Hannah's desire to have her family reunited, after the negotiations finished in Ghent, Gallatin and James set out for Geneva. Gallatin saw his birthplace for the first time since he had left on April 1, 1780, almost thirty-five years before. He returned as a hero and a man of peace to a republic that was formally joining the Swiss Confederation. Gallatin arrived on January 24, 1815, and spent a month in Geneva, where he was warmly received. During this time, he attended a memorial service for the French king Louis XVI in Saint-Germain Church, where he had been baptized, and he was seated in front of the congregation with the three lord mayors and nine state councillors. He was invited to numerous dinners in Geneva and at Coppet. Everyone found him accessible if not especially aristocratic in his manner—quite the opposite effect he produced on certain Americans! At one dinner he had everyone laughing at his story about American diplomacy, how in contrast to European habits of secrecy their instructions had been published and how the British had marked them up, writing "inadmissible, inadmissible" alongside the provisions. He and James left Geneva toward the end of February and arrived in Paris on March 7, 1815.

Gallatin learned then that Napoleon had escaped from Elba on February 26, 1815, and landed on the French mainland. At the same time, Gallatin was informed that President Madison had named him minister to France, to replace William Crawford. Days later he heard that, after the signing of the Treaty of Ghent but before news of it had reached America, General Andrew Jackson had turned back an attempted British invasion of New Orleans on January 8, 1815. Then the news reached them on March 20, 1815, that the Treaty of Ghent had been ratified by the Senate on February 16, 1815, but on that same day of March 20, 1815, Louis XVIII fled, and Napoleon Bonaparte reentered Paris and reclaimed control of France, which he was to rule famously for one hundred days.

Meanwhile, Gallatin had one more negotiation to conduct. The original instructions which had sent him to St. Petersburg charged Gallatin with effecting a commercial treaty with Great Britain. In London, he met with Lord Castlereagh; William Crawford, the departing American minister to Paris whom Gallatin was to replace; Henry Clay; and John Quincy Adams, who had been appointed minister in London after his tenure in St. Petersburg. These trade negotiations lasted from May to July and covered the freedom of trade between the two countries, reduction of discriminatory duties, and the appointment of consuls to each other's dependencies. Many provisions renewed those of Jay's Treaty that Gallatin had tried to obstruct when a freshman congressman. During this time, Crawford ordered the *Neptune* to depart because Bayard was deathly ill and he wanted to get him back to America. News reached London that Napoleon had been defeated at Waterloo on Sunday, June 18, 1815. Peace was now complete in Europe, and Louis XVIII was restored securely to the French throne. By July 2, 1815, the commercial treaty with Britain was ready, Gallatin had dinner that evening with Alexander Baring, and the treaty (styled as a "convention") was signed at the Board of Trade on July 3, 1815. Gallatin and his son James, together with Henry Clay and John Payne Todd, left England on the *Lorenzo*, sailing from Liverpool on July 22, 1815. He arrived in New York on September 1, 1815, more than two years and three months since he had last seen his wife and full family or had set foot on American soil.

Gallatin's greatest contribution to his country and the greatest achievement of his lifetime was the negotiation of the Treaty of Ghent—and its success, which he did not claim, was nonetheless largely his, as John Quincy Adams subsequently acknowledged. Had the negotiations failed, the growing strength of Great Britain meant that the situation of the United States—economic, diplomatic, military—might have remained fundamentally insecure for many decades in a nineteenth-century world dominated by the British Empire. Instead, the United States made peace with Britain on equal terms and eliminated sources of conflict while pushing sources of differences into future negotiations. In that sense, the United States won its second War of Independence. It would encounter no further foreign obstacles to its growth and prosperity as an independent nation. On this two-year odyssey to St. Petersburg, London, and Ghent, Gallatin endured discomfort, rejection, abandonment, confusion, and discord in his own camp, yet he won the respect and admiration of all whom he encountered. Gallatin's aristocratic, European upbringing and Swiss diligence and resilience enabled him to be a model American statesman.

[7]

AMERICAN MINISTER TO
FRANCE, 1816–1823

FOLLOWING the War of 1812, America truly became an independent country, increasingly free from European commercial, military, and political considerations. Gallatin was instrumental in creating the conditions for the United States to reach that status, but in the years that followed he became increasingly perplexed in trying to find his place in his adopted nation and felt more at home in Europe.

After arriving in New York in early September 1815, Gallatin wrote a friendly letter to President Madison, in which he thanked Madison for appointing him minister to France the previous March—this was the news Gallatin had received in Paris when he returned from Geneva and also learned of Napoleon's escape from Elba. Gallatin informed Madison that, despite the passage of six months, he had not yet decided whether to accept the offer:

> I received the account of my appointment to France with pleasure and gratitude, as an evidence of your undiminished friendship and of public satisfaction for my services. Whether I can or will accept I have not yet determined. The season is far advanced for taking Mrs. G. across the Atlantic, and I have had no time to ascertain what arrangement, if any, I can make for my children and private business during a second absence. The delay has been rather advantageous to the public, as it was best to have no minister at Paris during the late events.[1]

Gallatin's letter raises several questions. Taking his points in reverse order, it is at the very least open to debate whether it was "advantageous to the public" that the United States was without a minister in Paris during Napoleon's Hundred Days and the second Bourbon Restoration which placed Louis XVIII firmly on the French throne. From a diplomatic and economic standpoint, without foreknowledge of the turn that events would take or how American interests would be protected, it would surely have made more sense for the United States to have a senior representative in situ. Moreover, it is surprising that Gallatin, who was in Paris when the news came of Napoleon's escape from Elba, did not accept the appointment then and there (and postpone the relatively mundane London trade mission), precisely so as to be present in the midst of such important historical events, which would have unfolded before his eyes. Instead of expressing regret at missing those events, he opines to the president that his absence was advantageous. Gallatin again seems curiously oblivious to his own place in history and to the making of history around him. As to family concerns, Gallatin had been away for close to two years and had made provision for his children during that time, one of his sons was already with him, and Hannah had written to him earlier that she was prepared to join him in Europe. His slightly self-congratulatory and self-serving manner in his letter to Madison conveys the impression that, upon returning to a Washington where he had suffered so much contumely, he was now rather pleased to be back in demand.

Madison replied a few days later from Montpelier, taking Gallatin's letter entirely at face value. "I congratulate yourself and Mrs. Gallatin on your safe arrival and under circumstances which must console her so much for your prolonged absence." Madison went on to say, "I am not aware of any considerations that press for your decision as to the mission to Paris without the deliberation due to your private affairs."[2] Heeding this advice, Gallatin attended a banquet in New York in honor of himself and Henry Clay, went to the theater, and then repaired to Hannah's mother's house in Greenwich, Connecticut, where he remained for the next six weeks. He had a lot to think about. In addition to the possible position as minister to France, Pennsylvania Republicans asked him to become a congressman again, which he declined. On October 9, 1815, John Jacob Astor offered him the opportunity to go into business with him, which would have been a lucrative position.

GALLATIN VACILLATES ON WHETHER TO GO TO FRANCE

Gallatin returned to Washington in October for meetings with President Madison and Secretary of State Monroe. On November 23, 1815, he wrote to Secretary of State Monroe to decline the French mission and sent another letter to President Madison to explain why:

I have ultimately decided not to go to France, and write this day accordingly to the Secretary of State. I am fully sensible of the efforts you made to keep me in the Treasury, of the unpleasant situation in which my absence and that effort placed you, as well as of the friendly motives which, combined with your view of public utility, induced you to give me this last proof of your high regard and confidence. I feel truly grateful for every part of your conduct towards me before and since you were President, and I would have wished to have been able to evince my sense of it by a cheerful and thankful acceptance. But every consideration connected with private prudence and regard to my family forbids my doing it; and, considering the present depressed situation of France, no motive of public utility urges a contrary determination, even if, under other circumstances, my services could have been deemed useful at that court. As regards myself, I will briefly state that the compensation allowed to foreign ministers is incompetent to the support of a minister at Paris in the style in which he is expected to live, and which it is of some importance for the country that he should maintain; that my private resources are too scanty to supply the deficiency without making sacrifices which would leave my family at my death dependent upon others; that, supposing I could barely exist there for a few years, I would return with children having acquired expensive and foreign habits and lost the opportunities of entering into the active pursuits by which they must support themselves, and myself too old to assist and too poor to support them; and that a residence in France will at this time, both in a public and private view, be irksome and unpleasant to an American minister, affording no compensation for the sacrifices it would require. But I must add that these sacrifices would without hesitation have been made if the mission had in view any important and attainable object of public utility.[3]

In a letter to Jefferson on November 27, 1815, Gallatin provided a detailed explanation of his views of the French scene—"Our opinion of Bonaparte is precisely the same"—and reiterated more clearly still his decision to refuse the French mission:

Under different circumstances, without having any wish for a foreign mission or a residence in France, I might have accepted the appointment of minister there. But, satisfied that nothing can at this moment be effected in that country, and it being very reluctant to my feelings to be on a mission to a degraded monarch and to a nation under the yoke of foreign armies, I thought that I might, without any breach of public duty or of private grati-tude, consult my own convenience, and I have accordingly informed our government that I declined altogether the appointment.[4]

Just a few days later, on December 4, 1815, Secretary of State Monroe again urged Gallatin to accept: "We have been long in the public service together, engaged in the support of the same great cause, and it is distress-ing to me to see you withdraw."[5] He pressed his case once more on Decem-ber 16, 1815. Gallatin wrote to Monroe on December 26, 1815, again to de-cline the position formally, citing family reasons, his own frail health, and the inability to subsist in Paris on a minister's wages. On January 27, 1816, Monroe yet again pressed Gallatin to accept, quickly. Finally, on February 2, 1816, Gallatin caved in and assented to become minister of the United States to France. He explained his decision to Jefferson thus:

> After what I had written to you you could hardly have expected that I would have accepted the French mission. It was again offered to me in so friendly a manner and from so friendly motives that I was induced to accept. Nor will I conceal that I did not feel yet old enough, or had I phi-losophy enough, to go into retirement and abstract myself altogether from public affairs. I have no expectation, however, that in the present state of France I can be of any utility there, and hope that I will not make a long stay in that country.[6]

In March 1816, Gallatin returned to Washington to prepare for his new post, but at that very moment, President Madison offered him his old po-sition of secretary of the Treasury. Alexander Dallas, Gallatin's longtime friend, who, with his wife, originally introduced Gallatin to Hannah, had taken over the Treasury after Gallatin had vacated the post in February 1814 (and after an interlude by George Campbell), but he was ready to re-sign. Gallatin thought about it for a couple of days and then turned the offer down on the ground that he would no longer be able to manage the Treasury properly, so complex was the task. In the event, then, Madison appointed another friend of Gallatin's, the former minister to Paris Wil-liam Crawford. So while Gallatin succeeded Crawford in Paris, Crawford took up Gallatin's old job at the Treasury. Having been first named to the Paris post in March 1815, at the opening of Napoleon's Hundred Days, Gal-latin finally made preparations to sail to France.

Leaving the United States, Gallatin summed up his views on America in a letter that reveals how Federalist and how accepting of military power Gallatin had become:

> The war [of 1812] has been productive of evil and good, but I think the good preponderates. Independent of the loss of lives and the losses in property by individuals, the war has laid the foundation of permanent taxes and military establishment which the Republicans had deemed unfavorable to the happiness and free institutions of the country. But under our former system we were becoming too selfish, too much attached exclusively to the acquisition of wealth, above all too much confined in our political feelings to local and State objects. The war has renewed and reinstated the national feelings and character which the Revolution had given, and which were daily lessened.[7]

THE GALLATINS MOVE TO PARIS

Gallatin and his family sailed on the *Peacock* on June 11, 1816, more than nine months after he had returned from London. They made landfall at Le Havre on July 2, 1816.

Louis XVIII, king of France, had been exiled in Britain before he returned to France in 1814, when Bonaparte was shipped off to Elba. Talleyrand, who had served every French leader since Louis XVI, persuaded the victorious powers that restoring the monarchy under Louis XVIII was the best option for France and for the European balance of power that the Congress of Vienna meant to provide. Louis XVIII fled temporarily to Ghent during the Hundred Days of Napoleon's return from Elba. Once the king was definitively restored to the French throne, he reigned with considerable skill. He had no desire to be a constitutional monarch and hence eschewed symbols of democracy—in this way he distinguished himself from the British example; but he also granted sufficient powers to representative bodies and retained aspects of the recent revolutionary and Napoleonic eras so as not to provoke the French into anger. It had been twenty-seven years since the fall of the Bastille, and France had been sorely tested by its gory revolution and sanguinary wars. Louis XVIII acted as if the monarchy had not ended but had merely been inconveniently interrupted by events which he did not entirely seek to reverse. He reintroduced relatively inoffensive elements of the Old Regime, such as the royal white flag instead of the revolutionary tricolor, and reinstated the King's Court. But he left in place the Civil Code of Napoleon and, instead of a constitution, offered a charter to the people, which had the advantage of being granted by the king and not emanating from the populace. He created a Chamber of Peers, appointed by the king, which brought together the nobility of the Ancien Régime and the more newly prominent since then, and a lower legislative Chamber of Deputies. But neither of the chambers had sway over the government, which was appointed by the king, and only about ninety thousand people in France, chiefly the well-to-do, were granted the right to vote. The king did not find unwelcome the election of the *Chambre introuvable*, so named by the king because of its astonishingly high proportion of ultraroyalists. In 1815 and 1816 came the so-called White Terror, a wave of revenge by the monarchists against the former revolutionaries and supporters of Napoleon. This included massacres, deportations, and mass firings of civil servants. One of Napoleon's marshals, Ney, was condemned to death by the Chamber of Peers and executed by a firing squad. The White Terror caused a number of formerly powerful or prestigious men to flee into exile, such as the painter David, a favorite of Napoleon; the head of the Paris police, Fouché; and the former president of the Senate under Napoleon, Cambacérès.

Such was the France where the Gallatins landed. They arrived in Paris from Le Havre on July 9, 1816. A mere two days after arriving in the city, Gallatin had an audience of the king and presented his letters of credence. He received a gracious reception from the king, who, with his English-language skills honed in Britain, joked with Gallatin about his French accent. "Your French is very good," he apparently told the American minister, "but I think my English is better than yours!"

GALLATIN SEEKS SATISFACTION
OF AMERICA'S PRIOR CLAIMS

Gallatin's first order of business in his relations with the French government was to press claims of the American government for losses incurred during the Napoleonic years, arising from seizures and destruction that resulted from the Berlin and Milan decrees. This was a fairly far-fetched ambition, given the regime changes that France had undergone, and it occupied a good deal of the discussion that Gallatin had with the French government during his tenure, all the way to 1823. The French never denied or rejected the claims outright, but they did employ a strategy of vacillation, inattention, mild resistance, and deliberate if sometimes apologetic indecisiveness that rendered definitive action untenable.

Despite this murky nature of Franco-American diplomacy, Gallatin continued to work on the American claims. On August 30, 1816, he saw the Duc de Richelieu, who had succeeded Talleyrand as prime minister of France the previous year. In this meeting, Gallatin reviewed with Richelieu the history of the claims question, including the empty periods when Talleyrand was attending the Congress of Vienna and when William Crawford had returned to the United States (and when Gallatin, which he did not mention to Richelieu, was making up his mind whether to succeed William Crawford in Paris). Gallatin recorded Richelieu's response on this occasion:

> [H]e believed we would not be ultimately disappointed in our expectations, but . . . he hoped that, in the present situation of France, with which I must be well acquainted, we were not going to fill up the measure of embarrassments under which she now labored. . . . I requested him to explain precisely what he meant by our filling up the measure of her embarrassments. By demanding, he answered, immediate payment of what is due to you. On this I observed that the first point was the recognition of our claims, and, that, this once done, the time and mode of payment would be the subject of subsequent consideration, and must be arranged on principles of mutual accommodation. He then said that as soon as he had digested the papers connected with the subject he would lay it before the King and the council of ministers, and then invite me to another conference and communicate the result of their deliberations.[8]

A bit less than a month after that meeting, having heard nothing from Richelieu, Gallatin wrote to him again. Gallatin also wrote to Monroe to say,

> Much sensibility is, on every occasion, expressed on the subject of the hostility to the government of France, apparent in most of the American newspapers friendly to our Administration. This is not brought as an official complaint, the extent of the liberty of our press being well understood, but is stated as an evidence of an unfriendly disposition. I mention this because the several paragraphs in the *Moniteur,* though not entirely, may in some degree be considered as a kind of retaliation for certain pieces in the *National Intelligencer.*[9]

Here we enter onto classic terrain of diplomacy: the Americans had a precise and concrete issue to discuss, which was unwelcome to the French and which the French simply wished would go away; the Americans, however, having put this item at the top of their agenda, could not bring themselves to cross it off until it was settled; the French, therefore, in order to avoid addressing the issue (which would be unpleasant) and in order to avoid offending the Americans (which would be unpleasant), inject into the discussion, though not officially or as any kind of sine qua non, the overall feeling of the relationship, the ambient temperature, how they were getting along. This did not displace the main topic as such, but it did occupy some of the conversation.

Before things reached that point, Richelieu reinforced his position by multiplying his possible reasons for denying the American claims. On September 30, 1816, they met again in response to Gallatin's reminder, and Richelieu said that some of the claims were doubtful because the United States had retaliated and thus caused reciprocal damage to France. Gallatin parried this argument but could not dismiss it. Richelieu asked Gallatin what the Americans were doing about their claims against Britain. Gallatin said the British had given the Americans no satisfaction, but that was a different matter because the United States had actually gone to war against Britain.

> The Duke then stated that he was not authorized to enter into a negotiation for the purpose of providing an indemnity to the citizens of the United States for the captures and confiscations made by virtue of the Berlin and Milan decrees; that it was absolutely impossible for the present government of France to make compensation for the whole mass of injustice and injuries done by the former governments; that the whole territory, if sold, would not suffice for that object; that it had, therefore, been necessary to limit the measure of indemnity to the most flagrant cases, and that such had been the course adopted in the late treaties between France and the European powers.[10]

Thus did Richelieu introduce the concept of the comparability of claims against France by the United States with claims against France by other powers. In essence, Richelieu marked out three arguments: the diminished validity of American claims due to American retaliation against France, the nonsatisfaction of claims made by the United States against others, and the partial satisfaction of claims made by others against France. Simultaneously

Richelieu implicitly invited Gallatin to separate the American claims, precisely what Gallatin wished to avoid, in which case each claim could end up being the subject of a distinct negotiation, in which the first element would obviously be whether that particular claim was "flagrant" enough to be a claim at all. This is classic European statecraft at its best: Richelieu avoided the issue, protected his interests, and did his job without offending his interlocutor.

Then the other shoe dropped. On November 21, 1816, less than two months later, Gallatin had another meeting with Richelieu. In this meeting, Richelieu addressed Gallatin, American minister in Paris, about an application made by his counterpart, the French minister in Washington, Baron Hyde de Neuville, concerning the removal of the postmaster of the city of Baltimore, Maryland. On the previous July 4, 1816, while Gallatin was traveling from Le Havre to Paris, the Baltimore postmaster had made a patriotic Independence Day toast which the French believed was offensive to them. Hyde de Neuville therefore asked for the man to be dismissed. Now the matter was being raised in Paris as well as in Washington. Gallatin responded that it was impossible for the postmaster of Baltimore to be removed for this reason. Richelieu replied that while he fully understood freedom of speech in the United States, he found it incomprehensible that a government agent should be maintained in his functions when he had made derogatory public remarks about a friendly power. Richelieu said he had no wish to give offense but was merely stating the "kind of reparation which would be most natural, and which would be satisfactory." According to Gallatin, Richelieu added that

> the more precarious the situation of France might be supposed, the more important it was to take notice of any public insult, and to show that the sovereign of France was not a king of straw (the Duke's own words). It would not be in our interest, under the difficulties which she now had to encounter, that she should be vilified in the person of her monarch in the face of the world.[11]

Gallatin convinced Richelieu that the postmaster would not be dismissed, but Richelieu responded, again in Gallatin's words, "that the government of France could not certainly force ours to make them reparation for the insult given by that officer, and that they would be compelled to evince their dissatisfaction at our refusal in their own way."[12] In the coming months, Richelieu avoided the claims issue by not replying to Gallatin's missives and then, when pressed, stated, for the first time, that France did not think the United States was entitled to indemnity for Napoleon's actions.[13] While Richelieu was taking a hard line with Gallatin in Paris, the French minister in Washington, Hyde de Neuville, lightened the tone and warmed the relationship with the American government on his side of the Atlantic. In a letter to Gallatin, William Crawford wrote,

> Mr. de Neuville has conciliated the people of this place and the members of Congress very much during the winter by a prudent course of conduct. The newspapers have laid aside their asperity, and if the foolish affair of the toast at Baltimore could be well disposed of, I believe there would not arise any further cause of collision. The opinion which you state that he has given to the French Ministry corresponds with his declarations to Mr. Monroe on that subject. His wife is very amiable, and is highly respected for her excellent qualities. It is really ridiculous that the French Ministry should work up such a trifle into an object of such importance.[14]

In December 1816, Secretary of State James Monroe was elected president of the United States. In the virtual absence of Federalist opposition, he won the vote in the Electoral College by one hundred eighty-three to thirty-four. He took the oath of office on March 4, 1817. His Federalist opponent was the New York senator Rufus King, who went on to be minister to Great Britain. Monroe was supremely well qualified to be president: he had been in public service since 1782, minister to France under President Washington and to Britain under Jefferson, a U.S. senator from Virginia, twice governor of Virginia, secretary of war, and secretary of state. He was the last of the Virginians, after Washington, Jefferson, and Madison, to accede to the presidency. Given the harmony reigning within his own party, Monroe's two administrations came to be known as the "Era of Good Feelings." Monroe disappointed Gallatin, however, despite their mutual admiration and respect for each other, when he named John Quincy Adams as his secretary of state, thereby dashing Gallatin's hopes for that position. As a result, Gallatin continued as minister to France.

GALLATIN BROADENS HIS BRIEF TO OTHER EUROPEAN NEGOTIATIONS

In addition to pressing the American claims with the French government and trying to maintain harmonious relations with France, Gallatin, as a senior statesman, assisted his junior colleagues with their own responsibilities. In the early summer of 1817—Gallatin was in Geneva with his family—word reached him that his services were required on a negotiation with the kingdom of the Netherlands alongside William Eustis, the American minister there. So he returned via Paris to negotiate a trade treaty that would be similar to the convention which Gallatin had concluded with the British after the Treaty of Ghent, in 1815. This was part of the American policy to put in place open commercial agreements with key trading countries. On arriving in Brussels, Gallatin learned that the king of the Netherlands had decided that the negotiations should take place at The Hague, the royal seat, but that the court and the king would not be back there until September, so Gallatin and Eustis initiated discussions in Brussels with Baron de Nagel, the Dutch foreign minister, and then moved on to The Hague. The conferences on issues of international trade lasted four weeks but revealed that the Dutch were quite intransigent on what Gallatin regarded as fundamental issues, such as colonial preference—the adoption of advantageous terms of trade for commerce within an empire—and the subject of discriminatory duties. Having discovered just how deep their differences were, both sides decided, on a perfectly amicable basis, to abandon the discussions and refer the question of the usefulness of a commercial negotiation back to their governments. Although it would have been advantageous to conclude more positively, these trade treaties essentially aimed at creating better competitive conditions for both sides. Where one party had a structural competitive advantage, such as Dutch colonial preference within its empire, the other party's aims, such as the American desire for overall reciprocity, might simply be incompatible; but they did not constitute a bone of contention so strong as to sour the relation.

Gallatin's time in Paris was not all work and no play. For instance, he visited the soothing spa waters at Verrières-le-Buisson, a small town south of Paris. When not pressed by business, Gallatin frequented Parisian libraries and bookshops. And, most important, he spent time with his family. Hannah loved Paris, even if she found it slightly sinful, as when parties were held on the Sabbath. Gallatin excused her from a royal court reception in honor of the birth of the heir to the throne, the Duc de Bordeaux, because it was held on a Sunday. She righted the balance on that score by helping to establish the American Church in Paris. Their daughter, Frances, adored living in Paris, although as she grew up and began looking for an eligible man, she would have to face the fact that none of the Frenchmen she might be attracted to would be likely to take an interest in a bride without money for a dowry. James and Albert Rolaz thrived as well, even if Gallatin was concerned that they would turn out not to be American enough, the very worry he had cited to Madison before taking up the post.

In February 1818, Jefferson, nearing his seventy-fifth birthday, demonstrated that his mind was still very much in order, in a letter to Gallatin:

> A single measure in my own State has interested me much. Our Legislature some time ago appropriated a fund of a million and a half of dollars to a system of general education. After two or three projects proposed and put by, I have ventured to offer one, which, although not adopted, is printed and published for general consideration. It provides an elementary school in every neighborhood of fifty or sixty families, a college for the languages, mensuration, navigation, and geography within a day's ride of every man's house, and a central university of the sciences for the whole State, of eight, ten, or twelve professors. But it has to encounter ignorance, malice, egotism, fanaticism, religious, political, and local perversities.[15]

This was one point on which Gallatin never differed from Jefferson—the importance of education, the building of human infrastructure along with physical infrastructure. The ultimate founding of the University of Virginia was famously one of only three accomplishments in Jefferson's lifetime that he chose to have inscribed on his gravestone.

John Quincy Adams's replacement as minister to London was Richard Rush, whose father, Benjamin, had been a signatory of the Declaration of Independence. Rush was a Princeton graduate and a lawyer who had worked for Gallatin as comptroller of the Treasury in the Madison administration. Madison then made him attorney general. While continuing to occupy that position from March to September 1817 under Monroe's new administration, Rush also acted as secretary of state while John Quincy Adams ended his London mission and moved back to the United States. In this capacity, he negotiated with Sir Charles Bagot, the British minister in Washington, the agreement limiting American and British armed vessels on the Great Lakes that became known as the Rush-Bagot Agreement. He then moved on to London to replace John Quincy Adams.

The trade convention that Gallatin negotiated in England in 1815 after the Treaty of Ghent was set to expire four years later, in the summer of 1819. President Monroe requested an extension of eight years. Richard Rush asked Gallatin, as a senior American diplomat in Europe, to assist him with the negotiation of a new agreement with the British government.

The timing of this negotiation was made more urgent by the fact that Lord Castlereagh, the British foreign minister, was soon going to be leaving London. After the Congress of Vienna had settled outstanding disputes in Europe and reinstated the balance of power, a system of international governance was put in place that was not replicated until the League of Nations was attempted a century later. This system, known as the "Congress System," brought together representatives of the major powers at Aix-la-Chapelle in 1818, Carlsbad in 1819, Trappau in 1820, Laibach in 1821, and Verona in 1822. Although Gallatin did not attend these conferences, since the United States was not involved in the European system, his diplomacy in Europe was affected by them from time to time. The first occasion was August 1818, when Castlereagh was setting out for the Congress of Aix-la-Chapelle. Gallatin and his family hurried to arrive in London on August 16, 1818. On Saturday, August 22, 1818, Gallatin and Rush were invited to Castlereagh's country house for the weekend with their British counterparts, including Henry Goulburn, who had been one of the negotiators at Ghent and again during the discussions of the convention of 1815. Castlereagh was a grand host and most cordial. Rush met with Castlereagh in his office on September 1, 1818, as Castlereagh readied himself to go to Aix-la-Chapelle, and the negotiators then began work. Their contacts, meetings, notes, drafts, and the like continued through September and October, to little avail. Finally, in mid-October, Gallatin sent a note to Goulburn saying he would leave for Paris within five days. At this point they had agreed only on minor points. It was clear that Gallatin's note was designed to force the issue, and indeed within four days the negotiators agreed on a draft covering four significant issues. It renewed the 1815 convention and also included an agreement on the boundary between the United States and Canada in the west, up to the Rocky Mountains, and left for later the issue of the boundary of the Oregon territory reaching to the Pacific Ocean. This new convention was signed on October 20, 1818, in London and subsequently ratified by the Senate. Gallatin returned to Paris by October 27, 1818. Meanwhile, at Aix-la-Chapelle, Spain had been isolated by the other European powers: it had wanted to table the matter of its American colonies, which were then in revolt, but the other countries objected. Gallatin wrote to Adams from Paris that he was somewhat short of information following Aix-la-Chapelle because Richelieu and Pozzo di Borgo were not in Paris when he got back from London, but his analysis was that Austria and Prussia had no intention of intervening, that Russia and France were favorable to Spain but unwilling to be committed too far, and that although

Britain opposed a joint mediation by the major powers, it did not wish to be the cause of a mediation's not happening. The very nature of this discussion, though ultimately negative for the Spaniards, demonstrated the extent to which the Congress System attempted to resolve, by meeting on a regular basis, outstanding issues in international relations.[16] A couple of weeks later, Gallatin reported further on Aix-la-Chapelle: "The intimation that the independence of some of the Spanish colonies might be recognized by the United States has, as I expected, been received with much displeasure by Russia and by the Duke de Richelieu. By Lord Castlereagh it was considered as hasty measure."[17] Finally, Gallatin related that the proposal at Aix-la-Chapelle had been that the Duke of Wellington, who was in attendance as well as Castlereagh, should go to Spain—he had spent three years in Spain and Portugal fighting Napoleon in the Peninsular War—and, "charged with joint powers from the five great allies" (Austria, Britain, France, Prussia, and Russia), act as mediator between Spain and its American colonies. The project was abandoned.[18] All this information contributed to the intelligence of the Monroe administration, which was considering how to fashion appropriate American policy in the Americas, and testifies to the role that Gallatin now played of American senior statesman on pan-European affairs.

At the end of 1818, Jefferson again wrote to Gallatin with news from home. He mentioned in particular the capture of Pensacola, in Florida, by General Andrew Jackson the previous May.[19] While the Spanish-American colonies were in revolt and being discussed at Aix-la-Chapelle, the United States had conquered west Florida. Secretary of State John Quincy Adams was simultaneously negotiating the purchase of Florida with the Spanish, who protested against military action while they were in discussions. Ultimately, in February 1819, John Quincy Adams signed a treaty with Luis de Onís, the Spanish minister to the United States, in which Spain ceded Florida and the two countries agreed on a western border between the Vice-Royalty of New Spain and the Missouri Territory and the Oregon Country of the United States. During Monroe's administration, this activist diplomacy continued. Gallatin, from his Parisian perspective, reported to Adams in May 1819:

The Portuguese ambassador informs me that our treaty with Spain, having been laid before the Council of State at Madrid, had met in that body with strong opposition; that they having adjourned without coming to a decision, the King, under an impression that their opinion would be against the ratification, had concluded to ratify the treaty without their sanction; but that at the date of the last advices at Madrid the ratification had not yet taken place. Mr. Dessolle says that the treaty had occasioned warm debates, but seems to entertain no doubt of the final ratification.[20]

Gallatin continued to provide from Paris insights into Spanish politics and the question of ratification. Although the treaty was signed on February 22, 1819, in Washington, it was not ratified by Spain until October 24, 1820.

French-American Diplomacy Returns to the Forefront

Gallatin returned to a bilateral matter between France and the United States as France's maritime trade revived after the Napoleonic Wars. The duties and charges on American shipping, which had had negligible effect for some time, were now beginning to bite. As Gallatin wrote to Adams,

> The great inequality in favor of French vessels produced no effect so long as the French navigation remained in that state of nullity in which it was left at the close of the war. But everything has recovered here with un-exampled rapidity; and although we still preserve a great superiority in maritime affairs, it is not such as to counterbalance the difference in the rate of duties. American vessels are daily withdrawing from the trade, and if the evil is not corrected the whole of the commerce between the two countries will soon be carried on almost exclusively in French vessels.[21]

Gallatin recommended tough action on the part of the United States, even an amendment to the Constitution, but for the sake of swiftness he preferred that Congress should put in place a duty on French vessels of $12.50 per ton.[22] Congress meanwhile enacted a bill, to take effect in July 1820, imposing a duty of $18.00 per ton, far too punitive in Gallatin's view and bound to upset the French. In retaliation, the French enacted new and higher duties and enlarged the question to include other matters such as a leftover item from the treaty concluding the Louisiana Purchase. Baron Hyde de Neuville was sent back to Paris, then returned to Washington to negotiate directly with John Quincy Adams, the secretary of state. In the summer of 1821, Neuville and Adams put an end to the affair by moving the discriminatory duties to more moderate levels and then phasing them out. In the meantime Gallatin and Adams had differing interpretations on another matter that injected a sour note into the discussions: the seizure, of questionable legality, of the French ship *Apollon* while it might have been in Spanish, not American, waters on the St. Mary's River between Georgia and Spanish Florida (this was before the Adams-Onís Treaty entered into effect). In response to Spanish and French protests at this seizure, Adams, in blunt terms, said that since the Spanish did such a poor job at enforcing peace on the border, the Americans might as well do it themselves. Gallatin was summoned before Baron Pasquier, the French foreign minister, and offered his own interpretation of the incident—effectively parting ways from Adams, his chief. In a dispatch to Adams on July 2, 1821, Gallatin explained his view that Adams's defense was untenable, suggesting that the United States could hardly assert a right to seize another country's ship where and when it pleased. Gallatin also enclosed for Adams a copy of the letter that he had sent to Baron Pasquier,[23] in which Gallatin also departed from some of Adams's positions in the negotiation with Neuville.[24] The dispatch irritated Adams considerably, and as Gallatin already knew from the explosive arguments in Ghent between Adams and Clay, John Quincy Adams certainly had a temper. On November 8, 1821, Adams wrote in his diary,

> The most extraordinary part of Gallatin's conduct is that after a long argument to the French government upon grounds entirely new and different from those we had taken here, he gives us distinctly to understand that he considers all those grounds, ours and his own, as not worth a straw. I asked Calhoun to-day what he thought it could mean. He said perhaps it was the pride of opinion. I think it lies deeper. Gallatin is a man of first-rate talents, conscious and vain of them, and mortified in his ambition, checked, as it has been, after attaining the last step to the summit; timid in great perils, tortuous in his paths; born in Europe, disguising and yet betraying a supercilious prejudice of European superiority of intellect, and holding principles pliable to circumstances, occasionally mistaking the left for the right-handed wisdom.[25]

This passage says at least as much about Adams as it does about Gallatin, since Adams was clearly smarting under the lash of Gallatin's lessons while he, Adams, was actually secretary of state—and thus the embodiment of Gallatin's thwarted ambition.

What is interesting about the Neuville negotiations and the *Apollon* affair is less their specialized aspects than the illustration they give of two components of diplomacy: representation and negotiation. Throughout the Neuville negotiations and the *Apollon* affair, Gallatin had responsibility for the overall representation of the United States to the French government, while his own government was involved in negotiation with the representative of the French government in Washington. So Gallatin, as the American minister, would inevitably be held responsible for actions over which he could exercise no direct control. If negotiation is to take place by representatives within a bilateral relationship, the choice exists of conducting negotiations on the one side or on the other, but not both. This must ineluctably exclude the representative on the side where the negotiation is not taking place. And it confuses in one person the diplomatic duties of negotiation and representation. This is why the practice evolved of putting together separate, often specialized, delegations for specific negotiations, which can then be held outside the normal bilateral channels and can debate technicalities without prejudicing the friendly tone and well-functioning aspects of the overall relationship as maintained by the permanent representatives. That was not done in these instances, and so Gallatin was put in an awkward position vis-à-vis his home government and his host government.

GALLATIN PREPARES TO RETURN TO AMERICA AFTER SEVEN YEARS AWAY

During Gallatin's years in Paris, he often contemplated returning to the United States, and more than once his stay was extended. Gallatin was offered in 1822 the presidency of the Second Bank of the United States, which had been created in 1816 owing to the havoc of not having a central bank during the War of 1812—the very problem with which Gallatin had grappled during the loan of 1813—but he turned down this appointment, provoking mixed feelings on the part of his friend John Jacob Astor, who wrote to him, "I really think you will not like it so much in this country as you did, and I believe you had better remain where you are. For the interest of the United States Bank I am sorry that you will not take it. For your own sake I am glad. It is, as you say, a troublesome situation, and I doubt if much credit is to be got by it."[26] On November 13, 1822, Gallatin reported to John Quincy Adams that there was no hope that France would pay the claims that he had come over six years prior to negotiate: France's tactic had worked.[27] On the same day, he wrote to President Monroe to say how much he enjoyed being in Paris but requested permission to go to America in the spring of 1823 to arrange his personal affairs. He proposed a leave of absence only, for a period of about six months, after which he would return to Paris in the autumn and take up his duties again as minister.[28] By the spring of 1823, Monroe confirmed those arrangements, and on May 21, 1823, Gallatin and his family boarded the *Montano* at Le Havre, bound for New York.

After Gallatin's achievements at the apex of his power as secretary of the Treasury and negotiator of the end of the War of 1812, it is tempting to dismiss his seven years as minister to France as a generally idle interlude. In reality, he played the part of senior statesman with adroitness, steadiness, and thoroughness. True, he had made no Louisiana Purchase and signed no Treaty of Ghent, but that is precisely the point: out of the corridors of power, freed from the stresses and distractions of office, Gallatin, by his very standing, enhanced the overall French-American relationship, and indeed also the U.S. relationship with The Netherlands and Britain, while at the same time he dealt with the more recondite aspects of diplomacy with his usual assiduity. From a personal point of view, these had been delightful years, the happiest he had ever had. As he wrote to his old friend Badollet, "The last seven years I spent in Europe, though not the most useful, were the most pleasant of my life, both on account of my reception in Geneva, where I found many [of our] old and affectionate friends (Hentsch, Dumont, the Tronchins, Butiri, &c.) and from my standing with the first statesmen and men of merit in France and England."[29] After such an idyllic period, during which he had been associated with and appreciated by Europe's good and great, what lay ahead, when Gallatin returned to an America he had not seen for the better part of a decade, was far less certain.

[8]

SEARCHING FOR STABILITY, 1823–1829

THE Gallatins arrived in New York on June 23, 1823, in the midst of a heat wave at least as exhausting as the one Gallatin had known on his very first visit to the city in the summer of 1783, some forty years before. They went to stay with Hannah's mother, Mrs. Nicholson—Hannah's father had died while they were in Paris—at her house on the corner of Tenth Street and Sixth Avenue in Manhattan; and they rested there for a month. In July, Gallatin went to Washington, DC, with James. He determined that he could not afford to return to France the following spring, as had been his plan, and he informed John Quincy Adams of that during his trip.

The America where the Gallatins intended to remain had changed beyond recognition since the War of 1812. Expansion was the buzzword. Monroe had been reelected president and would remain in office until March 1825. During his two terms, five states were admitted to the Union: Mississippi and Alabama, part of the territory covered by the Yazoo Compromise that Gallatin had negotiated when secretary of the Treasury; Illinois; and famously Missouri, once the Missouri Compromise was reached, which also brought statehood to Maine and thus maintained the balance between slave states and free. Louisiana had already been made a state while Madison was president. Florida was acquired as a territory via the Adams-Onís treaty, though it did not become a state for another twenty years. In foreign affairs, Monroe recognized during his second term of office the Latin American republics of Colombia (which included the territories that are now Panama, Ecuador, and Venezuela), Mexico, Chile, Argentina, Brazil, the Federation of Central American States, and Peru. At the end of 1823, he promulgated the Monroe Doctrine, which barred European powers from intervening in the affairs of the American hemisphere. The doctrine had originally been suggested as a joint Anglo-American initiative by the British foreign secretary, Canning. In reaction, John Quincy Adams argued that the United States should act independently of Britain in the American hemisphere. The United States proceeded to proclaim the doctrine alone.

Gallatin, who agreed that the European powers should not interfere in Latin America, was nonetheless concerned that such unilateral action by the United States would find little favor with the British. It is often thought that the Monroe Doctrine was a mere statement of principle. In fact the Monroe Doctrine envisaged the use of American armed force to protect its interests in the Western Hemisphere (reinforced by the interventionist Roosevelt Corollary eighty years later).

During the second half of 1823, as these developments evolved in Washington, Gallatin returned to Friendship Hill. Never was his investment in western Pennsylvania worthwhile in the slightest, except for whatever residual Rousseauian satisfaction he might have derived from it. Now sixty-two years old, Gallatin had owned the property since 1786, for almost forty years. When he arrived back in Fayette County, Gallatin was not happy with what he found. He wrote to his daughter, Frances,

Notwithstanding all my exertions, you will find it hard enough when you come next spring to accommodate yourself to the privations and wildness of the country. Our house has been built by a new Irish carpenter, who was always head over heels and added much to the disorder inseparable from building. Being unacquainted with the Grecian architecture, he adopted an Hyberno-teutonic style, so that the outside of the house, with its port-hole-looking windows, has the appearance of Irish barracks, whilst the inside ornaments are similar to those of a Dutch tavern, and I must acknowledge that these form a singular contrast with the French marble chimney-pieces, paper, and mirrors. On one side of that mass of stones which Lucien calls "le château," and in full view as you approach it, is a wing consisting of the gable-end of a log house, with its chimney in front, and I could not pull it down, as it is the kitchen and dining-room where are daily fed two masons and plasterers, two attendants, two stonequarriers, two painters, a carpenter (besides three who board themselves), Lucien, Albert's black Peter, and Mr, Madame, Mesdemoiselles et les petits Buffle. The grounds are overgrown with elders, iron-weeds, stinking weeds, laurel, several varieties of briers, impenetrable thickets of brush, vines, and underwood, amongst which are discovered vestiges of old asparagus and new artichoke-beds, and now and then a spontaneous apple or peach tree. As to Albert, he has four guns, a pointer, three boats, two riding-horses, and a pet colt, smaller than a jackass, who feeds on the fragments of my old lilacs and altheafrutex. His own clothes adorn our parlor and only sitting-room in the old brick house; for the frame house is partly occupied by the Buffle family and partly encumbered by various boxes and Albert's billiard-table, the pockets of which are made with his stockings.[1]

GALLATIN IS TEMPTED INTO POLITICS AGAIN

Although Gallatin yearned to withdraw from politics and tend to his personal affairs, he was already being approached concerning the next presidential election by supporters of his old friend William Crawford. Monroe had served two terms and was not going to run again. The Virginians in the Republican Party wanted to nominate William Crawford, the man who had been minister to France before Gallatin and then secretary of the Treasury and who had been Gallatin's most faithful correspondent—providing background and insight on Washington politics—throughout Gallatin's years in Paris. In September 1823, Crawford suffered a stroke that resulted in partial paralysis and blindness, but the politicos paid no heed and felt sure he would improve. Sometime in midautumn, when Gallatin and Hannah were in Baltimore visiting her relatives the Montgomerys, he was approached about joining the ticket as Crawford's vice-presidential running mate. Crawford's doctors said he was out of danger, and in the first week of January, Gallatin went to go see him in Washington. He felt he was in a different world. He knew practically no one. He wrote to Hannah,

> [T]he place seems dull to me. . . . I hear nothing but election politics, and you know how unpleasant the subject is to me. . . . Mr. Crawford is mending slowly. His friends are not perfectly easy about his final recovery, and early adduced this to me as a reason why I should be made Vice-President. My answer was that I did not want the office, and would dislike to be proposed and not elected.[2]

Notwithstanding his reluctance, and the ill health of the candidate he was supposed to run alongside, Gallatin did not withdraw his name. In February 1824, the House Republicans conducted a caucus that nominated Crawford and Gallatin, but the following month, George Dallas, the son of Alexander Dallas who had been one of the secretaries in Gallatin's delegation at Ghent and who had become a political force himself, gave his backing to Andrew Jackson. As the year 1824 went on, John Quincy Adams emerged as a candidate; though not from Virginia, he would continue the tradition of the best and the brightest with world-class experience, including numerous secretaries of state (Jefferson, Madison, Monroe), moving up to the presidency. Gallatin continued to feel reluctant about running but did not decide to withdraw.

Meanwhile, the family was miserable at Friendship Hill. In July 1824, a year after they had returned from France, Gallatin wrote to his old friend Badollet,

> I have delayed much too long answering your letter of last year. I have ever since been on the wing, uncertain where I would fix myself. The habits of my wife and children, Albert's excepted, render this a very ineligible place of residence to them; but the impossibility of subsisting on my scanty income in one of our cities, and the necessity of attending to a valuable but mismanaged and unproductive property, have left me no choice; and we are all now here, including James's wife. My health and that of my daughter are delicate; the other members of the family are well. With the exception of James Nicholson, all my old friends are dead or confined by old age to their homes; there is not in this quarter the slightest improvement in the state of society, or indeed of any kind; but my children are good and very affectionate; neither of my sons, unfortunately, brought up to business. Albert, with considerable and varied talents and acquired knowledge, but as yet wanting perseverance and steadiness; James and Frances more fitted for a court than a wilderness; my wife just as she was twenty-four years ago.
>
> ... I will briefly state what has brought my name before the people for the office of Vice-President.[3]

Gallatin went on to explain how, despite his reticence, he had allowed himself to be sucked into the vice-presidential nomination:

> The friends of Mr. Crawford thought the persons proposed [as vice-presidential candidates] too obscure, and that my name would serve as a banner and show their nomination to be that of the old Republican party. I thought and still think that they were mistaken; that as a foreigner, as residuary legatee of the Federal[ist] hatred and as one whose services were forgotten and more recent ones though more useful but little known [Ghent and his other diplomatic missions], my name would be of no service to the cause. They insisted, and, being nominated both by the members of Congress and by the Legislature of Virginia, I could not honorably withdraw.[4]

Finally, in September 1824, as Republican political calculations continued to complicate, Martin van Buren asked Gallatin to withdraw, which he did with relief. In the end, the election went to the House of Representatives and was a three-way contest among Andrew Jackson, who had received the majority of the popular and electoral votes, John Quincy Adams, and William Crawford. Henry Clay, the Speaker of the House who had been with Gallatin and John Quincy Adams at Ghent, had also been a candidate but had not polled enough votes to be in the three-way runoff in the House. Crawford could not compete, owing to his stroke, so the contest came down to Jackson and Adams. Even though Jackson had won the elections, Clay threw the House vote to Adams, who became the sixth president of the United States on March 4, 1825, as a result of what Jackson, who succeeded Adams four years later, termed a corrupt bargain between Adams and Clay.

What is clear from Gallatin's letter to Badollet is that Gallatin was once again adrift. Just as he was in his early years in America, he was attracted to the country but unsure of his place there. He told Badollet that he missed the respect and consideration he could practically take for granted in Paris. There he was and always would be somebody. Back in America, others were coming along to replace him, and he might soon be forgotten. He wanted to be useful, but he also wanted to be recognized.[5]

His family was also growing up. James, who had thought about marriage with John Jacob Astor's youngest daughter, Eliza, in fact married the far less wealthy Josephine Mary Pascault in Baltimore in April 1824. Hannah adored her, however, and the couple made Albert and Hannah grandparents in February 1825 with the birth of their son, whom they named Albert for his grandfather: he was an Albert Gallatin who did go back and live in Geneva. Albert Rolaz became a lawyer, and Frances confessed that Gallatin's number two in the Paris embassy had proposed to her there, but nothing had come of it.

John Quincy Adams became president on March 4, 1825. Gallatin had some vague hope of being offered the Department of State, but subsequent correspondence between Adams and James Gallatin—they had of course known each other all throughout the Ghent negotiations—made plain that Adams never had any such intention. The position of secretary of the Treasury was proposed to William Crawford despite his incapacitated condition; he declined it. Rumors circulated that it would be offered to Gallatin, but this never happened, and Richard Rush, who had been

Gallatin's comptroller at the Treasury and then the minister to Britain with whom Gallatin negotiated the convention of 1818, occupied the office for the full four years of Adams's presidency. So in the spring of 1825 Gallatin found himself at Friendship Hill without any government position. Hannah finally just had too much of the place and convinced Gallatin to move away, even though he had spent ten thousand dollars to fix it up and settle in. He wrote to Badollet some years later,

> [A]lthough I should have been contented to live and die amongst the Monongahela hills, it must be acknowledged that, beyond the invaluable advantage of health, they afforded either to you or me but few intellectual or physical resources. Indeed, I must say that I do not know in the United States any spot which afforded less means to earn a bare subsistence for those who could not live by manual labor than the sequestered corner in which accident had first placed us.[6]

The reality was that he had chosen the wrong spot from the start and hung on far too long. Western Pennsylvania—barrenly beautiful but ultimately uninhabitable—would never be eastern Virginia, and Friendship Hill was certainly no Montpelier or Monticello. Gallatin needed a city and books and people and stimulation. He ought to have realized that long before, and he knew it; given the number of times he had contemplated returning to America from Paris, he had had ample opportunity to make decisions about where he would go and what he would do, and he had omitted repeatedly to seize that opportunity. Given how methodical and analytical Gallatin was about most things, his extraordinary nonchalance about the management of his own life is somewhat shocking. Although it might have been acceptable for an impetuous youth of nineteen wishing to satisfy his wanderlust, it became less and less justifiable in an accomplished statesman who owed a duty of care to his family. In October 1825, Gallatin and Hannah left Friendship Hill for the last time. James and Albert Rolaz were left to sell it as best they could; it took them seven years to find a buyer, and the sale price was thirty-five hundred dollars.

GALLATIN TAKES ON A NEW DIPLOMATIC ASSIGNMENT

When the Gallatins left Friendship Hill, they moved to a rented house in Baltimore. Hannah, Frances, and James were happy; Gallatin and Albert Rolaz hankered for the western Pennsylvania countryside. Gallatin was alarmed to find his expenses outstripping his income. He tried to cut back on the expenses; he ought to have been thinking about how to increase the income. During the year of 1825, he received a number of offers. In the spring, before the family had left New Geneva, the governor of Pennsylvania proposed to Gallatin that he become the commissioner of canals of the commonwealth, a pleasant offer but for an inferior position, which Gallatin declined. In November 1825, President John Quincy Adams invited Gallatin to become one of the American ministers at an inter-American congress which was to meet in Panama. The invitation was conveyed by Henry Clay, whom Adams had made his secretary of state. The two colleagues, who sparred at the Ghent negotiations, found unity after Clay delivered the presidency to Adams. Gallatin declined the inter-American offer, officially on the somewhat tenuous excuse that his knowledge of Spanish and the Latin American countries and officials was insufficient; he wrote privately to Clay to explain that his family did not want him to leave. Hannah was dead set against his going off once again on an open-ended mission. Then, in the spring of 1826, President Adams and Secretary of State Clay made Gallatin an offer of a special mission which interested him much more: to go to London to settle a number of issues, especially the Oregon border. He already had experience in negotiating with the British on the northern boundary between British North America (Canada) and the United States. He would join up with the permanent American minister to Britain, Rufus King. King had been a member of the Continental Congress, was a signer of the Constitution, a senator from New York, a candidate both for president and vice president, and twice minister to Great Britain. From Gallatin's standpoint, this negotiation and therefore his mission would have a finite purpose and tie up loose ends from his earlier assignments. While Gallatin was discussing the posting with Adams and Clay, Rufus King made known that he preferred to return to America. Gallatin wrote of his new assignment to Britain:

> There are important negotiations now pending between that country and the United States, and the state of Mr. King's health was such that he had requested that, for that purpose, an extraordinary minister might be united to him. Under those circumstances I was requested and agreed to go as special minister. Before my nomination was sent to the Senate, Mr. King resigned altogether his place, and his resignation arrived to this country and was accepted. The President, wishing to entrust me alone with the negotiation, and unwilling to nominate at once a special minister for that

purpose and an ordinary minister as successor to Mr. King, requested that I should go in the latter character, but with powers to negotiate, and with the understanding that I should be at liberty to return as soon as the negotiation was terminated, in same manner as if I had been appointed on a special mission. With that express understanding I have accepted.[7]

The only point of contention regarding Gallatin's mission was that he found his instructions too constricting. He wrote a long letter to Clay two days before his departure and a shorter one the next day to Adams: "I have this moment received your friendly letter of the 26th instant. I regret that I cannot say that my instructions are satisfactory. They are on almost every subject of the most peremptory nature, leaving no discretion on unimportant points, and making of me a mere machine."[8] Confident that he would have ample room to maneuver in one way or another, and having lodged his protest, Gallatin left with Hannah and Frances on July 1, 1826, from New York and arrived in London on August 7, 1826. While the Gallatins were at sea, Thomas Jefferson died at Monticello. Both Jefferson and John Adams breathed their last on July 4, 1826, the fiftieth anniversary of the signing of the Declaration of Independence.

FRUSTRATING NEGOTIATIONS IN LONDON

In London, George Canning was now again head of the Foreign Office. Canning, despite a troubled and impoverished childhood, had attended Eton and Oxford through the generosity of an uncle and had become a paragon of the British establishment and a pitiless practitioner of British statecraft. It was he who, in his first turn as foreign secretary from 1807 to 1809, had issued the Orders in Council that simultaneously thwarted Napoleon and stymied Jefferson, leading to the latter's fateful decision to initiate the embargo, all while Gallatin was secretary of the Treasury. Promptly upon Gallatin's arrival in London, new Orders in Council were issued interdicting intercourse in American vessels between the United States and British colonies in South America and the West Indies. As Gallatin wrote to Clay, this placed Gallatin "in a more difficult situation than had been anticipated."[9] Therefore, within mere weeks of his landing, Gallatin wrote to Canning to protest the new Orders in Council, which were, inter alia, in direct confrontation with the Monroe Doctrine. Gallatin had been right that Britain would not appreciate unilateral American action, and now Canning made that plain. His argument was that British colonies were not Britain itself, and America only had the right to trade with the colonies if Britain expressly permitted that. As these colonies were located in the Western Hemisphere, this represented a European influence in the zone which the Monroe Doctrine was supposed to ring fence. Once again, Britain bristled at the American upstarts who sought parity on the seas, whereas it had always been Canning's intention that Britain should enjoy exclusive maritime superiority over everyone else. Notwithstanding this disagreement, Gallatin had a pleasant meeting with Canning in London around mid-August, after which Canning left town.

Following Rufus King's departure from London, Gallatin was not only the special envoy for his negotiation but also the American minister to the Court of St. James's. On September 1, 1826, therefore, Gallatin went to Windsor to present his credentials to King George IV. England was nearing the peak of its imperial power, and London was booming. Frances, who by now was twenty-four years old, enjoyed herself. But Gallatin and Hannah were not happy. Partly this may have resulted from not committing to the mission for the long term. Had Gallatin accepted an open-ended embassy such as he had had in Paris, they would have had every incentive to ingratiate themselves in British society, to get to know the diplomatic corps, to cultivate professional and personal friendships as they had in Paris. There was also the question of their age—Gallatin was now sixty-five, and Hannah was about to be sixty—and they had a hard time being separated from their sons, whom they both missed terribly. James and Albert Rolaz wrote of their difficulty in unloading Friendship Hill, an albatross to the end. Two additional reasons compounded Gallatin and Hannah's dissatisfaction. In the first place, although Gallatin was well known to the governmental officials he was in contact with, he actually had no standing in Britain, nothing even remotely comparable to his prestige in France when he was minister there. His accomplishments on behalf of the United States were considerable, but they had largely been achieved in opposition to Britain. So Gallatin was doubly a foreigner, an American with a French accent with virtually no attachments to Britain except his friend Alexander Baring, himself considered in Britain to be highly Americanized. Furthermore, Gallatin had come to conduct a negotiation, his ministry included representation more or less in name only, and the issues for negotiation were arduous and complex and incited no real responsiveness from the British.

After Gallatin met with Canning in August and presented his letters of credence to the king, he had some initial contacts with his British counterparts in September. But these were not hopeful, and then his interlocutors left London. He wrote to Clay on September 22, 1826, with a summary of the situation as he found it and how it had changed since he was last negotiating in Britain:

> On three points we were perhaps vulnerable. 1. The delay in renewing the negotiation. 2. The omission of having revoked the restriction on the indirect intercourse when that of Great Britain had ceased. 3. Too long an adherence to the opposition to her right of laying protecting duties. This might have been given up as soon as the Act of 1825 had passed. These are the causes assigned for the late measures adopted towards the United States on that subject, and they have undoubtedly had a decisive effect as far as relates to the order in council, assisted as they were by the belief that our object was to compel this country to regulate the trade upon our own terms. But even this will not account for the refusal to negotiate and the apparent determination to exclude us altogether hereafter from a participation in the trade of the colonies. There is certainly an alteration in the disposition of this government since the year 1818, when I was last here. Lord Castlereagh and Mr. Robinson had it more at heart to cherish friendly relations than Mr. Canning and Mr. Huskisson. The difference may, however, be in the times rather than in the men. Treated in general with considerable arrogance till the last war, with great attention, if not respect, during the years that followed it, the United States are now an object of jealousy; and a policy founded on that feeling has been avowed.[10]

In early November, Canning said he was outraged by a report from a U.S. congressional committee earlier in 1826 staking claims to the Oregon Country, hitherto a condominium of the United States and British North America. In order to calm Canning down, Gallatin had to explain that the report had no value as government policy. Finally, in mid-November, Gallatin began structured meetings at the Foreign Office, starting with the Oregon boundary question, and throughout the autumn he addressed frequent dispatches to Secretary of State Clay. Once negotiation began, it became apparent that there were many more loose ends to be tied up than had been anticipated. Gallatin must have rued pushing off into the future some of the thorniest questions in his earlier discussions, because that future had now become his present. In addition to the Oregon question, they discussed the West India trade, the navigation of the St. Lawrence River, the boundary between New Brunswick and Maine, impressments, and the price to be paid for captured slaves, on which last point they actually agreed.

At the end of January 1827, having been in London just about six months, Gallatin wrote a letter to his son James with a full *tour d'horizon*:

We continue all well, and I anticipate nothing that can prevent our taking our departure about the middle of June. All that I can possibly do here must be terminated by that time, provided the instructions I have asked on some points be such as not to render another reference to Washington necessary. I have written to the Department of State accordingly, and asked for leave to return by that time, to which I presume no objection will be made, as it was explicitly understood that I should remain no longer than the pending negotiations required, and Mr. Adams's conjecture that they would occupy about twelve months is confirmed. I have written to him a private letter by the last packet, most earnestly entreating him both to direct the necessary instructions to be sent and to grant me leave to return. As you know him, and he has always shown kindness to you [Adams had held a favorable view of James Gallatin since the Ghent mission twelve years before], I wish you would join your solicitations to mine, either in writing or by waiting in person on him. There are many things which you may say or explain showing the importance of my return to my family. As to myself, whether it is the result of age (you know that in a fortnight I will enter my sixty-seventh year) or increased anxiety about you and your brother, my mind is enervated, and I feel that a longer absence would have a most serious effect upon me. As it is, though my health is tolerable, I hardly dare to hope that I will see you again. Nor will my return be any public loss. The United States want here a man of considerable talent, but he must be younger than I am and capable of going through great labor with more facility than I now possess. This is at all times the most laborious foreign mission. It is at this time, owing to the negotiations, one of the most laborious public offices. I cannot work neither as long nor do as much work in the same time as formerly. To think and to write, to see the true state of the question, and to state it, not with eloquence, but with perspicuity, all that formerly was done instantaneously and with ease is now attended with labor, requires time, and is not performed to my satisfaction. I believe that Mr. Lawrence will prove a useful public servant. Yet I have missed and do miss your assistance every day. I did not like French diplomacy; I cannot say that I admire that of this country. Some

of the French statesmen occasionally say what is not true (cordon sani-
taire); here they conceal the truth. The temper also towards us is bad. After all, though it is necessary to argue well, you may argue forever in vain;
strength and the opinion of your strength are the only efficient weapons.
We must either shut ourselves in our shell, as was attempted during the
Jefferson policy, and I might say mine, or we must support our rights and
pretensions by assuming at home a different attitude. I think that we are
now sufficiently numerous and rich for that purpose, and that with skill
our resources would be found adequate. But that is a subject requiring
more discussion than can be encompassed in a letter. I fear that you will
find this written in a too desponding mood; and I do not wish you to
despond as relates to yourself. . . . What you may, or rather ought to, do
about our lands [Friendship Hill and New Geneva], it belongs to you to
decide. They are yours and Albert's, and you must consider them as such,
keep or sacrifice, since there is no chance of a favorable sale at present,
as you shall think best. It is a troublesome and unproductive property,
which has plagued me all my life. I could not have vested my patrimony in
a more unprofitable manner.[11]

Things did not look up quickly thereafter. In March, President John
Quincy Adams wrote Gallatin an important and insightful letter which
both comforted Gallatin's position and paradoxically gave him the leeway
he needed to progress:

I have received from you several very kind and friendly letters, for which
the unremitted pressure of public business during the session of Congress
has not permitted me to make the due return of acknowledgment. The
march of time, which stays not for the convenience or the humors of men,
has closed the existence of that body for the present, and they have left
our relations with Great Britain precisely where they were.

The sudden and unexpected determination of the British government
to break off all negotiation concerning the colonial trade, and the contemporaneous measure of interdicting the vessels of the United States from
all their ports in the West Indies, as well as many others, has taken us so
much by surprise that a single short session of Congress has not been sufficient to mature the system by which we may most effectively meet this
new position assumed by the colonial monopoly of Great Britain. . . .

From the state of your negotiation upon the other subjects of interest in discussion between the two governments, as exhibited in your

latest despatches and letters, there is little encouragement to expect a satisfactory result regarding them. There are difficulties in the questions themselves,—difficulties still more serious in the exorbitant pretensions of Great Britain upon every point,—difficulties, to all appearances, insuperable in the temper which Great Britain now brings into the management of the controversy. For the causes of this present soreness of feeling we must doubtless look deeper than to the report of a committee of our House of Representatives or to the assertion by the late President that the American continents were no more subject to future colonization from Europe. As the assertion of this principle is an attitude which the American hemisphere must assume, it is one which no European has the right to question; and if the inference drawn from it of danger to existing colonies has any foundation, it can only be on the contingency of a war, which we shall by all possible means avoid. . . .

Upon the whole, if the same inflexible disposition which you have found prevailing upon the subject of the colonial trade, and of which indications so distinct have been given upon the boundary questions and the navigation of the St. Lawrence, should continue unabated, our last resource must be to agree upon the renewal for ten years of the Convention of 1818. This would probably now obtain the advice and consent of the Senate for ratification. On the colonial trade question the opposition here have taken the British side, and their bill in the Senate was concession unqualified but by a deceptive show of future resistance. But you must not conclude that the same spirit would be extended to anything in the shape of concession which you might send to us in a treaty. One inch of ground yielded on the northwest coast,—one step backward from the claim to the navigation of the St. Lawrence,—one hair's-breadth of compromise upon the article of impressment, would be certain to meet the reprobation of the Senate. In this temper of the parties, all we can hope to accomplish will be to adjourn controversies which we cannot adjust, and say to Britain, as the Abbé Bernis said to Cardinal Fleuri: Monseigneur, j'attendrai.

Your instructions will be forwarded in season that you may be subjected to no delay in bringing the negotiation to an issue; but I regret exceedingly the loss to the public of your continued services. The political and commercial system of Great Britain is undergoing great changes. It will certainly not stop at the stage where it now stands. The interdicting order in council of last July itself has the air of a start backwards by Mr. Huskisson from his own system to the old navigation laws. His whole system is experimental against deep-rooted prejudice and a delusion of past experience.[12]

GALLATIN MOVES THE NEGOTIATIONS TO AGREEMENT

John Quincy Adams's letter gave Gallatin everything he needed. He had the ability to walk away from the negotiations with the endorsement, even the encouragement, of the president of the United States. He had the ability to fall back on a crystal-clear view of what the Senate would and would not ratify: a priceless bargaining tool. He knew that his president understood not only the difficulty of these negotiations but the difficulty of any negotiation with the British in the current climate. Because he could now leave the room and leave the country with impunity, he had everything to play for and virtually no risk in doing so. On the British side, the news improved as well. On April 9, 1827, Lord Liverpool resigned as prime minister, and King George IV appointed Canning as prime minister the next day. It would have been several weeks after that that Gallatin received Adams's letter of late March and knew the flexibility he had, about the time Gallatin attended a dinner with Canning and Alexander von Humboldt. The testy British negotiator Huskisson saw his health worsen again, and he was replaced. All the while, Gallatin made progress in small steps, just by showing up and continuing the talks. Then, on August 8, 1827, Canning died. The king named Viscount Goderich as prime minister. Already a treaty was signed on August 6, 1827, continuing the commercial convention—the same negotiation Gallatin had conducted after Ghent in 1815 and among all the topics the easiest one to agree on. We see once again the result of Gallatin's diligence and resilience; once again we see him operating to effect a rapprochement of the two sides by focusing first on matters on which they can actually agree—and postponing, sometimes well into the future, matters on which they could not agree. On the same day as the commercial convention was signed, August, 6, 1827, a convention that in essence merely renewed an earlier agreement was signed perpetuating the joint occupancy of the Oregon Country by Britain and the United States. Gallatin felt this was the best he could do. The renewal convention lessened British-American tensions in the territory, and the two countries finally reached peaceful agreement on the Oregon-Canada boundary in 1846. On September 29, 1827, in the absence of an agreement settling a dispute concerning the Maine-Canada boundary, a treaty was signed that referred the determination of the boundary to a friendly sovereign acceptable as a decision-maker to both sides. That question also took decades to solve and was ultimately negotiated by Gallatin's friend Alexander Baring. For the time being, however, Gallatin's job was done, and he could go home.

The journey was a difficult one. Gallatin, Hannah, and Frances embarked on a packet ship, the *Sylvanus Jackson,* on October 8, 1827. As a smaller and lighter vessel, it was meant to be faster, but it was also susceptible to wild movement in storms. They endured seventeen stormy days in a row during the passage across. When they finally landed in New York after almost two months at sea, on November 29, 1827, the family moved into the American Hotel at Broadway and Park Place, about a block from City Hall. On December 5, 1827, Gallatin wrote a private letter to President John Quincy Adams. He said he would have remained another year in England, as the president had wished, had it not been for family reasons. The president replied to Gallatin from Washington on December 12, 1827, saying,

I regret exceedingly for the public interest that you found yourself under the necessity of coming home. At the time of your arrival in England, although I do not believe they had a deliberate purpose of coming to a rupture with us, they were undoubtedly in a waspish temper, and Mr. Canning had determined to play off upon us one of his flourishes for effect. . . . But, whatever it was, your convention upon the slave indemnities first turned the tide of feeling and soothed irritations on both sides. You gained an ascendancy over him by suffering him to fancy himself victorious on some points, by the forbearance to expose too glaringly his absurdities, and his position, from the time of Lord Liverpool's political demise, warned him that he had enemies enough upon his hands without seeking this *querelle d'Allemand* with us. . . . Mr. Canning was so fond of creating worlds that, under his administration, the turn of a straw would have plunged Great Britain into a war with any nation upon earth. His successors will be more prudent, and I hope more pacific. . . . Altogether, if your conventions are ratified, I shall indulge a strong hope that our relations with Great Britain generally will become more friendly than they have lately been. But I know only that I shall feel most sensibly the loss of your presence at London, and can form no more earnest wish than that your successor may acquire the same influence of reason and good temper which you did exercise, and that it may be applied with as salutary effect to the future discussions between the two governments. I remain, with great respect and attachment, your friend.[13]

DIPLOMATIC BUSINESS STILL TO DO AT HOME

With this praise from the president, and an appreciative analysis of his negotiating tactics, Albert Gallatin concluded his last mission abroad for his country. But this was not the end of his diplomatic negotiations, for after the Senate ratified the treaties he had brought back to America, Gallatin was asked to continue to work on the issues he had negotiated in London, but from within the United States. In February 1828, Secretary of State Clay requested Gallatin to prepare the American case for the presentation of the Maine–New Brunswick boundary dispute to a friendly sovereign, which was where Gallatin had agreed to leave the question in his negotiations with the British. Nobody knew the question better than he, of course (right up to the fact that the northern Maine border was the very place where he had stayed within two months of coming to the United States almost half a century before). Gallatin launched into this assignment with his usual verve, and it occupied his time for virtually all the rest of 1828 and 1829. By the end of 1828 he had created a vast sense of purpose for this mission and was clearly in his element. He wrote to Hannah from Washington on December 16, 1828:

I have used every possible endeavor to terminate our business earlier than the day on which it must necessarily be concluded; I have attended to nothing else, and owe now thirty and more visits, yet I do not expect to have done before the 1st of January. I cannot rise early, the days are short, the details very complex, new materials coming in to the last moment, a great mass of papers to read, selections to make, several transcribers and draughtsmen to direct, and, independent of age, the whole much retarded by my being obliged to abstain from writing [because he had hurt his arm].[14]

During this mission, Andrew Jackson was elected president of the United States and assumed office on March 4, 1829. Martin Van Buren was his secretary of state, and Gallatin reported to him on the mission. Indeed, on inauguration day itself, Gallatin wrote to Van Buren saying he would accept returning as minister to France. The Maine–New Brunswick boundary question was going to be referred to the king of the Netherlands, and it would have been useful for Gallatin to be in Europe when the king deliberated on the outcome. Van Buren never put forward such an offer, and when Jackson arrived in the presidency, he made so many wholesale changes—an echo of the question of removals with which Jefferson and Gallatin had grappled in 1801 but handled swiftly and brutally by Jackson—that the question never again arose.

Gallatin had a low opinion of Andrew Jackson, whom he found a crude bully, but was nonetheless invited to dinner at the White House in late November 1829. He was confined by a cold, and so Albert Rolaz represented him at the president's. Gallatin remained in Washington after recovering from his cold and paid an unscheduled visit to John Quincy Adams on New Year's Day 1830. The Maine–New Brunswick report was printed in final form just the day before, and Gallatin gave a copy to the ex-president. Gallatin's public career was over.

Once again, Gallatin had taken what looked like a period of drift and doubt and turned it into an era of performance and distinction. He did this by throwing himself into activities that stimulated his interests and gave him an outlet for his abilities. In this rather haphazard way, he not only succeeded in landing on his feet; he managed to stay in the flow of great events and realize great achievements. Yet this method of operating was indecisive and inefficient. It was heavily dependent on the right offer coming along at the right time, it immobilized him for long periods, it required intense travel, and it represented only one assignment at a time, with no clear path for the future. It must have been intensely frustrating to Hannah, who found her husband so wrapped up in his work but in ever-unpredictable circumstances and timing. There is evidence in Gallatin's writing and thinking that perhaps he too felt he should cease to wait for another main chance but instead settle down and, rather than search for stability, just accept it where he found it. Finally, at the age of seventy, he put down roots in one place, in New York City.

[9]

THE CAPSTONES OF A CAREER, 1830–1849

GALLATIN'S years in New York from 1830 to 1849 were to be the last and among the happiest of his life: he was settled and surrounded by his family, and he earned a decent living. He was able to influence opinions and events without having to bear the burden of executing the policies he recommended, particularly through intellectual interests in fields that he selected. The fruits of these pursuits appeared in published pamphlets and studies and, importantly, in the establishment of educational institutions that have endured until this day.

The family took a house at 113 Bleecker Street when they returned from London in 1828, then moved to the suburbs, then moved four more times—always on the first of May (probably owing to the lease terminating on that date)—until they moved into 57 Bleecker Street, near the corner of Crosby Street, where they remained. On April 6, 1830, Frances married Byam Kerby Stevens after seven years of courtship. Stevens came from a wealthy and prominent business family, and the couple raised five sons and two daughters. Seven years after that marriage, Albert Rolaz married his brother-in-law's niece, Mary Lucille Stevens, on November 8, 1837.

In late 1829, Gallatin was invited to join a gentlemen's eating society, known as "The Club," limited to a dozen members meeting once a week for dinner, of whom, at the time Gallatin was invited, three were lawyers, three were professors at Columbia, two were businessmen, one an Episcopal priest, another a Protestant minister, and the last a doctor, John Augustine Smith, who had been president of William and Mary College (Jefferson's alma mater) and was the member who invited Gallatin. The place Gallatin occupied had belonged to Samuel F. B. Morse, the founder and president of the National Academy of Design, who was later known as the inventor of the telegraph and the Morse code. Morse left New York to paint in Europe. One can imagine Gallatin fitting very comfortably into the informal intellectual discussions of The Club.

New York City in the 1830s and '40s proved to be the perfect place for Gallatin, brimming with opportunities and excitement for the elder statesman. For example, in April 1830 the editor of the highly prestigious *American Quarterly Review*, Robert Walsh, Jr., wrote to Gallatin to ask if he would be willing to contribute an article on currency. Congressman George McDuffie, of the Ways and Means Committee, had just prepared a report on the renewal of the charter of the Second Bank of the United States, to which President Jackson was dead opposed. Walsh was a partisan of Nicholas Biddle, the president of the Bank of the United States; this was the job that Gallatin had refused at the end of his mission to France, in 1822, and it was given to Biddle instead.

After Gallatin accepted Walsh's offer to write the article, Biddle carried on a lively correspondence with Gallatin, sent him a mass of information, and dispatched his own nephew to act as Gallatin's research assistant on the project. Gallatin simply did not know how to take a complex subject and treat it superficially. He spent months working on his treatise, missing deadlines along the way. But the final product was a masterpiece. The piece was published in the *American Quarterly Review* issue of December 1830, then republished in February 1831 with additions. The original article in the *American Quarterly Review* occupied eighty-seven pages, and the final document, published as *Considerations on the Currency and Banking System of the United States* ran to one hundred eleven pages including notes and tables. This latter pamphlet was sent at the expense of the Bank of the United States to opinion-shapers and decision-makers. Gallatin declined any compensation for the article, however. *Banks and Currency,* to use its short name, recommended a system not dissimilar to that of France, which Alexander Baring and Gallatin had agreed seemed to be especially robust. Transposed to the United States, that would mean gold and silver coin circulating as currency, in fixed ratios, and a single national bank responsible for the issue of paper currency and open-market operations on behalf of the U.S. Treasury. In the midst of debate over the renewal of the charter of the Second Bank of the United States, which President Andrew Jackson vetoed on July 10, 1832, this stance reinforced Gallatin's reputation as a partisan of the Bank of the United States as an institution. That narrow focus tended to obscure the larger message of his paper. In fact, his recommendations were implemented when the gold standard and the Federal Reserve System were adopted in the early twentieth century.

GALLATIN BECOMES THE FIRST PRESIDENT OF THE COUNCIL OF NEW YORK UNIVERSITY

Gallatin took a leading role in the inception of a new educational institution in New York City, New York University. Two establishments in Britain—University College London, founded in 1827, and King's College London, founded in 1829, both of which evolved into the University of London—provided educational opportunities to students from families in the expanding middle class, not focused exclusively on the aristocracy. A number of influential persons in New York gathered to promote a similar idea under the name of New York University. Gallatin had long held the idea that education for all was essential, going back to his experience in Congress in 1796 and as secretary of the Treasury in laying out the townships in the Ohio territory, which were to include schools. There was also the example of Thomas Jefferson and his proposal to found a series of educational institutions in Virginia, which Jefferson had related to Gallatin in his letter of February 1818, during the Paris embassy. On December 16, 1829, a meeting was held at the house of the Reverend James M. Mathews, who was then pastor of the South Dutch Reformed Church. In attendance at the meeting was the Reverend J. M. Wainwright, then rector of Grace Church (and later Episcopal bishop of New York). These were the two clergymen who belonged to The Club. The December 1829 meeting agreed unanimously that a broad-based university was desirable and determined to invite representatives of some of New York's leading institutions—the Athenaeum learned society, the New-York Historical Society, and the Lyceum of Natural History—to a later and larger meeting, which was held at the New-York Historical Society on January 6, 1830. Fundraising and other preparations continued over the course of the year, and as that process unfolded Gallatin was approached in September 1830 by John Delafield, a banker who had participated in the discussions from the beginning. We do not know whether Gallatin also learned of the New York University project at the dinner meetings of The Club. Gallatin's name was added by hand to the list of the subscribers, who contributed a total of $54,300. These men formed the Council of New York University in October, and at the council's first meeting on October 18, 1830, Gallatin was elected the first president of the council. New York University was formally chartered via an act of the New York State legislature on April 21, 1831, and received its first students in 1832.

Gallatin had misgivings about the financial plans—he viewed the projected investments as too ambitious for the resources likely to be available—and, apparently, he had a concern that the curriculum would be narrowed to religious studies and students at the expense of a broader education for a broader student body. On October 22, 1831, he resigned as president of the council, citing poor health, but wrote later to Badollet,

> I had another favorite object in view, in which I have failed. My wish was to devote what may remain of my life to the establishment, in this immense and fast-growing city, of a general system of rational and practical education fitted for all and gratuitously opened to all. For it appeared to me impossible to preserve our democratic institutions and the right of universal suffrage unless we could raise the standard of *general* education and the mind of the laboring classes nearer to the level of those born under more favorable circumstances. I became accordingly the president of the council of a new university, originally established on the most liberal principles. But finding that the object was no longer the same, that a certain portion of the clergy had obtained the control, and that their object, though laudable, was special and quite distinct from mine, I resigned at the end of one year rather than to struggle, probably in vain, for what was nearly unattainable.[1]

Although Gallatin might have felt that he failed at the time, New York University subsequently evolved into an institution offering a very broad-based education to a very diverse student body. In remembrance of Gallatin, there exists at New York University the Gallatin School of Individualized Study, while the university's information-services website for students is named "Albert" in Gallatin's honor—a gesture he would no doubt have enormously appreciated.

GALLATIN AND BANKING AND DEFENDING FREE TRADE

Yet another endeavor involved Gallatin's good friend John Jacob Astor. Astor came with his brother to America in the years after the War of Independence, and he made a fortune in fur trading along the whole area of what became the border between Canada and the United States. He was by all accounts Gallatin's best American friend—they were both European and were born two years apart—and Astor was always thoroughly interested from a business point of view in the border issues that Gallatin was called on to negotiate, but there is no suggestion that Gallatin ever committed any impropriety with the information that was entrusted to him. Astor was becoming active in the property market in New York when Gallatin moved to the city. He had already proposed to Gallatin that they go into business together in the autumn of 1815, when Gallatin came back from Ghent and was considering Madison's offer to become minister to France. Astor renewed the idea in March 1827—when Gallatin was in London trying to accelerate discussions with the British—and proposed to Gallatin that they think about starting a transatlantic merchant bank. Now another opportunity arose. The New York legislature had granted in April 1829 the charter for a new bank, but the individuals who had sought and obtained the charter were unable to find investors to subscribe to the bank's capital. They approached John Jacob Astor, who still had in mind the concept of a merchant bank that he had put to Gallatin. Astor agreed to capitalize the bank with $750,000 on the condition that Gallatin be named president. Gallatin accepted the position and a low salary of two thousand dollars a year. It was called the National Bank of New York.

On another issue relevant to the times, freedom of international commerce, Gallatin was to take a leading role while in private life. Henry Clay was the champion of what was known as the "American System," which consisted of letting domestic American business flourish behind a wall of protective tariffs. Gallatin was a longstanding free-trader, against protectionism and protectionist tariffs. In 1828 John Quincy Adams signed what became known as the Tariff of Abominations, and in the run-up to the 1832 presidential election a hot debate developed over whether the states had to accede to federal tariffs that hurt their regions.

In September 1831, Philadelphia held a convention of free-traders. It charged a committee, of which Gallatin was named chairman, with the task of writing a paper, styled a memorial, to be presented to Congress, in defense of the free-trade positions. The final version of the memorial ran to ninety pages and bore every similarity to a report from the secretary of the Treasury. Its rationale was adopted as the standard of the free-traders. During this period, Henry Clay decided to challenge Andrew Jackson in the upcoming 1832 election for the presidency. Clay, it will be recalled, was from Kentucky and had been a brilliant young Speaker of the House and War Hawk before the War of 1812. Along with John Quincy Adams, he had been one of the American commissioners at Ghent—Gallatin had kept them from each other's throats. Clay returned to the House of Representatives as a member from Kentucky and Speaker of the House and, it will also be recalled, threw the 1824 election in the House against Andrew Jackson and in favor of John Quincy Adams, thus earning Clay his position as secretary of state. Despite his diplomatic experience in Ghent and as secretary of state, Clay was an ardent nationalist. After leaving his position as secretary of state, Clay was elected as a U.S. senator from Kentucky, the platform from which he intended to challenge Andrew Jackson for the presidency. Clay advocated the American System of high tariffs to protect American domestic industry from foreign competition, and this was a pillar of his political credo. When the free-trade paper from Gallatin's committee—with all its aura of an official document and the presumption that it had come at least in part from Gallatin's pen—was presented to Congress, Clay, on February 2, 1832, included in his speech defending the American System the following remarks about Albert Gallatin:

> The gentleman to whom I am about to allude, although long a resident of this country, has no feelings, no attachments, no sympathies, no principles in common with our people. Near fifty years ago Pennsylvania took him to her bosom, and warmed and cherished and honored him; and how does he manifest his gratitude? By aiming a vital blow at a system endeared to her by a thorough conviction that it is indispensable to her prosperity. He has filled, at home and abroad, some of the highest offices under this government during thirty years, and he is still at heart an alien. The authority of his name has been invoked, and the labors of his pen, in the form of a memorial to Congress, have been engaged, to overthrow the American system and to substitute the foreign. Go home to your native Europe, and there inculcate upon her sovereigns your Utopian doctrines of free trade, and when you have prevailed upon them to unseal their ports and freely admit the produce of Pennsylvania and other States, come back, and we shall be prepared to become converts and to adopt your faith![2]

Even making allowances for the excesses of political rhetoric, this contumely surpassed the bounds of civilized discourse and showed, like John Quincy Adams's diary remark, just how deeply Gallatin's penetrating method and brilliance were resented, despite a lifetime of service to the United States—and despite the achievements they had accomplished together, not least during the negotiations at Ghent.

GALLATIN'S INTEREST IN NATIVE AMERICAN
ETHNOLOGY AND LINGUISTICS

In the latter part of 1832, Gallatin returned to a hobby he had adopted some years before, namely, the ethnology and linguistics of what were then known as American Indians and today are known in the United States as Native Americans and in Canada as Native People. It appears that this idea originated as a suggestion to Gallatin by Alexander von Humboldt in Paris in 1823. Humboldt requested that Gallatin prepare an essay on the subject, and although the essay itself was not published as a separate piece, it was cited favorably in the introduction to Adriano Balbi's *Atlas ethnographique du globe,* which was published in Paris in 1826. When Gallatin was back in the United States after the Paris mission, living in Baltimore in the latter half of 1825 (after the family had left Friendship Hill but before Gallatin was tapped for the London mission), he began collating Native American vocabularies and then, in Washington, DC, where a delegation of Native Americans from the South were present, expanding his lists. He suggested to the War Department that it circulate a basic vocabulary of about six hundred Native American words, which was done. Gallatin published a table of all the tribes of Native Americans in the United States. Some people have questioned why, with his background, he would undertake such a pursuit. Gallatin himself never provided a detailed explanation, but there are several plausible rationales.

First, as Balbi's *Atlas* demonstrates, it was in the spirit of the times to delve into the customs and conditions of native peoples, in Africa, India, and elsewhere in the British Empire, so why not add to that the native peoples of the United States? This spirit was possibly a source of Humboldt's original proposal. Beyond that, Gallatin had met Native Americans from his very first days in Massachusetts, and he lived among them at Machias in Maine in 1780 and 1781. Perhaps this was a chance to answer questions he had harbored for a long time. Many of the Indian tribes had conducted longstanding relations with the French and, after all, had been the allies of France against the British during the French and Indian War. The fur trade of Gallatin's friend John Jacob Astor had long dealt with Native Americans. This was also a period in the life of the United States when Native Americans were subjected to especially bad treatment. Andrew Jackson, now president of the United States, led the invasion of Florida during the First Seminole War, and the Second Seminole War was, as Gallatin picked up his studies of the subject, just around the corner. Moreover, on May 26,

1830, Jackson signed the Indian Removal Act. The purpose of the act was less brutal than its execution, as it was intended to assuage disputes with certain states, especially Georgia. But the practice of Indian removal, even when agreed to, was barbaric and extreme. The Native Americans were herded, in a movement called the Trail of Tears, often with few or no possessions, into Oklahoma, whose name means "red people" in the Choctaw language.

The treatment of the Native Americans was therefore highly topical when Gallatin began his study of the question. And it is typical of Gallatin that, if he was unable to find an authoritative work on a subject of interest, he set out to create it himself; this was, after all, precisely what he had done, to the annoyance of Hamilton, with the *Sketch of the Finances of the United States* as far back as 1796; so his method was entirely consistent. Lastly, just as the *Sketch* may have been inspired by a request that Jefferson made to Madison for more accurate information with which to attack the Federalists, so Gallatin's interest in Native Americans may have been prompted by a word from Jefferson some years before. While Gallatin was minister in Paris, Jefferson wrote to him, in November 1818, about an exchange he had had with Monroe:

> Emigration to the West and South is going on beyond anything imaginable. The President told me lately that the sales of public lands within the last year would amount to ten millions of dollars. There is only one passage in his message which I disapprove, and which I trust will not be approved by our legislators. It is that which proposes to subject the Indians to our laws without their consent. A little patience and a little money are so rapidly producing their voluntary removal across the Mississippi, that I hope this immorality will not be permitted to stain our history.[3]

Jefferson had himself compiled a classification of Native American tribes in his *Notes on Virginia* in 1801. Whatever Jefferson's caprices, Gallatin was forever and genuinely his humble and obedient servant; and Gallatin paid a silent tribute to Jefferson by taking up the issue of the Native Americans.

Toward the end of 1831, George Folsom, the chair of the publications committee of the American Antiquarian Society, based in Worcester, Massachusetts, having seen the reference in the introduction to Balbi's *Atlas*, wrote to Gallatin to ask if he had anything further to offer on the subject. This was just the incentive that Gallatin needed to produce a new magnum opus. For the next year and a half, Gallatin plunged into the subject, and in 1836 his study, which ran to four hundred twenty-two pages and had appended an ethnological map and numerous vocabularies, was published by the American Antiquarian Society under the title *A Synopsis of the Indian Tribes within the United States East of the Rocky Mountains and in the British and Russian Possessions of North America*. The work, which he had prepared from sources and without, on this occasion, undertaking any travel, was met with acclaim by American and European ethnologists, a striking accomplishment for a seventy-five-year-old man making his opening bow on the subject.

GALLATIN'S MISGIVINGS ABOUT HIS ADOPTED COUNTRY

Aside from the lamentable Native American question, these were exciting times in the United States and in New York. In November 1832, the first streetcar made its appearance on the streets of New York City. The *New York Sun* began as a daily newspaper in September 1833, followed by the *New York Herald* in May 1835 and the *New York Tribune* in April 1841. The population of New York doubled in the two decades of Gallatin's residence there, and the United States also increased in size, adding Arkansas, Florida, Texas, Iowa, and Wisconsin as states. The growth was so fast and so brash that Gallatin worried about his children's prospects in such an atmosphere, and he wondered, in a letter to his old friend Jean Badollet, whether it would not be better to educate his grandson in Geneva, "rather than to leave him to struggle in this most energetic country, where the strong in mind and character overset everybody else, and where consideration and respectability are not at all in proportion to virtue and merit."[4] "Every day's experience convinces us that the most unprincipled men are often the most successful. In this country there is much more morality and less of integrity than on the continent of Europe."[5]

As if to vindicate this feeling, Gallatin stayed in touch with his contacts in Geneva through correspondence during these years. He wrote a long response to an inquiry from Geneva about the appropriateness of making investments in the United States, a document that was a virtual primer on American finance. He wrote to a school friend recalling a prize that the friend had won at the Academy of Geneva and a walk they had taken together in Cologne in 1815 when Gallatin was on his way from St. Petersburg to London and Ghent. He introduced his son-in-law, Byam Kerby Stevens, and explained that he would be bringing Byam's son, Gallatin's grandson, to Geneva for school for a few years and would be making the trip with some nephews: would they please welcome his family members and take his grandson a bit under their wing? He discouraged another friend from his idea to immigrate to the United States, expressing the same sorts of hesitations about living in America that he had expressed to Badollet. He said the Genevans would have no standing; instead he recommended France, reversing his own choice in 1780. As he had written earlier to Badollet, "I believe emigration, when not compulsory, to be always an error, and you are the only person that I ever induced to take that step."[6] Indeed in these closing decades of his life, Gallatin looked back more and more often to his experiences in Geneva and early in his career. He drafted in these years a number of letters and short essays—and, sadly, no account of greater length—from which some of the description earlier in this story is drawn.

America's boom experienced a setback in the 1830s with a weakening of its financial system. President Jackson refused to recharter the Second Bank of the United States, but in news that ought to have been music to the ears of Gallatin, the United States repaid its national debt. The combination of these circumstances produced a plethora of liquidity and a profusion of new banks, more than three hundred from 1830 to 1837, all with money to lend. This resulted in a classic credit bubble, with all the symptoms of easy money, ever-reducing credit quality of borrowers, and, ultimately, a wave of defaults. In March 1837, this led to a banking panic, and on May 10, 1837, the New York banks stopped making payments in cash. Thereupon, all banks in the United States followed suit. This was the Panic of 1837.

Gallatin played a central role in unwinding the banking crisis. He and two other bankers were appointed in mid-August by the New York banks to approach the banks of the states throughout the United States to propose a conference to agree on a date to resume payments, which had to be done within a year, or the New York banks, under state law, would be dissolved. The banks of the other states, led by Pennsylvania, where the old Bank of the United States had been rechartered and was effectively bankrupt, followed by the banks in Baltimore and Boston, declined this proposal. Gallatin, leading the New York banks, called the conference anyway, and the non–New York banks were obliged to attend, lest New York act without them. In the end they reached no agreement, and New York did act alone, resuming payments on May 10, 1838, just in time to avoid dissolution. Gallatin deployed his legendary talent as a negotiator and as a parliamentarian. A year later, he resigned as president of the National Bank of

New York. The bank's officers gave him a dinner at Delmonico's in thanks for his seven years of leadership. Even more gratifying was the fact that his son James, who had worked side by side with his father on so many occasions since the Treaty of Ghent more than twenty years before, was elected president of the bank to succeed him. Gallatin wrote a hundred-page essay in 1841 entitled "Suggestions on the Banks and Currency of the Several United States—in Reference Principally to the Suspension of Specie Payments," his contribution to the understanding of what had caused the Panic of 1837 and what could prevent another one, chiefly that the public authorities should avoid encouraging speculation and prevent the public from overborrowing.

OLD ISSUES AND OLD FRIENDS COME BACK TO THE FORE

Gallatin also produced an important paper in 1840 entitled "The Right of the United States of America to the North-Eastern Boundary Claimed by Them, Principally Extracted from Statements Laid before the King of the Netherlands." The king's arbitration had been recognized by the British but not by the state of Maine. Gallatin revised and rewrote his argumentation of 1830 in forty thousand words, with almost as much in the way of appendices, plus maps. This was printed and sent to decision-makers in Britain. In 1842, his old friend Alexander Baring, now Lord Ashburton, came to the United States to make the final negotiation of that issue with Daniel Webster, the secretary of state. It had been thirty-seven years since he and Gallatin arranged together the financing of the Louisiana Purchase. The letters of these men are impressive and moving.

Ashburton wrote to Gallatin on April 12, 1842, from Washington, DC:

> My first destination was to approach America through New York, but the winds decided otherwise, and I was landed at Annapolis. In one respect only this was a disappointment, and a serious one. I should have much wished to seek you out in your retreat to renew an old and highly-valued acquaintance and, I believe and hope I may add, friendship; to talk over with you the Old and the New World, their follies and their wisdom, their present and by-gone actors, all which nobody understands so well as you do, and, what is more rare, nobody that has crossed my passage in life has appeared to me to judge with the same candid impartiality. This pleasure of meeting you is, I trust, only deferred. I shall, if I live to accomplish my

work here, certainly not leave the country without an attempt to find you out and to draw a little wisdom from the best well, though it may be too late for my use in the work I have in hand and very much at heart.

You will probably be surprised at my undertaking this task at my period of life, and when I am left to my own thoughts I am sometimes surprised myself at my rashness. People here stare when I tell them that I listened to the debates in Congress on Mr. Jay's treaty in 1795, and seem to think that some antediluvian has come among them out of his grave. The truth is that I was tempted by my great anxiety in the cause, and the extreme importance which I have always attached to the maintenance of peace between our countries. The latter circumstance induced my political friends to press this appointment upon me, and with much hesitation, founded solely upon my health and age, I yielded. In short, here I am. My reception has been everything I could expect or wish; but your experience will tell you that little can be inferred from this until real business is entered upon. I can only say that it shall not be my fault if we do not continue to live on better terms than we have lately done, and, if I do not misunderstand the present very anomalous state of parties here, or misinterpret public opinion generally, there appears to be no class of politicians of any respectable character indisposed to peace with us on reasonable terms. I expect and desire to obtain no other, and my present character of a diplomatist is so new to me that I know no other course but candor and plain-dealing. The most inexpert protocolist would beat me hollow at such work. I rely on your good wishes, my dear sir, though I can have nothing else, and that you will believe me unfeignedly yours.[7]

Gallatin replied from New York on April 20, 1842:

Your not landing here was as great disappointment to me as to you. I have survived all my early friends, all my political associates; and out of my own family no one remains for whom I have a higher regard or feel a more sincere attachment than yourself. If you cannot come here, I will make an effort and see you at Washington. Your mission is in every respect a most auspicious event. To all those who know you it affords a decisive proof of the sincere wish on the part of your government to attempt a settlement of our differences as far as practicable; at all events, to prevent an unnatural, and on both sides absurd and disgraceful, war. There are but few intrinsic difficulties of any magnitude in the way. Incautious commitments, pride, prejudices, selfish or party feelings present more serious obstacles. You have one of a peculiar kind to encounter. Our President is supported by neither of the two great political parties of the country, and is hated by that which elected him, and which has gained a temporary ascendancy. He must, in fact, negotiate with the Senate before he can agree with you on any subject. It is the first time that we have been in that situation, which is somewhat similar to that of France; witness your late treaty, which the French Administration concluded and dared not ratify. It may be that under those circumstances our government may think it more eligible to make separate conventions for each of the subjects on which you may agree than to blend them in one instrument. The greatest difficulties may be found in settling the two questions in which both parties have in my humble opinion the least personal or separate interest, viz., the right of visitation on the African seas for the purpose only of ascertaining the nationality of the vessel; and the North-Western boundary. I have no reason, however, to believe that the Administration, left to itself, will be intractable on any subject whatever; I hope that higher motives will prevail over too sensitive or local feelings, and I place the greatest reliance on your sound judgment, thorough knowledge of the subject, straightforwardness, and ardent desire to preserve peace and cement friendship between the two kindred nations. You cannot apply your faculties to a more useful or nobler purpose. I am now in my 82d year, and on taking a retrospective view of my long career I derive the greatest consolation for my many faults and errors from the consciousness that I ever was a minister of peace, from the fact that the twenty last years of my political life were almost exclusively employed in preventing the war as long as I could, in assisting in a speedy restoration of peace, and in settling subsequently as many of the points of difference as was at the time practicable. May God prosper your efforts and enable you to consummate the holy work![8]

The Webster-Ashburton Treaty settled disputed issues relating to the U.S.-Canadian border and the terms of joint British and American rights on the Great Lakes. It was signed on August 9, 1842, and the two old friends met in New York as Lord Ashburton made his way home.

In October 1842, Gallatin became a member of the New-York Historical Society. That November, Gallatin founded the American Ethnological Society in New York and became its first president, furthering his interest in Native American ethnology and linguistics and earning him the honor of being known as the father of American ethnology. In February 1843, the New-York Historical Society elected Gallatin as its president; he prepared and delivered an address that was published in the organization's *Proceedings* for that year. In late 1843, intimations were made that he was being considered for the position of secretary of the Treasury, which he characterized as "insanity."[9] In April 1844, he presided at a meeting protesting the potential annexation of Texas, then at war with Mexico, as an act that would implicitly put the United States into a position of being at war and, worse, the first war of conquest in its history and, if Texas were admitted as a state, would spread slavery further throughout the United States. That meeting was raucous, full of tumult and shouting, and he could hardly be heard, but Gallatin's speech was reported in the press. The United States did annex Texas, which led to the Mexican-American War. Gallatin published in 1847 an essay called "Peace with Mexico," of which ninety thousand copies were distributed around the country He continued to write on the subject of ethnology and of boundaries and on the Mexican situation. In 1845 he completed a three-hundred-page study entitled *Notes on the Semi-Civilized Nations of Mexico, Yucatan and Central America,* which was published in the *Transactions of the American Ethnological Society.* In January 1846, the *National Intelligencer* printed a piece entitled "Letters of Albert Gallatin on the Oregon Question." In 1848, following "Peace with Mexico," Gallatin prepared a companion study entitled "War Expenses." And in 1848 he wrote an essay "Hale's Indians of North-West America, and Vocabularies of North America: With an Introduction," also published in the *Transactions of the American Ethnological Society.* This is a high level of varied activity for a man in his eighties. Gallatin now occupied a place of merit as a public intellectual on some of the most burning issues of the day, ones with which he had long experience. He created for himself, in New York City, a new, stimulating, and valuable last career.

Yet Gallatin was very old, and finally he began to fade. In the first half of 1848, his friends John Quincy Adams, John Jacob Astor, and Lord Ashburton all died. In the latter half of the year, Gallatin was generally confined to his room. In the spring of 1849, Hannah died. When she departed, to all intents and purposes, his life was at an end. At the age of eighty-eight Albert Gallatin died in the arms of his daughter, Frances, on August 12, 1849, and was buried three days later in the Nicholson vault in the graveyard of Trinity Church on Broadway at the end of Wall Street.

CONCLUSION

Gauging Gallatin's Greatness

WAS Gallatin a great man? Greatness is most frequently measured by accomplishments, and on that basis it is hard to challenge Gallatin's entitlement to the description. Suppose Gallatin had not been Jefferson's secretary of the Treasury or had not been present at Ghent. Gallatin brought to the Treasury a level of professionalism and attention to detail that had been lacking theretofore. And if the American commissioners at Ghent had been left to their own devices without Gallatin, as they very nearly were, their nationalism (Clay) and obduracy (Adams) would probably have resulted not only in a fracture within the American delegation but in an utter inability to communicate with the British. The United States was not winning the War of 1812, and Britain was possessed, after its Napoleonic victories, of bottomless reserves of military and commercial strength. Had the issues between the two countries not been resolved by tactful, shrewd, and highly skilled diplomacy—including postponing many of those issues for later discussion, some of which rebounded to Gallatin as they reemerged—the United States simply would not have achieved the same degree of independence or have cleared the way for its future expansion. Gallatin's deft suggestion of draft treaties on both sides established the equality of the parties and put the talks in a more positive mode. These two achievements alone would have earned Gallatin his greatness, and as this book has shown, they were accompanied by many more.

Greatness can also be measured by character. On that scale Gallatin scores at least as highly as he does when judged on accomplishments. He took on challenges, overcame hardships, prized rather than snatched victory from the jaws of multiple defeats, faced down enemies, cherished friends, revered his family, adhered to his principles, trusted his methods, and held to his ethics, all to the end. To be sure, he had character flaws: he was hopelessly obstinate in trying to make a success of Friendship Hill;

[167]

his approach to the study of complex questions was so profound as to lack a lightness of touch; he was unable to refrain from pointing out to others the flaws which he found in their thinking, whereas he might have let slip some illogicality simply in order to smooth relations, and that earned him the resentment of some of the people he admired most.

Finally, his greatness can be measured by his faithfulness to two sometimes conflicting and sometimes complementary cultures: he spanned the divide between the Europe he came from and the America he helped to shape. It is particularly fortunate that he ended up in New York, where both his European erudition and his American ambition were accepted as compatible and not contradictory. Gallatin led a long and active life by accepting challenges, by taking risks, and by being willing to innovate: all thought of as "American" virtues. At the same time, he held fast to a set of European values that made him a civilized man by the standards of any epoch. Gallatin lived to old age by combining the most salient characteristics of a well-lived life: the willingness to work, an interest in people, a love of ideas, a sense of purpose based on his own standards for himself, and no fear. Gallatin is thus an excellent example of an American and a Swiss.

NOTES

LETTERS originally in French have been translated by the author and are indicated in the notes by [F].

NOTES TO THE INTRODUCTION

1. Edward Gibbon, *Memoirs* (London: Routledge, 1891), 151.

NOTES TO CHAPTER 1

1. "Genealogy of the Gallatin Family," Albert Gallatin Papers [hereafter AGP].
2. Ibid.
3. Albert Gallatin to Ebenezer Dodge, January 21, 1847, AGP; email from Martine Piquet at the Archives d'État, November 26, 2009, citing Charles Borgeaud, *Histoire de l'Université de Genève* (Geneva: Georg & Co., 1900).
4. Catherine Pictet to Albert Gallatin, Geneva, May 28, 1780, AGP, [F].
5. Albert Gallatin to Horace-Bénédict de Saussure, Geneva, May 28, 1779, Bibliothèque de Genève, [F].
6. Edward Gibbon, *The History of the Decline and Fall of the Roman Empire* (New York: Harper & Brothers, 1841), xxviii.
7. Albert Gallatin to Jean Badollet, Boston, October 1, 1783, AGP, [F].
8. Paul-Michel Gallatin to Albert Gallatin, Geneva, May 21, 1780, AGP, [F].
9. Catherine Pictet to Albert Gallatin, Geneva, May 28, 1790, AGP, [F].
10. Catherine Pictet to Frances Kinloch, Geneva, May 26, 1780, AGP, [F].
11. Benjamin Franklin to the Duc de la Rochefoucauld d'Enville, Passy, May 24, 1780, in Henry Adams, *The Life of Albert Gallatin* (Philadelphia: Lippincott, 1880), 24.
12. Catherine Pictet to Albert Gallatin, Geneva, May 31, 1780, AGP, [F].
13. Albert Gallatin to Jean Badollet, Pimbeuf, May 16, 1780, AGP, [F].
14. Albert Gallatin, notes on Gallatin coat of arms, 1848, AGP.

NOTES TO CHAPTER 2

1. Albert Gallatin to Jean Badollet, Boston, September 14, 1780, AGP, [F].

2. Catherine Pictet to Albert Gallatin, Geneva, December 26, 1782, AGP, [F].
3. Albert Gallatin to Jean Badollet, Philadelphia, October 1, 1783, AGP, [F].
4. Albert Gallatin to William Maxwell, New York, February 15, 1848, AGP.
5. "Draft of Report of the Harrisburg Conference of September 3, 1788," in Henry Adams, ed., *The Writings of Albert Gallatin*, 3 vols. (Philadelphia: Lippincott, 1879), 1:1–2; and Adams, *Life of Albert Gallatin*, 78–79.
6. Albert Gallatin to Jean Badollet, Richmond, May 4, 1789, AGP, [F].
7. Albert Gallatin to Alexander Addison, Friendship Hill, October 7, 1789, AGP.
8. Albert Gallatin to Charles Brown, New York, March 1, 1838, AGP.
9. Albert Gallatin to Jean Badollet, Philadelphia, March 8, 1790, AGP, [F].
10. Catherine Pictet to Albert Gallatin, Geneva, July 1, 1790, AGP, [F].
11. Albert Gallatin Biographical Sketch, 1849, AGP.
12. *The Speech of Albert Gallatin*, January 3, 1795, in Adams, *Writings of Albert Gallatin*, 3:6–7.
13. Albert Gallatin to Jean Badollet, Philadelphia, December 18, 1792, AGP.
14. Catherine Pictet to Albert Gallatin, Geneva, November 6, 1792, AGP, [F].

Notes to Chapter 3

1. Albert Gallatin Biographical Sketch, 1849, AGP.
2. Albert Gallatin to Jean Badollet, Philadelphia, July 30, 1793, AGP.
3. Albert Gallatin to Hannah Nicholson, Philadelphia, August 25, 1793, in Adams, *Life of Albert Gallatin*, 103–104.
4. Albert Gallatin to Jean Badollet, Philadelphia, February 1, 1794, AGP.
5. Alexander Hamilton to the Senate of the United States, Treasury Department, Philadelphia, February 22, 1794, in Adams, *Life of Albert Gallatin*, 117 footnote.
6. Albert Gallatin to Thomas Clare, Philadelphia, March 5, 1794, AGP.
7. Albert Gallatin Biographical Sketch 1849, AGP.
8. Albert Gallatin to Hannah Nicholson Gallatin, Catskill Landing, April 22, 1795, in Adams, *Life of Albert Gallatin*, 146–147.
9. Albert Gallatin to Hannah Nicholson Gallatin, Philadelphia, June 29, 1795, in Adams, *Life of Albert Gallatin*, 151.
10. Albert Gallatin to Hannah Nicholson Gallatin, Philadelphia, September 29, 1795, in Adams, *Life of Albert Gallatin*, 153.
11. Thomas Jefferson to James Madison, March 6, 1796, James Madison Papers, Library of Congress.
12. Albert Gallatin, *A Sketch of the Finances of the United States*, in Adams, *Writings of Albert Gallatin*, 3:145.
13. Albert Gallatin to Hannah Nicholson Gallatin, Philadelphia, January 24, 1797, in Adams, *Life of Albert Gallatin*, 182.
14. Albert Gallatin to Hannah Nicholson Gallatin, Philadelphia, December 7,

1798, January 4, 1799, and January 18, 1799, in Adams, *Life of Albert Gallatin,* 221–223, 225, 226.

15. Albert Gallatin to Lewis F. de Lesdernier, Philadelphia, May 25, 1798, in Adams, *Writings of Albert Gallatin,* 1:15.

16. Albert Gallatin to Henry A. Muhlenberg, New York, May 8, 1848, AGP.

17. Albert Gallatin to Hannah Nicholson Gallatin, Washington City, February 17, 1801, AGP.

NOTES TO CHAPTER 4

1. Albert Gallatin to Hannah Nicholson Gallatin, Washington City, January 15, 1801, AGP.

2. Thomas Jefferson to Albert Gallatin, Washington City, June 3, 1801, AGP.

3. Albert Gallatin to Maria Nicholson, Washington City, March 12, 1801, AGP.

4. Thomas Jefferson to Robert R. Livingston, April 12, 1802, Thomas Jefferson Papers, Library of Congress.

5. Ibid.

6. Albert Gallatin to Thomas Jefferson, Washington City, January 13, 1803, Thomas Jefferson Papers, Library of Congress.

NOTES TO CHAPTER 5

1. *History of Congress, Foreign Relations,* House of Representatives, November 1808, 514.

2. Albert Gallatin to Thomas Jefferson, Washington City, January 18, 1803, Thomas Jefferson Papers, Library of Congress.

3. Thomas Jefferson to Albert Gallatin, Monticello, October 11, 1809, AGP.

4. Albert Gallatin to Thomas Jefferson, Washington, DC, November 8, 1809, AGP.

5. Albert Gallatin to James Madison, Washington, DC, [March 4, 1811?], AGP.

6. Albert Gallatin to Thomas Jefferson, Washington, DC, December 18, 1812, AGP.

7. Albert Gallatin to James W. Nicholson, Philadelphia, May 5, 1813, AGP.

NOTES TO CHAPTER 6

1. Albert Gallatin to Baring Brothers, Gothenburg, June 22, 1813, AGP.

2. Alexander Baring to Albert Gallatin, London, July 22, 1813, AGP.

3. Albert Gallatin to Alexander Baring, St. Petersburg, August 27, 1813, AGP.

4. Albert Gallatin to James Monroe, St. Petersburg, August 28, 1813, AGP.

5. Albert Gallatin to Alexander Baring, St. Petersburg, October 18, 1813, AGP.

6. Alexander Baring to Albert Gallatin, London, October 12, 1813, AGP.

7. Albert Gallatin to James Monroe, St. Petersburg, November 21, 1813, AGP.

8. Alexander Baring to Albert Gallatin, London, December 14, 1813, AGP.

9. Albert Gallatin to Alexander Baring, St. Petersburg, January 7, 1814, AGP.

10. Albert Gallatin and James A. Bayard to James Monroe, London, May 6, 1814, AGP.

11. Albert Gallatin to James Monroe, Ghent, August 20, 1814, AGP.

12. Albert Gallatin to James Monroe, Ghent, October 26, 1814, AGP.

13. Hannah Nicholson Gallatin to Albert Gallatin, Philadelphia, December 1, 1814, AGP.

Notes to Chapter 7

1. Albert Gallatin to James Madison, New York, September 4, 1815, AGP.

2. James Madison to Albert Gallatin, Montpelier, September 11, 1815, AGP.

3. Albert Gallatin to James Madison New York, November 23, 1815, AGP.

4. Albert Gallatin to Thomas Jefferson, New York, November 27, 1815, AGP.

5. James Monroe to Albert Gallatin, Washington City, December 4, 1815, AGP.

6. Albert Gallatin to Thomas Jefferson, Washington City, April 1, 1816, AGP.

7. Albert Gallatin to Matthew Lyon, New York, May 7, 1816, AGP.

8. Albert Gallatin to James Monroe, Paris, September 12, 1816, AGP.

9. Albert Gallatin to James Monroe, Paris, September 25, 1816, AGP.

10. Albert Gallatin to James Monroe, Paris, October 14, 1816, AGP.

11. Albert Gallatin to James Monroe, Paris, November 21, 1816, AGP.

12. Ibid.

13. Albert Gallatin to James Monroe, Paris, January 20, 1817, AGP.

14. A. J. Crawford to Albert Gallatin, Washington City, March 12, 1817, AGP.

15. Thomas Jefferson to Albert Gallatin, Monticello, February 15, 1818, AGP.

16. Albert Gallatin to John Quincy Adams, Paris, November 5, 1818, AGP.

17. Albert Gallatin to John Quincy Adams, Paris, November 21, 1818, AGP.

18. Albert Gallatin to John Quincy Adams, Paris, January 4, 1819, AGP.

19. Thomas Jefferson to Albert Gallatin, Monticello, November 24, 1818, AGP.

20. Albert Gallatin to John Quincy Adams, Paris, May 24, 1819, AGP.

21. Albert Gallatin to John Quincy Adams, Paris, October 25, 1819, AGP.

22. Ibid.

23. Albert Gallatin to John Quincy Adams, Paris, July 2, 1821, AGP.

24. Albert Gallatin to John Quincy Adams, Paris, September 26, 1821, AGP.

25. John Quincy Adams diary entry, November 8, 1821, in Adams, *Life of Albert Gallatin,* 576.

26. John Jacob Astor to Albert Gallatin, New York, October 18, 1822, AGP.

27. Albert Gallatin to John Quincy Adams, Paris, November 13, 1822, AGP.

28. Albert Gallatin to James Monroe, Paris, November 13, 1822, AGP.

29. Albert Gallatin to Jean Badollet, New Geneva, July 29, 1824, AGP.

Notes to Chapter 8

1. Albert Gallatin to Frances Gallatin, New Geneva, September 17, 1823, in Adams, *Life of Albert Gallatin,* 539–540.
2. Albert Gallatin to Hannah Nicholson Gallatin, Washington, January 24, 1824, in Adams, *Life of Albert Gallatin,* 594.
3. Albert Gallatin to Jean Badollet, New Geneva, July 29, 1824, AGP.
4. Ibid.
5. Ibid.
6. Albert Gallatin to Jean Badollet, New York, February 7, 1833, AGP.
7. Albert Gallatin to unidentified, Baltimore, May 12, 1826, in Adams, *Life of Albert Gallatin,* 613.
8. Albert Gallatin to John Quincy Adams, New York, June 30, 1826, AGP.
9. Albert Gallatin to Henry Clay, London, August 28, 1826, AGP.
10. Albert Gallatin to Henry Clay, London, September 22, 1826, AGP.
11. Albert Gallatin to James Gallatin, London, January 13, 1827, in Adams, *Life of Albert Gallatin,* 621–623.
12. John Quincy Adams to Albert Gallatin, Washington City, March 20, 1827, AGP.
13. John Quincy Adams to Albert Gallatin, Washington City, December 12, 1827, AGP.
14. Albert Gallatin to Hannah Nicholson Gallatin, Washington City, December 16, 1828, in Adams, *Life of Albert Gallatin,* 629–630.

Notes to Chapter 9

1. Albert Gallatin to Jean Badollet, New York, February 7, 1833, in Adams, *Life of Albert Gallatin,* 648.
2. Henry Clay, speech in the U.S. Senate, in Adams, *Life of Albert Gallatin,* 641.
3. Thomas Jefferson to Albert Gallatin, Monticello, November 24, 1818, AGP.
4. Albert Gallatin to Jean Badollet, New York, February 3, 1834, AGP.
5. Albert Gallatin to Jean Badollet, New Geneva, March 18, 1825, in Adams, *Life of Albert Gallatin,* 610.
6. Ibid.
7. Lord Ashburton to Albert Gallatin, Washington City, April 12, 1842, AGP.
8. Albert Gallatin to Lord Ashburton, New York, April 20, 1842, AGP.
9. Albert Gallatin to Albert Davy, New York, December 28, 1843, AGP.

A Note on Sources

THE Albert Gallatin Papers constitute the backbone of the original sources consulted for this book and are available on microfilm at the New-York Historical Society. The Papers of Albert Gallatin result from a project sponsored by New York University in 1970 and are available at the Library of Congress and the New-York Historical Society. There is a small archive of Gallatin papers at the Bibliothèque de Genève. The Archives d'État in Geneva provided background via email and copies of archive material by mail. So far as is possible, I have tried to limit the citations in the text to original source material only, mainly correspondence and published papers.

Among secondary sources (see details of the publications in the bibliography that follows), two books stand out for their exhaustive research: Henry Adams's *Life of Albert Gallatin,* which is the bible of Gallatin biographies and of irreplaceable value for anyone wishing to write a life of Gallatin; and Raymond Walters's biography, which contains a wealth of detail and context. Readers are advised to avoid the *Diary of James Gallatin, Secretary to Albert Gallatin, a Great Peacemaker,* which is not listed in the bibliography. It is almost certainly a fanciful invention, copying much of Adams's *Life* for its context, perpetrated by Albert Gallatin's great-grandson James, as described in Walters's paper "The James Gallatin Diary: A Fraud?" cited in the bibliography. Ewing's enthusiastic biography seems to be based on that *Diary* in too large part. John Austin Stevens's *Albert Gallatin* is a readable and to all appearances reliable account by a distant relative of Gallatin's wife. Benedict von Tscharner's recent slim biography is a compact and accessible account from a Swiss diplomat's urbane and admiring perspective. Adams published the *Writings of Albert Gallatin* in three volumes around the same time as his *Life of Albert Gallatin.* The *Writings* contain much of the most interesting material in the Albert Gallatin Papers and have the virtue of being typeset and printed, and so are much more legible. I have sought to anchor the narrative as much as possible using primary sources but have also relied on the biographies—by Adams,

Stevens, and Walters, in particular—in constructing the story. Some of the shorter pieces, such as Rappard's paper, which covers Gallatin's return to Geneva in 1815, are helpful in filling in the gaps.

With regard to background history, Dufour's *Histoire de Genève* is a dense account of the history of Geneva. Osborne's section on Calvin and the Reformation is helpful in situating their importance. For American history, Remini is highly readable, Morison remains a standard that is hard to beat, and Channing's work from the early twentieth century is a model of old-school erudition. Jones's commemorative edition of the centenary history of New York University is of the same style and quality.

Many of the other sources listed in the bibliography have been consulted. All are listed so as to provide as complete as possible a picture of the information on Gallatin that is up to date for his two hundred fiftieth anniversary.

BIBLIOGRAPHY

MANUSCRIPT COLLECTIONS

Albert Gallatin Papers, New-York Historical Society.

American State Papers: Documents, Legislative and Executive of the Congress of the United States, 38 vols. (Washington, DC: Gales and Seaton, 1833–1861); and *Foreign Relations,* 6 vols. (Washington, DC: Gales and Seaton, 1832–1859).

Annals of Congress: The Debates and Proceedings in the Congress of the United States, 42 vols. (Washington, DC: Gales and Seaton, 1833–1861). Includes most of his Gallatin's speeches in the House of Representatives.

Archives d'État, Geneva, Switzerland.

Bibliothèque de Genève, Geneva, Switzerland.

James Madison Papers, Library of Congress.

James Monroe Papers, Library of Congress.

Papers of Albert Gallatin. In Carl E. Prince, *Guide to the Microfilm Edition of the Papers of Albert Gallatin,* sponsored by New York University, the National Historical Publications Commission, 1970. Available at the Library of Congress and at the New-York Historical Society.

Thomas Jefferson Papers, Library of Congress.

BOOKS AND ARTICLES

Abegg, Bruno, and Barbara Lüthi. *Small Number, Big Impact: Swiss Immigration to the USA.* Translated by Rafaël Newmann. Zürich: Verlag Neue Züricher Zeitung, 2006.

Adams, Henry. *The Life of Albert Gallatin.* Philadelphia: Lippincott, 1880.

Adams, Henry, ed. *The Writings of Albert Gallatin.* 3 vols. Philadelphia: Lippincott, 1879.

Aitken, Thomas. *Albert Gallatin: Early America's Swiss-Born Statesman.* New York: Vantage, 1985.

Ammon, Harry. *James Monroe: The Quest for National Identity.* New York: McGraw-Hill, 1971.

Asselain, Jean-Charles. *Histoire économique de la France du XVIIIe siècle à nos jours: 1. De l'Ancien Régime à la Première Guerre mondiale.* Paris: Editions du Seuil, 1984.

Bacon, William Plumb. *Ancestry of Albert Gallatin, born Geneva, Switzerland, January 29, 1761; died New York, August 12, 1849, and of Hannah Nicholson, born New York, September 11, 1766; died New York, May 14, 1849, with a list of their descendants to the second and third generation.* New York: Press of Tobias A. Wright, 1916.

Badollet, John Louis. *The Correspondence of John Badollet and Albert Gallatin, 1804–1836.* Edited by Gayle Thornbrough. Indianapolis: Indiana Historical Society, 1963.

Balinky, Alexander. *Albert Gallatin: Fiscal Theories and Policies.* New Brunswick, NJ: Rutgers University Press, 1958.

Bieder, Robert E. *Science Encounters the American Indian, 1820–1880: The Early Years of American Ethnology.* Norman: Univerisity of Oklahoma Press, 1986.

Bouquet, Jean-Jacques. *Histoire de la Suisse.* Paris: Presses Universitaires de France, 1995.

Bryen, G. J., III. *Albert Gallatin: Diplomat.* Cambridge, Ohio, 1984.

Burrows, Edwin G. *Albert Gallatin and the Political Economy of Republicanism, 1761–1800.* Edited by Harold Hyman and Stuart Bruchey. New York: Garland, 1986.

———. "Notes on Settling America: Albert Gallatin, New England, and the American Revolution." *New England Quarterly* 58, no. 4 (September 1985): 442–453.

Cachia-Riedl, Markus Claudius. "Albert Gallatin and the Politics of the New Nation." Ph.D. dissertation, University of California at Berkeley, 1998.

Caldwell, Lynton K. *The Administrative Theories of Hamilton and Jefferson.* Chicago: University of Chicago Press, 1944.

Channing, Edward. *A History of the United States: Federalists and Republicans.* Vol. 4. New York: Macmillan, 1920.

Chernow, Ron. *Alexander Hamilton.* New York: Penguin, 2004.

Churchill, Winston S. *A History of the English-Speaking Peoples,* vol. 3, *The Age of Revolution.* New York: Dodd, Mead, 1957.

Clark, Sir George. *English History: A Survey.* Oxford, UK: Clarendon, 1971.

Cottret, Bernard. *Calvin: A Biography.* Translated by Wallace M. McDonald. Grand Rapids, MI: Eerdmans, 2000.

Dufour, Alfred. *Histoire de Genève.* Paris: Presses Universitaires de France, 1997.

Dungan, Nicholas. "France in America 1608–2008 and the Notion of Nationality." New York: privately printed, 2008.

Esdaile, Charles. *Napoleon's Wars: An International History, 1803–1815.* New York: Viking, 2007.

Ewing, Frank. *America's Forgotten Statesman: Albert Gallatin.* New York: Vantage, 1959.

Ferguson, E. James, ed. *Selected Writings of Albert Gallatin.* Indianapolis: Bobbs-Merrill, 1967.

Ferguson, Russell J. *Early Western Pennsylvania Politics, 1773–1823*. Pittsburgh: University of Pittsburgh Press, 1938.

Fleming, Dolores A. "A Critique of the James Gallatin Diary." Privately printed, 1982.

———. *Historic Furnishings Report, Friendship Hill National Historic Site,* Harpers Ferry Center, National Park Service, 1985.

Ford, Franklin L. *Europe, 1780–1830*. 2nd ed. London: Longman, 1989.

Gallatin, Albert. "Campbell's Report." November 22, 1808. *State Papers: Foreign Relations,* 3:259–262.

———. *Considerations on the Currency and Banking System of the United States.* First printed in the *American Quarterly Review* of December 1830. Reprinted, with additions, Philadelphia: Carey A Lea, 1831.

———. "Correspondence as Commissioner for Negotiating a Treaty of Commerce with Great Britain, 1815." *State Papers: Foreign Relations,* 4:7–18.

———. "Correspondence as Commissioner for Negotiating a Treaty of Peace with Great Britain, 1814." *State Papers: Foreign Relations,* 3:705–726, 730–748; 4:810.

———. "Hale's Indians of North-West America and Vocabularies of North America, with an Introduction." *Transactions of the American Ethnological Society* 2. New York, 1848.

———. "Inaugural Address Delivered before the New-York Historical Society. February 7, 1843." *Proceedings of the New-York Historical Society,* 1843.

———. "Memoir on the North-Eastern Boundary in Connection with Jay's Map." *Proceedings of the New-York Historical Society,* 1843.

———. "Memorial of the Committee appointed by the Free Trade Convention held in Philadelphia in September and October 1831, to prepare and present a memorial to Congress remonstrating against the existing tariff of duties." New York: William A. Mercein, 1832.

———. "Notes on the Semi-Civilized Nations of Mexico, Yucatan, and Central America." *Transactions of the American Ethnological Society* 1. New York, 1845.

———. *The Oregon Question,* with an appendix on *War Expenses*. A series of articles published in the *National Intelligencer;* reprinted in New York: Bartlett and Welford, 1846.

———. "Peace with Mexico." New York: Bartlett A Welford, 1817.

———. *The Right of the United States of America to the North-Eastern Boundary Claimed by Them, Principally Extracted from the Statements Laid before the King of the Netherlands.* New York, 1840.

———. Special reports and communications of the secretary of the Treasury to Congress during the years of 1801–1813:

"On Internal Improvements (Roads and Canals)." April 4, 1808. *State Papers: Miscellaneous,* 1:724–741.

"On Specific Appropriations." March 1, 1802. *State Papers: Finance,* 1:755–757.

"On the Admission of Ohio, and the Disposition to Be Made of the Proceeds of the Public Lands (National Road)." Letter to William B. Giles, Chairman of Committee, February 13, 1802. *State Papers: Miscellaneous,* 1:327.

"On the Amicable Settlement of the Limits of the State of Georgia (Yazoo Claims)." February 16 and April 26, 1803. *State Papers: Public Lands,* 1:125–132.

"On the Renewal of the Charter of the Bank of the United States." March 2, 1809. *State Papers: Finance,* 2:351–353. On the same subject: January 30, 1811. *State Papers: Finance,* 2:481.

"On the subject of the Public Debt, and the Provisions for its Redemption." March 31, 1802. *State Papers: Finance,* 1:746–749.

———. *A Sketch of the Finances of the United States.* New York: William A. Davis, 1796.

———. "Speech at the Reception of La Fayette at Uniontown, Pa., May 26, 1825." *National Intelligencer,* June 11, 1825.

———. *Suggestions on the Banks and Currency of the Several United States, in Reference Principally to the Suspension of Specie Payments.* New York: Wiley A. Putnam, 1841.

———. *Views of the Public Debt, Receipts and Expenditures of the United States.* Philadelphia: Matthew Carey, 1800.

Gallatin, Albert Eugene. *Gallatin Iconography.* Boston: privately printed, 1934.

———. *The Portraits of Albert Gallatin.* New York: De Vinne, 1911.

Goodrich, Carter. "The Gallatin Plan after One Hundred and Fifty Years." *Proceedings of the American Philosophical Society,* 1958: 436–441.

Gordon, Bruce F. *Calvin.* New Haven, CT: Yale University Press, 2009.

Gray, Francine du Plessix. *Madame de Stael: The First Modern Woman.* New York: Atlas, 2008.

Grueningen, John Paul von. *The Swiss in the United States.* Madison, WI: Swiss-American Historical Society, 1940.

Heinlein, Jay C. "Albert Gallatin: A Pioneer in Public Administration." *William and Mary Quarterly,* 3rd ser., January 1950: 64–94.

Hildebrand, Philipp M. "Albert Gallatin, One of the Financial Founding Fathers: What Can We Learn from Him Today?" Swiss National Bank, September 10, 2008.

Hitchens, Christopher. *Thomas Jefferson: Author of America.* New York: HarperCollins, 2005.

Johnson, Paul. *George Washington: The Founding Father.* New York: HarperCollins, 2005.

Jones, Theodore Francis, ed. *New York University, 1832–1932.* New York: New York University Press, 1933.

Kissinger, Henry A. *A World Restored: Metternich, Castlereagh and the Problems of Peace, 1812–1822.* London: Phoenix. First published by Weidenfeld & Nicolson, 1957.

———. *Diplomacy*. New York: Simon and Schuster, 1994.

Kuntz, Joëlle. *Switzerland: How an Apline Pass Became a Country*. Geneva: Historiator Editions, 2008.

Kuppenheimer, L. B. *Albert Gallatin's Vision of Democratic Stability: An Interpretive Profile*. Westport, CT: Praeger, 1996.

Labouchère, G. "L'annexion de la Louisiane aux Etats-Unis et les maisons Hope et Baring." *Revue d'histoire diplomatique* 30: 423–455.

Lafaber, Walter. *The American Age: United States Foreign Policy at Home and Abroad Since 1750*. New York: Norton, 1989.

Levasseur, Auguste. *Lafayette in America in 1824 and 1825*. Vol. 2. Philadelphia, 1829.

Lodge, Henry Cabot. *Albert Gallatin*. New York: Charles Scribner's Sons, 1879.

Lowther, Minnie Kendall. *Historic Friendship Hill: Home of Albert Gallatin*. Rutland, VT: Tuttle, 1928.

Mai, Chien Tseng. "The Fiscal Policies of Albert Gallatin." New York: Columbia University, 1930.

Malone, Dumas. *Jefferson and His Time*, vol. 4, *Jefferson the President: First Term, 1801–1805*. Boston: Little, Brown, 1970.

———. *Jefferson and His Time*, vol. 5, *Jefferson the President: Second Term, 1805–1809*. Boston: Little, Brown, 1970.

Mannix, Richard. "Gallatin, Jefferson, and the Embargo of 1808." *Diplomatic History*, 1979: 151–172.

March, John B., and Scott Jacobs. *Historic Structure Report, Architectural Data Section, Friendship Hill National Historic Site*. Denver Service Center, National Park Service, September 1984.

McKee, Larry. *Historic Structure Report, Archeological Data Section, Friendship Hill National Historic Site*. Denver Service Center (Applied Archeology Center), National Park Service and the American University, March 1989.

Meacham, Jon. *American Lion: Andrew Jackson in the White House*. New York: Random House, 2008.

Merk, Frederick. *Albert Gallatin and the Oregon Problem: A Study in Anglo-American Diplomacy*. Cambridge, MA: Harvard University Press, 1950.

Morison, Samuel Eliot. *The Oxford History of the American People*. New York: Oxford University Press, 1965.

Murray, Meridith A. *To Live and Die Amongst the Monongahela Hills: The Story of Albert Gallatin and Friendship Hill*. Eastern National, 1999.

O'Brien, Dennis H. "Albert Gallatin and Southwestern Pennsylvania." West Virginia University, 1982.

Osborne, Roger. *Civilization: A New History of the Western World*. New York: Pegasus Books, 2006.

Peter, Marc. *Une amie de Voltaire: Madame Gallatin*. Lausanne: SPES, 1975.

Prominent Americans of Swiss Origin: A Compilation Prepared by the Swiss-American Historical Society. New York: James T. White, 1932.

Rakove, Jack N. *James Madison and the Creation of the American Republic.* Edited by Oscar Handlin. New York: HarperCollins, 1990.

Rappard, William E. *Albert Gallatin: Citoyen de Genève, Ministre des Etats-Unis.* Genève: Imprimerie Central, 1917.

Remini, Robert V. *A Short History of the United States.* New York: HarperCollins, 2008.

Stevens, John Austin. *Albert Gallatin.* Boston: Hougthton Mifflin, 1883.

Torres, Louis. *Special History Report: Albert Gallatin, Statesman, Diplomat, Humanitarian, Scientist.* Friendship Hill National Historic Site, Denver, Colorado. U.S. Department of the Interior, National Park Service, 1991.

Tscharner, Benedict von. *Albert Gallatin (1761–1849): Geneva's American Statesman.* Translated by Caterine Pierre. Gollion: Éditions Infolio and Editions de Penthe, 2008.

Unrau, Harlan D. *Albert Gallatin: Statesman, Diplomat, Humanitarian, Scientist.* Friendship Hill National Historic Site, Historic Resource Study, Historical Data Section, Denver Service Center, National Park Service, September 1981.

Walters, Raymond, Jr. *Albert Gallatin: Jeffersonian Financier and Diplomat.* New York: Macmillan, 1975.

———. "The James Gallatin Diary: A Fraud?" *American Historical Association* 62, no. 4 (July): 878–885.

White, Leonard D. *The Jeffersonians.* New York: Macmillan, 1951.

Wood, Gordon S. *Empire of Liberty: A History of the Early Republic, 1789–1815.* New York: Oxford University Press, 2009.

Wright, Robert E., and David J. Cowen. *Financial Founding Fathers: The Men Who Made America Rich.* Chicago: University of Chicago Press, 2006.

Ziegler, Philip. *The Sixth Great Power: A History of One of the Greatest of All Banking Families, the House of Barings, 1762–1929.* New York: Knopf, 1988.

INDEX

About the Author

Nicholas Dungan is a transatlantic expert, senior advisor to the French Institute of International and Strategic Relations, former president of the French-American Foundation in New York, and former associate fellow of the Royal Institute of International Affairs at Chatham House in London. He is a frequent media commentator on international relations, politics, business, and finance. An investment banker in his prior career, Dungan is a graduate of St. Paul's School, Stanford University, and Sciences Po Paris.